This is both a seminal and profound body of work.

Over the past century the evangelical church has become global; in fact, the majority of its adherents (over 65 percent) now live in the Majority World. As the church has grown, we are beginning to see the emergence of a new generation of indigenous missionary leaders who are seeking to wed missiological reflection and praxis in a way that both challenges Western perspectives and brings fresh life to the mission of the global church. Eraston Kighoma is one such leader.

This work has much to commend it, offering deep and challenging insights into the Christian attitude to suffering, war and adversity, as well as highlighting fresh and renewed models of contextual mission. It has been written by someone who has sought to live out these principles in difficult circumstances. The humble reader will therefore be rebuked, enriched and challenged by reading this significant work.

Lindsay Brown, DDiv
Former General Secretary, IFES
Former International Director, Lausanne Movement

Eraston Kighoma has produced a comprehensive study attempting "to develop an understanding of church, mission and ministry in the context of war and the theology that underlies the church's action."

Dr. Kighoma has himself lived in a context of war since the early 1990s in the DRC. He has had the courage and the calling to remain in that environment with his family, believing that the gospel could and should make a difference. Through the lives and testimonies of Eraston and many others whom he has discipled, this difference is evidenced through their courage and, at times, deep pain as they have sought to reconcile God's goodness in the midst of terrible acts of war.

This is a unique and important piece of research and I commend it to everyone seeking to understand the role of intentional discipleship and mission in the context of war.

Malcolm McGregor
Former SIM International Director
Associate Director for Pastoral Care, Scholars Programme, Langham Partnership

Humanity is complex and human tragedy such as war gives us a prism by which we can better understand our lived realities. This is the heart of this work where the author has meticulously examined discipleship in the context of war. He argues that in a time of war and violence, God demonstrates his mission through the local church pastor. Thus, the author rejects the simplistic narrative that the experience of the Christian leader in a time of war and suffering is a story of survival. While recognizing that war is tragic and devastating to humanity, the author identifies a silver lining to bring discipleship to bear in such times of tragedy. The DRC is well known for its great natural resources but the country is also a reservoir of much knowledge that informs and equips scholars, researchers and other leaders in navigating matters of discipleship and leadership in the context of war. I highly recommend this work for scholars and graduate students as well as seasoned researchers and policy makers around the globe.

David Ngaruiya, PhD
Deputy Vice Chancellor, Academic Affairs,
International Leadership University, Nairobi, Kenya

This is a ground-breaking consideration of the response of one Christian community to two decades of war in Eastern Congo. It contains probing analysis and argues convincingly that the experience of war has had a profound influence on Baptist mission, on local theologies and on the church community's attitude to violence. The nature of that impact is set out in what is a rich multi-dimensional investigation. Although this book is rooted in a particular context, the missiological insights it offers are important for many parts of the world in which violence is the dark background against which Christian witness takes place. I am delighted to commend Eraston Kighoma's crucial study.

Ian M. Randall, PhD
Research Associate,
Cambridge Centre for Christianity Worldwide
Senior Research Fellow,
International Baptist Theological Study Centre, Amsterdam, The Netherlands

Church and Mission in the Context of War

A Descriptive Missiological Study of the Response of the Baptist Church in Central Africa to the War in Eastern Congo between 1990 and 2011

Eraston Kambale Kighoma

MONOGRAPHS

© 2021 Eraston Kambale Kighoma

Published 2021 by Langham Monographs
An imprint of Langham Publishing
www.langhampublishing.org

Langham Publishing and its imprints are a ministry of Langham Partnership

Langham Partnership
PO Box 296, Carlisle, Cumbria, CA3 9WZ, UK
www.langham.org

ISBNs:
978-1-83973-062-7 Print
978-1-83973-517-2 ePub
978-1-83973-518-9 Mobi
978-1-83973-519-6 PDF

Eraston Kambale Kighoma has asserted his right under the Copyright, Designs and Patents Act, 1988 to be identified as the Author of this work.

All rights reserved. No part of this publication may be reproduced, stored in a retrieval system or transmitted, in any form or by any means, electronic, mechanical, photocopying, recording or otherwise, without the prior written permission of the publisher or the Copyright Licensing Agency.

Requests to reuse content from Langham Publishing are processed through PLSclear. Please visit www.plsclear.com to complete your request.

All Scripture quotations, unless otherwise indicated, are taken from the Holy Bible, New International Version®, NIV®. Copyright ©1973, 1978, 1984, 2011 by Biblica, Inc.™ Used by permission of Zondervan.

Scripture quotations marked (ESV) are from The Holy Bible, English Standard Version® (ESV®), copyright © 2001 by Crossway, a publishing ministry of Good News Publishers. Used by permission. All rights reserved.

Scripture quotations marked (HCSB) are taken from the Holman Christian Standard Bible®, Copyright © 1999, 2000, 2002, 2003, 2009 by Holman Bible Publishers. Used by permission. Holman Christian Standard Bible®, Holman CSB®, and HCSB® are federally registered trademarks of Holman Bible Publishers.

Scripture quotations marked (NASB) are taken from the New American Standard Bible®, Copyright © 1960, 1962, 1963, 1968, 1971, 1972, 1973, 1975, 1977, 1995 by The Lockman Foundation. Used by permission.

British Library Cataloguing-in-Publication Data
A catalogue record for this book is available from the British Library

ISBN: 978-1-83973-062-7

Cover & Book Design: projectluz.com

Langham Partnership actively supports theological dialogue and an author's right to publish but does not necessarily endorse the views and opinions set forth here or in works referenced within this publication, nor can we guarantee technical and grammatical correctness. Langham Partnership does not accept any responsibility or liability to persons or property as a consequence of the reading, use or interpretation of its published content.

*This study is dedicated to
my wife,
Judith Mwengenindi,
to our three children,
Stone, Keren and Elysée Hadisi,
and to all men and women who have dedicated
their lives to mission in the context of war.*

Contents

Acknowledgements xv
Abstract xvii
List of Abbreviations xix
Chapter 1 1
  Introduction
  1.1 Background 1
  1.2 Problem Statement 3
  1.3 Objectives 6
  1.4 Purpose and Value 6
  1.5 Limitations and Delimitations 7
  1.6 Presuppositions 8
  1.7 Conceptual Framework 9
  1.8 Design and Methodology 10
    1.8.1 Research Design 10
    1.8.2 Population and Sampling 17
    1.8.3 Data Collection 18
    1.8.4 Data Analysis 20
    1.8.5 Validation and Verification 21
  1.9 Summary 21

Chapter 2 23
  Church, Mission, and War – Literature Review
  2.1 Introduction 23
  2.2 Theories and Views on War 23
    2.2.1 Just War Theory 23
    2.2.2 Pacifism theory 26
    2.2.3 Crusade/Holy War 27
    2.2.4 Nonviolence Theory 28
    2.2.5 The Church Fathers on War 30
    2.2.6 Protestant Reformers and War 31
    2.2.7 Toward a Theory of Church Survival in the Context of War 31
  2.3 Church Missions and Wars 32
    2.3.1 Identity Conflicts and the Transmission of the Christian Faith 32

  2.3.2 Church Growth during Wartime 43
  2.3.3 African Wars Framework: Ethnic Clashes and Wars
    in Eastern Congo 46
  2.3.4 Direct Results of War 48
 2.4 Views on Migration and Mission 50
 2.5 War – an Avenue for Church Missions 52
 2.6 Church Mission: Advocating for Peace, Justice and Harmony 55
  2.6.1 The Church and War 55
  2.6.2 War and Social Development 56
 2.7 Summary and Gaps in Existing Literature 57

Chapter 3 61
Church, Mission, and War – Biblical Perspectives
 3.1 Introduction 61
 3.2 Biblical View of Missions 62
  3.2.1 Missions and War in the Old Testament 62
  3.2.2 Church Missions in the Gospels 65
  3.2.3 Church Mission in Pauline Writings 70
  3.2.4 Conclusion 72
 3.3 Matthew 5:38–45: Not War but Peace as the Christian
  Response to War 74
  3.3.1 Introduction 74
  3.3.2 Structure 74
  3.3.3 Context of Matthew 5:38–45 74
  3.3.4 Historical Background and Authorship 75
  3.3.5 Retaliation and Nonviolence (5:38–43) 77
  3.3.6 Love of the Enemy (5:43–45) 82
  3.3.7 Conclusion and Theological Meaning of
    Matthew 5:38–45 88
 3.4 Acts 18:1–4: Power, Identity Conflict and Migration and
  Missions 89
  3.4.1 Introduction 89
  3.4.2 Context of Acts 18:1–4 89
  3.4.3 Historical Background of Acts 18:1–4 89
  3.4.4 Analysis and Comment 91
  3.4.5 Conclusion and Theological Meaning of Acts 18:1–4 98
 3.5 Hebrews 10:32–34: The Experience of War Provides
  Guidance for a Suffering Church and Discipleship 99
  3.5.1 Introduction 99
  3.5.2 Context of Hebrews 10:32–34 100
  3.5.3 Historical Background of Hebrews 10 101

3.5.4 Christians and Vengeance 103
3.5.5 The Value of Church's Past Experience in Context
(Hebrews 10:32–34) 104
3.5.6 Church Survival during Hardship 105
3.5.7 Conclusion and Theological Meaning of
Hebrews 10:32–34 111
3.6 Summary 112

Chapter 4 115
Historical and Ethnical Context of Eastern Congo from 1990 to 2011
4.1 Introduction 115
4.2 Ethnic Violence and War in Eastern Congo: Root Causes 116
4.3 Ethnic Wars in the Early 1990s (1990–1994) 120
4.4 Eastern Congo between 1994 and 1996 125
4.5 First Congo War/AFDL (1996–1997) 127
4.6 The Second Congo War (1998–2003) 130
4.7 Transitional Government and Elections (2003–2006) 135
4.8 Eastern Congo between 2006 and 28 November 2011 139
4.9 Congo War Against Women and Children 144
4.10 Eastern Congo and a Mining War 146
4.11 Conclusion 149

Chapter 5 157
The Nature of Church Missions before and during the War
5.1 Introduction 157
5.2 Demographic Information 157
5.2.1 Codes and Usage 158
5.3 Nature of Missions before the War 159
5.3.1 Oral Witness before the War 159
5.3.2 Discipleship before the War 162
5.3.3 Involvement in Social Concerns before War 165
5.4 The Nature of Missions during the War 166
5.4.1 Oral Witness during the War 166
5.4.2 Discipleship during the War 172
5.4.3 Involvement in Social Concerns during War 179
5.5 Summary 183

Chapter 6 187
Christian Leaders' Experiences of Missions before and during the War
6.1 Introduction 187
6.2 Experiences of Christian Leaders Involved in Missions in
the Context of War 188

  6.2.1 Stories of Christian Leaders Involved in Missions
during War 188
  6.2.2 Personal Suffering Related to Missions during War 195
  6.2.3 Family's Suffering during the War 197
  6.2.4 Suffering of Church Members during the War 198
  6.2.5 Effects of the War on Witnessing, Discipleship and
Social Involvement 201
 6.3 The Effect of the War on the Understanding of Church
Missions 204
  6.3.1 Christian Leaders' Understanding of Church
Missions before the War 204
  6.3.2 Church Leaders' Understanding of Church Missions
during the War 205
  6.3.3 Effects of War on Christian Leaders' Practice of
Church Missions 211
  6.3.4 Participants' Suggestions for the Improvement of
Missions 213
 6.4 Church Position on War 216
  6.4.1 Church Position on War before the War 216
  6.4.2 The Church's Position on War during the War 217
 6.5 Summary 221
  6.5.1 Experience of Church Leaders Involved in Church
Missions during the War 221
  6.5.2 The Effect of the Experience of War on the
Understanding of the Church's Missions 222
  6.5.3 The Church's Position on War before and during the
War 223
  6.5.4 Church's Survival during War from the View of
Respondents 224
  6.5.5 Survival of the Church during War 225

Chapter 7 229
Toward an Understanding of Church and Mission in the Context of War
 7.1 Introduction 229
 7.2 The Experience of Missions in Eastern Congo and the
Biblical Perspectives on the Response to Violence and War 230
  7.2.1 Tensions between the Local Missiologies and
Matthew 5:38–45 230
  7.2.2 Tensions between the Local Missiologies and
Acts 18:1–4 232

  7.2.3 Tensions between the Local Missiologies and
    Hebrews 10:32–34 234
 7.3 Missions in Eastern Congo and Contemporary
   Missiological Models 239
  7.3.1 David Bosch's Emerging Model and Kenosis Theology ...239
  7.3.2 Samuel Escobar's Migration Model.....................................244
  7.3.3 Stephen Bevans' Model of Constants in Context 248
 7.4 Summary 251

Chapter 8 259
 Conclusion
 8.1 Introduction 259
 8.2 Summary of Research 259
  8.2.1 Relationship between the Missions of the CBCA
   before and during the War in the Period between
   1990 to 2011 259
  8.2.2 The Effects of the War in Eastern Congo between
   1990 and 2011 on the Understanding and Practices
   of Missions in the CBCA...263
 8.3 Contribution of the Research to Missions 270
 8.4 Recommendations for Further Studies.......................................272
 8.5 Conclusion 273

Appendix A 275
 Face-To-Face Interview Guide
  I. Nature of Missions 276
  II. Experience of Church leaders undertaking church
   missions during the war...278
  III. How did the experience of war affect the
   understanding of church missions in Eastern Congo?........278
  IV. What contemporary, contextual mission theory that
   incorporates experiential, biblical and missiological
   perspective can be developed based on the experience
   of the church in Eastern Congo and a biblical model? 279
  V. What else would you like me to know? 279

Appendix B..281
 Focus Groups Interview Guide

Bibliography 283

List of Tables

Table 1: Face to face participants' understanding of missions before the war...204

Table 2: FGD Participants' understanding of missions before the war 205

Table 3: Face to face respondents' understanding of missions during war........206

Table 4: FGD participants' understanding of missions during war..................207

Table 5: Change in pastors' understanding of missions as a result of the experience of war 208

Table 6: Change in FGD participants' understanding of war as a result of the experience of war...210

Table 7: Face to face interview respondents' current missional practices resulting from their experience of war. 211

Table 8: Face to face participants' suggestions for improvements for effective church missions in the context of war..................................213

Table 9: FGD participants' suggestions for improvements for effective church missions in the context of war 214

Table 10: Church's position on war before the war 216

Table 11: Church's position on war during the war...218

List of Figures

Figure 1: Conceptual framework of missions in the context of war...................10

Figure 2: Effect of war on women and children in Eastern Congo 199

Acknowledgements

I first want to thank the almighty God for his grace and for enabling me to complete this study. I then would like to extend my gratitude to Langham Partnership for funding my doctoral studies and for pastoral care provided throughout the process.

For the academic work, my supervisor, Professor David K. Ngaruiya, International Leadership University (ILU-Kenya), deserves particular thanks for his careful guidance, support and tenacious resolve for academic excellence throughout the period and his mentorship. I am also thankful to Dr. Johannes Malherbe of the South African Theological Seminary (SATS), for co-supervising this work and the insights he provided to me in Nairobi. It has guided my first steps on this study journey. My heartfelt gratitude goes to Professor Elizabeth Mburu and her office, Department of Theology at ILU-Kenya, for the encouragement and the technical support during my doctoral education. I am also thankful to Dr. Cathy Ross at the University of Oxford for her valuable guidance during my research visit at Wycliffe Hall, Oxford University, and to the leadership of Wycliffe Hall for the grant that helped me to make progress in the writing of this work. My gratitude goes to the board of CIMR, my mission organization, for support and encouragement, as well as Chappelle CBCA Goma-Ouest, my home church, for encouragement and prayers.

I also express my gratitude to Lindsay Brown and his friends, to the late Rev. Mbusa K.Thaluliva, Rev. Estone Kasereka, Ando and Nesmy Mvé, Agnes and Milly Ibanda, Richard and Nicolette Bayunda, Jean Baptiste Kasekwa, John Allert and his family, Chris Britain and Nadine Britain, Fr. Emmanuel Tavuliandanda, my father Pastor Jean Hadisi Karondwa and others for their support of my research.

My acknowledgements cannot be concluded without mentioning my dear and loving wife, Judith Mwengenindi, and our children Stone Kighoma, Keren Kighoma and Elysée Hadisi Kighoma for the love, patience and support received from them during the period of my study. I will always be grateful for their decision to allow me to take three more years for doctoral research in addition to the previous years away from home when I, prior to that, studied to obtain my other formal qualifications. They have always prayed for me and provided encouragement in times when I needed their comfort the most. I will always cherish the daily evening prayer sessions in our home. The successful completion of the work is testimony to the fact that our prayers were heard by our good Lord.

Abstract

This work is a missiological study about the response of the Baptist Church in Central Africa to the war in Eastern Congo. The study explores the church's understanding of, and approach to, mission before and during the war in the period between 1990 and 2011. It compares and contrasts the results with the understanding of, and approach to, missions before the war. It concludes that the experience of war informed the nature of missions and the development of local theologies, the experience and method of missions, the church's attitude toward violence and the church's survival during the war.

This study involves a combination of descriptive, contextual and integrative approaches, which emphasize attention to culture and intercultural dynamics. It integrates methods and insights from various fields of theological study. The research process comprises face-to-face interviews and focus group discussions for data collection. It also makes use of exegesis and a theological assessment of Matthew 5:38–45, Acts 18:1–4 and Hebrews 10:32–34 in order to identify the response of the church to the war, including the four steps of historical research as advocated by Deiros[1] to establish a historical and contextual basis for the study.

The completion of the church's missiological task during war depends on the way Christian leaders contextualize the transmission of the Christian message, disciple and strategically organize the routine of church life. The church's response to war in Eastern Congo is in action, both in ministry and mission, undergirded by theology. The latter is shaped in and by war, as sharing the gospel was confined to the church's pulpit and, as a result of war, the church shifted from being a mission force in the mission field to a force

---

1. Deiros, "Historical Research," 136–40.

in contextual discipleship that needed to address growth, hope and social concerns including poverty and peaceful coexistence. Rather than accepting the Christian leaders' experience of war as a survival story, the study argues for a demonstration of God in mission through the church pastor fulfilling his mission. It is the reconstruction of church missions centered on the Christian leader in the context of violence and suffering, thus a story of God incarnate, silent during violence and suffering but present through the local church pastor. The response of the church in action and theology that developed from the local experience of missions is linked with the biblical responses to church, violence and war. Therefore, this study integrates the local theologies that guide the church practice with theoretical models of church missions and biblical teaching on Christian responses to the church, violence and war. Consequently, the church's appropriate missiological response to war must draw on insights gained from an understanding of church and mission in the context of war.

List of Abbreviations

ADF	Allied Democratic Forces
ADF/Nalu	Allied Democratic Force and National Army for the Liberation
AFDL	Alliance des Forces Démocratiques pour la Libération du Congo-Zaïre
ALiR	Alliance pour la Libération du Rwanda (Alliance for the Liberation of Rwanda)
APRED-RGL	Action pour la Promotion de la Paix, la Réconciliation et le Développement Durable dans la Sous-Région des Grands Lacs
CBCA	Communauté Baptiste au Centre de l'Afrique (The Baptist Church in Central Africa)
CCC	Church of Christ in Congo
CEBCE	Communauté des Eglises Baptistes du Congo-Est (Community of Baptist Churches of Eastern Congo)
CNDP	Congrès National pour la Défense du Peuple
CNS	Conférence Nationale Souveraine
ECC	Eglise du Christ au Congo
ECZ	Eglise du Christ au Zaire
DRC	Democratic Republic of the Congo
FAC	Forces Armées Congolaises (Congolese Armed Forces)
FAR	Forces Armées Rwandaises (Rwandese Armed Forces)
FARDC	Forces Armées de la République Démocratique du Congo (Congolese armed forces)
FGD	Focus Group Discussion

IDP	Internally displaced person / people
ILU	International Leadership University
IRRI	International Refugee Rights Initiative
JPIC	Justice, Peace and Integrity of Creation (Justice, Paix et Sauvegarde de la Création)
LRA	Lord's Resistance Army
MAGRIVI	Mutuelles des Agriculteurs de Virunga
MONUC	Mission de l'Organisation des Nations Unies en Republique Démocratique du Congo
MONUSCO	Mission de l'Organisation des Nations Unies pour la Stabilisation en RD Congo
MP	Member of Parliament
MPA	Metal Processing Association
MPC	Mining and Processing Congo
M23	Mouvement du 23 Mars
NIF	National and Integrationist Front
NGO	Non-governmental Organization
NLF	National Liberation Front
OCHA :	United Nations for the Coordination of Humanitarian Affairs
OECD	Organization for Economic Co-operation and Development
PARECO	Coalition des patriotes résistants Congolais
RCD	Rassemblement Congolais pour la Démocratie (Rally for Congolese Democracy)
RCD-KML	Rassemblement congolais pour la démocratie-Kisangani Mouvement de liberation
RCD-ML	Rassemblement congolais pour la démocratie-Mouvement de libération
RPA	Rwanda Patriotic Army
SADC	Southen African Development Community
SNPC	Synergie Nationale pour la Paix et la Concorde(National Synergy for Peace and Concord)
UPDF	Uganda People's Defence Forces

CHAPTER 1

Introduction

1.1 Background

This study focuses on the response of the Baptist Church in Central Africa (CBCA) to the wars in Eastern DRC (Democratic Republic of Congo) from 1990 to 2011. This chapter presents the background of the research topic, describes the problem statement, the research objectives, purpose and value, limitations, presuppositions, research questions, the definition of key terms, the conceptual framework, as well as indications of the research design and methodology. This study is an attempt to develop an understanding of church mission and ministry in the context of war and the theology that underlies the church's action.

Since the arrival of the first missionaries in the DRC, the church has always been busy organizing church activities. Since 1990, the country has gone through civil war due to political and ethnic conflicts. The church, which is over a century old, has been working in this context of war during the last two decades in the Eastern Congo region. During these decades of war, from 28 November 1990 to the election in 2011, God was at work in that region through the church, which survived and continued to grow as it brought hope to its members.

The war has exposed communities to internal displacements, migration, rape, food scarcity, poverty and famine, among other challenges. Population movements not only affected both the rural areas and the cities but also aggravated identity conflicts. Describing the situation of Goma, in Eastern Congo, Vlassenroot and Karen Buscher say that

> This reality . . . of a frontier zone has a remarkable impact on the process of local urban identity formation; the city's location has evoked the emerging of multiple, strongly pronounced social identities that reflect the characteristics of contestation and mobility.[1]

Regarding the context, Jacob Kavunkal suggests it is "a truly holistic approach to Christian ministry rooted in biblical truth as being essential to church missions today."[2]

David Barrett shows that Christians in the DRC were 1.4 percent of the total country population in 1909.[3] This number grew to 90.3 percent in the mid-1970s with a growth rate of 3 percent annually between 1970 and 1980, 93 percent in mid-1975, 94.5 percent in mid-1980 and was estimated to be 97 percent in the year 2000. It appears that during the peaceful era of Mobutu Sese Seko's rule since 1961, the number of Christian adherents, though increasing at 3 percent annually, did not increase as fast as it did during the last two decades of the twentieth century. This period includes the time of the civil revolt in Congo that marked the decline of the Sese Seko era in the 1980s and introduced the first decade of war in Eastern Congo in 1990s.

A. Scott Moreau, Harold Netland and Charles van Engen state that "the deteriorating economic situation sparked rioting in the early 1990s and led to the withdrawal of expatriate missions personnel from some part of the country" including Eastern Congo and that "some of the largest refugee camps result from the ethnic strife in Rwanda."[4] It is curious that after the expatriate missions personnel left, "despite these problems, the vitality of the church sets it within the top ten non-western nations sending out their own missionaries for cross-cultural ministry both within and beyond their borders" and that while the response to the Christian message continues to be high "the numerically growing church has been criticized for not influencing as it should in such endemic evils."[5] During the same period, it was estimated that only 44 of the 445 missionaries in Congo from 39 agencies were sent

---

1. Vlassenroot and Buscher, *City as Frontier*, 2.
2. Kavunkal, "Christian Mission," 46.
3. Barrett, *World Christianity Encyclopedia*, 758.
4. Moreau, Netland and Van Engen, *Evangelical Dictionary*, 267.
5. Moreau, Netland and Van Engen, 267.

abroad. At the same time, it was estimated that 650 missionaries were in the DRC from 76 agencies representing 26 countries in the world, including USA, UK, Australia and Nigeria.[6]

The CBCA, formerly the Baptist Church in Kivu (Communauté Baptiste au Kivu-CBK), which mainly works in Eastern Congo, had 280 congregations with a total of 97,250 members in the year 2001 and sixteen years later, in 2017, had more than 450,000 members, including the children, in 404 parishes under the leadership of 704 ordained pastors, 180 retired pastors and caring for 130 widows of deceased pastors. Since 2001, this church has planted 170 new churches while war was going on.[7]

From the above data, it is clear that even during the very dark period of war God has used the church as it struggled to fulfill the Great Commission and make disciples as stated in Matthew 28:18–20. This study, therefore, raises the question of how the church survived the war in Eastern Congo while, according to the critics, it is irrelevant whether it had any "influence in the endemic evils" of war.[8] This question will be addressed as part of the response to the main concern of the study, namely, the relationship between the CBCA's missions before and during the war in Eastern Congo in the period 1990 to 2011.

1.2 Problem Statement

Current theologies of missions do not adequately deal with the realities of war and social disruption as a context for mission. There is, therefore, little understanding of, and guidance for, a church like the CBCA that has been deeply affected by the recent war in the Eastern DRC.

While God has called and equipped his church to transform society and advance his kingdom on earth, wars have continued their destructive course. For example,

> the disintegration that followed the collapse of the DRC and its armed forces in the 1990s reduced the state's capacity to deal with the effects of poverty and environmental destruction,

---

6. Johnstone and Mandryk, *Operation World*, 199.
7. "Brief Survey on the CBCA."
8. Moreau, Netland and Van Engen, *Evangelical Dictionary*, 267.

and also exposed the country to external invasion, occupation and plunder.[9]

The country has been acknowledged as "the rape capital of the world" because "while the country was trapped in conflicts, the use of rape as a weapon of war was rampant and unyielding"[10] to the extent that "over 200,000 rapes have been reported since the war started."[11] Even in the DRC, one of the most Christian nations of the world, the church could not prevent recurring waves of war or their underlying causes. How does the church in the DRC understand this reality and how has it responded to these wars?

The main research question is as follows: How has the war in Eastern Congo between 1990 and 2011 affected the understanding and practice of missions in the CBCA?

The following six research questions emerge from the main research question and will be addressed in the chapters as indicated:

1. What can we learn from earlier Christian views regarding the church encountering violence and war? (Chapter 2)
2. What was the situation in the church and the nature of the war in Eastern Congo between 1990 and 2011? (Chapter 3)
3. What can we learn from the Bible regarding Christian responses to church, violence and war? (Chapter 4)
4. How did the CBCA respond to the wars between 1990 and 2011? (Chapters 5 and 6)
5. What are the implications for our understanding of church encountering war? (Chapter 7)
6. What are the implications of this study for the church in the DRC and beyond? (Chapter 8)

The major focus is not merely on issues of survival, but on how the church deals with the inherent tension between a world torn apart by warfare and the command to expand God's kingdom.

There is not much literature that exists on the experience of the church in the context of war in African Christianity, except scholars such as David Bosch and Isaiah Dau who have written on missions and suffering.[12] It will be

---

9. Nzogola-Ntalaja, "International Dimensions," 118.
10. Brown, "Rape as a Weapon," 24.
11. Burrow, *Violence against Women*, 26.
12. Bosch, "Vulnerability of Mission," 363; Dau, "Following Jesus."

shown that the survival of the church in Eastern Congo brought new insights to the church's mission and ministry. These insights were gained through the experience of the church during the war in Eastern Congo, but especially the war in and around Goma.

The term "missions" "describes the specific church's efforts to carry out the task of mission in the world."[13] Hence, interrogating "the church's relationship with the world is a missionary concern."[14] This study, therefore, agrees with Ott and his colleagues who advocate for "a dialogue between the biblical text and missionary context."[15] It appears that with that dialogue when "speaking of church mission one is speaking of the church's relationship to the world and the purposes for which God sends the church, his people, into the world."[16] The nature and task of church missions vary with the context as the church transmits the consistent message of the gospel of Christ. For example, "whilst the local population enjoyed the healing and preaching ministry of Simon Kimbangu,"[17] in the colonial context the people faced higher taxes from the Belgium administration, but during the post-World War I period after 1921, the Kimbanguism theology developed and led to his followers' revolt against the Belgium power and taxes. This theology consisted of interpreting the biblical message into a language that was meaningful to Africans but taking into account the values of their culture. This made Kimbangu develop forms of thought and action that made sense to his own people and communities. Kimbangu's preaching is now known to have been one of the factors that led to the end of the colonial era.[18]

By trying to establish how the church managed to maintain its missiological task during the war, the study will compare the state of church missions before and during the war. The descriptive missiological study of the response of the CBCA to the war in Eastern Congo aims to identify continuities and discontinuities between the church's missions before and during the war in Eastern Congo in the period 1990 to 2011.

---

13. Ott, Strauss and Tennent, *Encountering Theology of Mission*, xv.
14. Ott, *Mission of the Church*, xv.
15. Ott, Strauss and Tennent, *Encountering Theology of Mission*, xix.
16. Ott, *Mission of the Church*, xv.
17. Jesse, "Missiological Study," 30.
18. Jesse, 30–32.

1.3 Objectives

In order to find an answer to the main research question, the following objectives are set for this study:

1. To Draw on existing knowledge from earlier Christian views regarding the church's encounter with violence and war that can be applied to the contemporary context of war.
2. To describe the context of the CBCA and war in Eastern Congo between 1990 and 2011.
3. To identify the biblical Christian response to violence and war.
4. To describe the CBCA's response to the wars from 1990 to 2011 by
   (a) identifying the nature of missions before and during the war in Eastern Congo from 1990 to 2011, and
   (b) synthesizing the experiences of Christian leaders involved in missions in the context of war.
5. To discuss the implications for our understanding of church's encounter with war.
6. To determine the implications of the study for the CBCA in the DRC and beyond.

1.4 Purpose and Value

The purpose of this research is to document the relationships that can be established between the CBCA's missions before and during the war in Eastern Congo in the period 1990 to 2011. The study is primarily a descriptive and evaluative project. It seeks to describe the church's response in its historical context and to assess it theologically.

The value of this study is that it contributes to an understanding of the church in action, its ministry and mission and provides an understanding of the theology that underlies the church's mission in the context of the war. In order to show that, it avails itself of information from African scholars and missionaries where and when relevant to the topic. The insight gained from the experience of war in Eastern Congo will allow a greater contribution toward the existing theories of missions. The study will also reveal what has been missing in existing theories of war and the church's understanding of its missionary task in the context of war. The mandate to make disciples of all nations is not limited to the action of making converts as the role of the church in society in the face of war and violence is translated by its actions (ministry and mission) and the theology that underlies these actions. The documented stories of Christian leaders involved in missions before and during the war in Eastern Congo will bring new insight into how ministry is to be conducted in the context of war.

1.5 Limitations and Delimitations

The data collection focuses on (1) the assessment of the topic from the perspective of biblical experiences or texts and (2) empirical data on Eastern Congo. The study of the ethnic and geographic context of Eastern Congo will cover the period from 1990 to 2011. It will particularly focus on the so-called war "of liberation" that was led by the AFDL Movement in 1996 and some inter-ethnic clashes around Goma such as the so-called "Kanyarwanda" war that occurred in 1990. The interest here is the connection with the political war in Eastern Congo. The historical and ethnic context is very important, because many authors have written on the war in Eastern Congo portraying it, for their political agenda, as far from the truth and reality of its context. This study will provide a different perspective on that truth and reality.

Eastern Congo is commonly considered as consisting of a North Kivu, South Kivu, Maniema and Oriental province. However, only a few selected locations or areas were targeted by the study due to their level of vulnerability to war from 1990 to 2011, namely, Goma town, Masisi territory and Rutshuru territory. The wars to be investigated will be the outbreaks/conflicts of the war around Goma town. Reference to the war in Bunia will be made as a way to cross-check the information in order to see whether the church survived the war due to its ethnic character or whether it "became defensive and withdrew from the world" during the wars and found its refuge and "comfort in becoming sanctuaries, places of refuge in hostile environment(s)"[19] or for any other reason.

Due to the complexity of the Church Corporation in Congo, the study will only focus on the CBCA (referred to as "the church") with specific attention paid to its three church districts in Goma, Buturande and Bambo. The

---

19. Mwikamba, "Shift in Mission," 12.

local church of CBCA Bunia in the Oriental province will also be selected for data collection for the reason mentioned above. It will capture the experiences of Christian leaders involved in mission before and during the war in Eastern Congo.

In this work "missions" is used "to describe various specific efforts of the church to carry out the task of mission in the world, usually related to the spread of the Gospel and the expansion of the Kingdom of God"[20] and, therefore, it is "everything the church is sent in the world to do."[21] The scope of missions in this work is also limited to the variables in the conceptual framework of oral witness, discipleship and involvement in social concerns.

1.6 Presuppositions

The presuppositions that underlie the study are the following:

1. Ethnic conflicts are acknowledged to be one of the critical causes of the perpetuation of war in Eastern Congo, which has challenged the church's understanding of its unity in Christ.
2. Different wars over the two decades of study had different causes although it remains connected to ethnicity which provided a long-term opportunity for the church to define itself in the context of war.
3. Scripture is adequate in addressing human realities such as war, ethnicity, migrations and everything that pertains to war.
4. Church mission is done according to an existing understanding of the nature of mission, which may be either explicit (written) or not. Due to a context of war a written and developed understanding of mission will be limited.
5. This book will concentrate on wars carried out in Eastern Congo. The former Kivu province that was split into three provinces (i.e. North Kivu, South Kivu and Maniema) plus the former Eastern, Oriental Province are commonly known as Eastern Congo. Goma, the capital city and the most affected city in the North

---

20. Ott, Strauss and Tennent, *Encountering Theology of Mission*, xv.
21. Beals, *People for His Name*, 3.

Kivu province is the crossroad for understanding the war in Eastern Congo.

1.7 Conceptual Framework

In this study, the conceptual framework "limits the conceptual elements to be covered."[22] A conceptual framework being "a concise description of the phenomenon under study accompanied by a graphic or visual depiction of the major variables of the study"[23] has been chosen to present a sketch revealing the possible interactions between dependent and independent variables.

In the sketch (figure 1 below), the study focuses on "the feasibility to control all the causes (independents variables) that may be affecting an outcome (dependent variable)."[24] It identifies the accurate and reliable formation of relationships among the experience of war, which is the independent variable, and the church missions, which is the dependent variable. An independent variable is defined as "an explanatory variable that can affect other (dependent) variables but cannot be affected by them."[25] The background variables consist of an ensemble of church's elements (ministry and mission). In this case, the Christian leader is central to lead the church response (i.e. the action and the theology) that involve church members in the implementation of the programs under existing church systems in order to accomplish the task of missions.

The experience of war is characterized by the war, clashes and violence that cause displacements, suffering and poverty. It is assumed that violence, suffering and poverty are sub-variables of, and causes and effects of, war. They together, therefore, constitute the context of war in which the church in Eastern Congo has been undertaken its missions. In other words, the dramatic cycle of conflicts, war, violence, migration and poverty form the context being explored. It is in that context of war that the church's response to the war represented in the sketch (figure 1) is represented in terms of the church action in ministry and mission and the theology that underlies the

---

22. Smith, *Academic Writing*, 142.
23. Mugenda, *Social Science*, 111.
24. Elliston, *Introduction to Missiological Research*, 77.
25. "Background Variable," Oxford Reference.

action. The study will proceed from the biblical views of missions discussed in chapter 4 to identify the oral witness, discipleship and involvement in social concerns as sub-variables of the independent variable, which is missions.

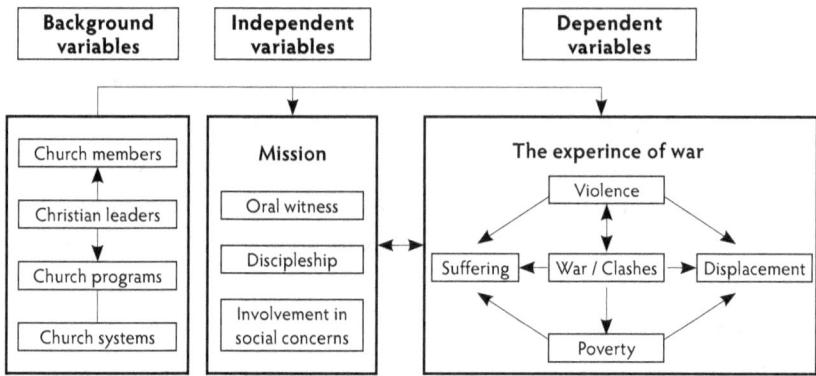

Figure 1: Conceptual framework of missions in the context of war

1.8 Design and Methodology

1.8.1 Research Design

Methodologies in research can differ depending on the field of research. Each methodology has its strengths as well as its weaknesses. This is a study in missiology, using a combination of descriptive, integrative and contextual methods or approaches. The use of descriptive research, which generally serves in theory development, provides needed information for the evaluative research part of the study[26] with the aim of leading the researcher in the discussion of the implication of an understanding of church and mission in the context of war.

The descriptive study involves the rigorous analysis of the research problem using a missiological research design approach. This approach "is an iterative process among five basic components: (1) the central research issue, (2) review of precedents research, (3) research methods, (4) findings and (5) recommendations."[27] Through that process, the study seeks to integrate

---

26. See Elliston, *Introduction to Missiological Research*, 68.
27. Elliston, xxi.

methods and insights from various fields of theological study. Elliston states that "descriptive research takes several significantly different forms and is supported by a wider range of research methods."[28] This research on church, war and mission is a church-related and integrative research as it includes historical research, survey with interviews and focus group discussions, exegetical studies and theological research.[29] In this way, the researcher does missiology as a contextual theology reflecting on the church mission as it expresses itself in contemporary praxis.[30]

The study purposively made use of descriptive methods, including survey research and historical research, the two strengthened by exegesis and theological assessment. The former is essential in interviews and focus group discussions; the latter supports this church-related research.[31] The evaluation part of the research used a kind of exegetical study in order to identify the biblical responses to war and violence. The methods used also agree with Stuart Bate's suggestions about the method in contextual missiology which presupposes that the reflection journey affirms theology as history, takes into account contextual theology, brings in the understanding of church and reflection as the guiding anthropology.[32]

This integrative approach to theological studies has been applied within systematic theology[33] and in practical theology of mission.[34] Scholars are also giving attention to issues of history and context in their exploration of the meaning of the biblical text, though we do not yet see a widely accepted integrative approach. An integrative approach is a helpful tool in this study.

This blend of integrative and contextual theology resembles Bevans' synthetic model of contextual theology quite closely. It gives special attention to culture and intercultural dynamics. God's revelation is "operative in one's own context, calling men and women to perfect that context through cultural

---

28. Elliston, 68.

29. See Elliston, 68.

30. See Bate, "Method in Contextual Missiology," 150.

31. Elliston, *Introduction to Missiological Research*, 68; Schensul, LeCompte, Nastasi, and Borgatti, *Enhanced Ethnographic Methods*, 51–114

32. Bate, "Method in Contextual Missiology," 150–85.

33. For example, Lewis and Demarest, *Integrative Theology*.

34. For example, Cameron, *Resourcing Mission*; Cameron and Duce, *Researching Practice*; Elliston, *Introduction to Missiological Research*; Browning, *Fundamental Practical Theology*.

transformation and social change."³⁵ One of the weaknesses of Bevans' summarized model is its limitation to systematic theological reflection. His recent idea of "the six constants of mission"³⁶ gives a wider understanding of his contextual theology of mission with an emphasis on the church and its mission strategy and a "model developed as a prophetic dialogue" in its "particular context where faith is to be preached."³⁷

The descriptive approach used in the study takes into account integrative theology. According to Lewis and Demarest, "the method of integrative theology is biblically grounded, historically related, culturally sensitive, person-centered, and profoundly related to life."³⁸ This

> method seeks to involve the reader (of the Scripture) in six distinct steps . . . defining the problem for inquiry, learning alternative approaches from scholars, discovering and formulating a coherent summary of biblical teaching, apologetic interaction, and applying these convictions to Christians and ministry.³⁹

The study also acknowledges that Lewis and Demarest have limitations for they focus mostly on doctrine, whereas Bevans focuses on contextual theology and considers both the biblical context of the message and the particular context of the message's recipient.⁴⁰

The study, therefore, gives full attention to the specific context of the CBCA encountering war in the Eastern Congo from 1990 to 2011. It includes an empirical survey of the experiences and views of a sample of church leaders within this context. It engages the opinions of other Christians encountering or reflecting on similar realities (through a combination of historical perspective and literature review). It also engages a number of biblical passages relevant to the same realities. These diverse views are finally integrated into an updated understanding of issues related to church, war and missions as well as suggestions about their implications for the practice of the church. It is to be noted that the process of theological assessment of biblical texts

---

35. Bevans, *Models of Contextual Theology*, 84–5.
36. Bevans, Constants in Context, 317–18.
37. Bevans, 332, 350.
38. Lewis and Demarest, *Integrative Theology*, 9.
39. Lewis and Demarest, 26.
40. Bevans, *Models of Contextual Theology*, 84–85.

is related, in some ways, to the steps of integrative theology. In this case, for example, the researcher identified the issue for each of the biblical texts, assessed the issue based on various biblical and theological scholarship, and identified the relevance for the text in the context of war in Eastern Congo.

Although Lewis and Demarest describe the integrative approach to theology as being culturally sensitive and person-centered, the methodology used in this study is stronger in context.[41] For example, critical contextualization calls for "the exegesis of culture, the exegesis of Scripture and the Hermeneutical bridge, and a critical response."[42] The fact that missiology, while "primarily focused on God's mission for humankind, ranges across three areas: the physical environment in which people live, their socio-cultural environment, and their spiritual environment"[43] requires missiological research to employ other methods that allowed the researcher to understand the church's missions in that particular context.

The introductory chapter of the study states the background, the problem statement, the research objectives and research questions, its values as well as the study limitations and the conceptual framework of the study. In this section, the design and methodology were presented and discussed. Chapter 2 presents the literature review as it is considered to be a better way to present "the review of precedent research"[44] and draws existing knowledge from earlier Christian views regarding the church encountering violence and war that can be applied to the contemporary context of war. The biblical view of missions (see chapter 4) is also written from different scholars' points of view. At this level, the aim of the study is to establish gaps in existing knowledge on missions in the context as stipulated earlier.

The historical and ethnic context of Eastern Congo (see chapter 3) was done prior to field data collection in order to describe the context regarding the church and war in Eastern Congo between 1990 and 2011. Historical research being part of contextual missiology, the construction of this chapter (presenting the context of the research) did not utilize the "SEE, JUDGE, ACT

---

41. Lewis and Demarest, *Integrative Theology*, 9.
42. Hiebert, *Anthropological Reflections*, 89.
43. Elliston, *Introduction to Missiological Research*, 3.
44. Elliston, xxi.

methodology"[45] but found a more appropriate historical research method that helped to picture the referred context of war. The information for chapter 4 was adopted in accordance with the following four steps of historical research: "heuristic step," "critique step," "synthesis step" and "exposition step."[46] The aim is to draw the connection between wars in Eastern Congo. This sets the foundation or describes the context being addressed by the study in order to avoid misunderstanding by the reader who may have read some books written with a political agenda. Since historical research "explores the crossing of cultural and religious boundaries with regards to mission history,"[47] the last four chapters connect the historical and ethnic context of Eastern Congo with the understanding of the church in that context of war.

The study also attempts to reflect upon the experience of faith that is lived in a particular context.[48] That reflection consists of a theological assessment (chapter 4) focusing on biblical texts taken from the NT (Matt 5:38–45, Acts 18:1–4 and Heb 10:32–34) and draws the biblical responses to church, war and violence. The strength of these passages is that they help to assess (1) Jesus's attitude and position on war; (2) the early Christians' experience of war and the movement that occurred in the church, assessing the church's mission both in the new locations where church members had migrated and that of the remnant church; then (3) the mission of the young church's "planting" experience during war by focusing on the early Christians' experience in Hebrews. It presents an analysis of the effects of the misuse of power in the Roman Empire with the experience of the believers' displacement under Caesar's edict in Acts 18. Possible connections with ethnicity in the Roman church in Romans is involved in the assessment at this level. In Mathew 5:38–45, Jesus refers to the retaliation law of conflict and the prevention of clashes or war in Exodus 21:24 and Leviticus 24:20 which also appear in the Hammurabi code, which existed before Moses. Hebrews 10:32–34 mainly deals with the survival of the Christian faith and enduring sufferings as one of the outcomes of war.

---

45. Bate, "Method in Contextual Missiology," 150–85.
46. Deiros, "Historical Research," 136–40.
47. Simon, "Mission as Frontier-Crossing," 97.
48. See Bate, "Method in Contextual Missiology," 150–85.

Knowing that the mission of the church expresses itself in praxis, Bate adopted Bevans's praxis model and chose a "missiological circle" and a "pastoral circle" to collect information.[49] However, in this study, the use of "narrative inquiry" is preferred and is "applied to in-depth interviews"[50] and gave room to qualitative data collection "to allow the researcher assemble a composite picture of a group's experiences."[51] Information from these interviews and information from focus group discussions will be used in the construction of chapter 5 and chapter 6. This step identifies the nature of mission before and during the war in response to the question on how the CBCA responded to the recent wars between 1990 and 2011. It also captures the stories of the experience of missions before the war commenced in 1990 and the stories of the experience of missions during the war from 1990 to 2011.

Since interviews on the nature of mission were mainly in-depth interviews, only four long-serving pastors in the selected churches from the three selected church districts were included in the study as respondents. Two of the four from each church were those who pastored the church before the war and the other two were selected as those who pastored the same church during the war from 1990 to 2011. Focus group discussions involved church leaders of the churches selected to be part of the research.

The method in contextual missiology or theology involves "understanding church,"[52] which requires experience and contextual theology. Accordingly, it was decided to develop and propose a chapter titled "Toward an Understanding of Church and Mission in the Context of War" based on the experience of the church in Eastern Congo. Chapter 7 provides the implications of the researcher's understanding of the church's encounter with war. A critical comparison of the church's undertaking of missions before and during the war was evaluated through the lenses of the biblical responses of the church to war and violence together with the theoretical models of missions. This critical analysis, discussion and theological reflection agree that

---

49. Bate, 150–185; Bevans, *Models of Contextual Theology*, 63.
50. Marshall and Rossman, *Designing Qualitative Research*, 153.
51. LeCompte and Schensul, *Designing and Conducting*, 118.
52. Bate, "Method in Contextual Missiology," 150–185.

"theology arises from reflection on experience."[53] It includes the following (numbering corresponds with that of the sections headings in chapter 7):

- 7.2. The experience of missions in Eastern Congo and the biblical responses to church, violence and war
- 7.2.1. Tensions between the local missiologies and Matthew 5:38–45
- 7.2.2. Tensions between the local missiologies and Acts 18:1–4
- 7.2.3. Tensions between the local missiologies and Hebrews 10:32–34
- 7.3. Missions in Eastern Congo and Contemporary Missiological Models
- 7.3.1. David Bosch's emerging models and kenosis theology
- 7.3.2. Samuel Escobar's migration model
- 7.3.3. Stephen Bevans's model of constants in context

Schreiter's definition of a "local theology" as "the reflection of Christians upon the Gospel in light of their own circumstances" is considered as most applicable to this study and "much more attention is paid to how those circumstances shaped the response to the Gospel."[54] Local theologies identified from the experience of the church in Eastern Congo were compared and contrasted with insights from the theological assessment of the missions' biblical response to church, war and violence. By so doing, the researcher, for example, discusses the tensions between local theologies and Matthew 5:38–45 and explores the impact of worldview on theology and syncretism.

With regard to theoretical models of missions, the models of Bosch, Escobar and Bevans were chosen because these scholars and their work represent the wider theological thinking that has made key contributions to the debate of the contextualization of the gospel especially in the area of missiology in the context of violence, suffering and migration.[55] Bosch's "emerging model of missions" in *Transforming Mission* and his "kenosis theology" concept in his lecture on "The Vulnerability of Mission" are used to make

---

53. Lukose, *Contextual Missiology*, 275.

54. Schreiter, *Constructing Local Theologies*, 1.

55. Bosch, *Transforming Mission*; "Vulnerability of Mission"; Escobar, *Time for Mission*; and Bevans, *Constants in Context*; "Themes and Questions."

sense of the war in question.⁵⁶ Samuel Escobar was chosen for his "migration model," which presents strengths and gaps to be filled by the experience of the church in Eastern Congo.⁵⁷ The choice of Bevans was motivated by two reasons: first, Bevans is a Catholic mission scholar who introduced the thinking about "mission being a prophetic dialogue."⁵⁸ It was decided, after thinking through the meaning of that dialogue, that its ecclesiological aspect brings to the debate the need for a philosophy of mission as a response to the context. And second, Bevans's idea of mission as prophetic dialogue is foundational to his suggestion of a model of mission in a migrant context has been used to compare and contrast the experience of the eastern Congolese internally displaced churches.⁵⁹

1.8.2 Population and Sampling

According to Celia Reaves, a "population consists of every member of a particular group, and you could measure every member of a particular group."⁶⁰ This study has Eastern Congo as its specific focus area and the CBCA as its specific study group. Pastors who had pastored churches before and during the war and other church leaders are the target population for the study. Two local churches, in each of the three selected church districts, Goma, Buturande and Bambo, are involved as the field for data collection. The first church in Bunia town (CBCA Bunia) is incorporated for the specific reason of verifying whether there is any relationship between ethnicity and the survival of the church during war. Therefore, the seven local churches selected are CBCA Virunga and CBCA Birere in the Goma district, CBCA Buturande and CBCA Rwanguba in the Buturande district, CBCA Bambo and CBCA Mutanda in the Bambo district and CBCA Bunia in the Beni district.

Sampling for the qualitative aspect of the research is purposive. This approach allows the researcher to access information that applies to the research objectives. A minimum of four pastors who pastored each of the seven local churches participated in the research. Apart from the total of forty-three

---

56. Bosch, *Transforming Mission*, 363–367; "Vulnerability of Mission," 357.
57. Escobar, *Time for Mission*.
58. Bevans, *Constants in Context*, 322.
59. Bevans, "Themes and Questions," 13.
60. Celia Reaves, *Quantitative Research*, 94.

pastors, a maximum of twenty-two people in each of the selected churches who are or have been in church leadership participated in group discussions. These were both male and female and were all Christian leaders and representative of the women's ministry, children's ministry, deacons, elders, men's ministry, youth ministry and from the current pastoral team. This chosen sample was relevant to this study, which bore a qualitative character and focused on the CBCA church leaders of the church districts involved in the study. Even though Congolese churches may be clouded with members, it is good to note that church members were not concerned as participants in the study. Therefore, the selected participants to this study, from selected churches rural areas and only two from Goma and one from Bunia, constitute a sample that is relevant to this particular study.

1.8.3 Data Collection

In-depth interviews, narrative inquiries and group interviews were used to collect field data while biblical exegesis was used for the theological assessment and the historical research techniques: heuristic step, critic step, synthesis step and exposition step – all used to collect data for historical and ethnic contextual understanding. The data collection techniques used are the following.

Interviews

An interview consists of "two people talking together about some topic which is of interest to them both."[61] The in-depth interviews in the study are mainly semi-structured interviews. The guides for the semi-structured interviews were "pre-formulated with open-ended questions and the answers can be fully expanded at the discretion of both the interviewer and the interviewee."[62] It allowed the researcher to follow leads arising during the interview while keeping the focus on the topic variables. Two kinds of interviews were conducted by the researcher: individual interviews and group interviews.

The first kind of interview, individual, targeted pastors who pastored local churches before the war began in 1990 and those who pastored the same

---

61. LeCompte and Schensul, *Designing and Conducting*, 17.
62. Schensul, Schensul and LeCompte, *Essential Ethnographic Methods*, 149.

churches during the war. Open-ended interview questions were used to guide the recipients to identify the nature of missions before the war.

A focus group discussion was held with church leaders of each of the recipients' churches selected to be part of the research. This, being a setting "where the researcher works with several people simultaneously, rather than just one,"[63] helped to triangulate the information and strengthen the information concerning the nature of mission during wartime. It is important to note that focus groups mainly dealt with the war period. Three focus group discussions were done on a triangulation basis in each of the local churches. So, in each of the churches, the participants who formed focus group discussions represented three categories: pastors who served in the church during the war period, women leaders of the target areas, and targeted members of the church. Each group had a maximum of ten to twelve people. Focus group discussions were conducted after the interviews. Both interviews and focus group discussions were recorded and then accurately transcribed by the researcher.

Narrative inquiry

In this approach, "narratives obtained from different people and sources can be used to assemble a composite picture of a group's experiences."[64] Narrative inquiry was "applied to in-depth interviews"[65] to capture the experiences or synthesize the experiences of Christian leaders involved in missions in the context of war. Therefore, "it involves a mutual and sincere collaboration for a full participation in the storytelling, retelling, and reliving of personal experiences"[66] from pastors involved, resulting from the openness and trust between the researcher and pastors being interviewed. Field notes, interview transcriptions or any audio tape recording was used to capture the experiences of the participants. Prior to the interview, the researcher asked for permission to record the information and undertook to provide the information to be published. Research participants were given appropriate and accessible information about the purpose, methods and intended use of the research

---

63. Punch, *Introduction*, 171.
64. LeCompte and Schensul, *Designing and Conducting*, 118.
65. Marshall and Rossman, *Designing Qualitative Research*, 153.
66. Marshall and Rossman, 153.

in order to obtain their consent and voluntary participation.[67] The researcher made sure confidentiality has been kept and consequently omitted the names of the participants. This was because "research ethics involve requirements on daily work, the protection of dignity of subjects and the publication of the information in the research."[68]

Historical research techniques

This approach was used only to write the chapter on the historical and ethnic context of Eastern Congo (chapter 4). It followed four techniques, which constitute the four steps of historical research: (1) the heuristic step, which "as a technique, deals with the establishment of rules to obtain evidence from the documents that give testimony of past events. To obtain evidence from documents means to transform them into sources"[69]; (2) the critique step, which is mainly the stage that helped the researcher to critically and qualitatively analyze the information; (3) the synthesis step "which consists of the coherent ordaining of the material collected and the resulting historic 'construction' or 'creation'"[70]; and (4) the exposition step, in which the researcher put the results obtained through historical research in the form of a detailed and extensive written document, which is the literary work constituting the chapter on the historical and ethnic context of Eastern Congo between 1990 and 2011.

Archive and secondary data

Relevant secondary data was obtained from documents at the head office of CBCA in Goma, the three church districts' office archives and local church archives. These were, for example, statistical data, letters, constitution, reports and church minutes.

1.8.4 Data Analysis

Data analysis focused on a systematic analysis of qualitative information accessed from interviews and focus group discussions. The researcher used

---

67. cf. Halej, "Ethics in Primary Research," 3.
68. Fouka and Mantzorou, "What Are Major Ethical Issues," 3.
69. Deiros, "Historical Research," 136.
70. Deiros, 137.

the Weft QDA Software for the analysis of qualitative data. The SPSS package was used in case of any quantitative information.

1.8.5 Validation and Verification

Validity is key to the measurement of information used in a research. Measurement validity means "the extent to which an instrument measures what it claimed to measure; an indicator is valid to the extent that it empirically represents the concept it reports to measure."[71] The methods used for data collection are reliable for the qualitative research.

To increase the level of validity and reliability of the information, the researcher made sure participants were selected with respect to eligibility criteria, which were those who pastored a church for at least five consecutive years in a period of time before or during war and leaders (men and women) who had led the church for at least one term. The researcher used a semi-structured interview that took care of the triangulation approach in the designing of interview questions with respect to variables being surveyed.

Prior to field data collection, the researcher organized training for his research assistants to help familiarize them with the research tools and techniques and the manipulation of qualitative data, software and the use of any available data recorder. During the whole process from data collection to data analysis, the researcher cross-checked information given to avoid possible bias that may have occurred in the process and affect data interpretation. The researcher made sure each pastor was interviewed in the language they felt comfortable with, and questionnaires/checklists were translated into Kiswahili and French.

Furthermore, validity was sought in the process of verification in historical research as well. The researcher compared information from different sources using triangulation.

1.9 Summary

Chapter 1 of this work identifies the major problem to be investigated and the design and methodology applied. This study develops an understanding of the church's response to war and violence and the theology that underlies

---

71. Punch, *Introduction*, 97.

the church's action (ministry and mission). This understanding is extracted from an examination of the way the eastern Congolese church experienced the war. The study focused on the mission of the church and exploring how this was affected by the war.

This chapter identifies the need to add to the existing little understanding of missions and guidance for the eastern Congolese affected by war. This church called and carried out the task of mission in the context of the Congolese destructive wars in the period between 1990 to 2011, although it did survive the war, it dealt with tension between a world affected by warfare and its mandate to make disciples. A central research question addresses the issue of how the war in Eastern Congo between 1990 and 2011 affected the understanding and practice of missions in the CBCA. Six focused research questions are presented as means that the study will use to draw the structured way to respond to the research main question.

The next chapter presents the literature review and is followed by a presentation of a biblical view of missions in chapter 3. As indicated earlier in the methodological section, chapter 4 will focus on the historical and ethnic context of Eastern Congo and describe the context within which the study should be understood, thus responding to the first research question. Responses to question 4 are found in the two chapters dealing with the description of church missions in the context of war in Eastern Congo (chapters 6 and 7). In relation to question 5, chapter 8 presents a contemporary model for missions in the context of war that incorporates experiential, biblical and missiological perspectives based on the experience of the church in Eastern Congo and the biblical model. The concluding chapter, therefore, summarizes the study and its results and presents the implications of the study for the church in the DRC.

CHAPTER 2

Church, Mission, and War – Literature Review

2.1 Introduction

Much has been written on the subject of church and war from various perspectives. This chapter examines literature related to church and war in order to draw existing knowledge from earlier Christian views regarding the church encountering violence and war that can be applied to the contemporary context of war. The particular focus is on theories and views on war, church missions and war, views on migration and mission and war as an avenue for church missions and advocating for peace and justice. The chapter concludes with a summary of the key points and identifies some gaps in existing knowledge.

2.2 Theories and Views on War

2.2.1 Just War Theory

According to Michael Buttler, "Military philosophy dating at least to the works of Sun Tzu has characterized the war as a definitive experience in international relations and an inherently political act."[1] According to him, "few

---

1. Buttler, "U.S. Military Intervention in Crisis," 226.

subjects receive more attention or invite more controversy than the study of war and its causes, import, and justifications."[2]

One of the most popular theories on war is the "just war" theory. R. A. Markus presents this theory as Augustine's legacy to the medieval period. According to Augustine's early ideas, "human society, being part of the universe, must be ordered in terms of the same hierarchies of sensible and intelligible, of bodies, souls and God."[3] This, however, cannot be taken as a foundation for the just war theory. This church father clearly was trying to think critically about his ideas of the *City of God* in which he might have advocated for "a decisive turning away from the readiness with which others were prepared to identify themselves with values and institutions of the society."[4] Instead, as Markus observes, "Augustine did not repudiate the possibility, even the necessity, of fighting a 'just war'; . . . what he came to repudiate was a whole set of attitudes . . . which encouraged Christians to invest wars with a religious significance."[5] The context in which Augustine served was also that of Roman Empire dictatorship.

Trying to demonstrate Augustine's association with the just war theory, Thomas Aquinas specified the three conditions set by Augustine for a just war: legitimate authority must be received from the sovereign, a just cause for the attack must be present, and a rightful intention should guide the proceedings.[6] To a certain extent, these conditions introduce the idea of Christian individuals who are involved in the military, politics and the like who had the responsibility to provide peace and security in order to ensure that any war they enroll in is a "just war." The idea also excludes the aspect of church/Christian self-defense because war was given a sovereign aspect.[7]

It is clear that Augustine was encouraging Christians to promote Christian distinctiveness, not by a Christian "pacifism" but a serious involvement in defending the integrity and good values that have to govern a nation. So, he is not telling the church to take up arms and overthrow the government. On the contrary, he encourages Christians to fight for righteousness, justice and

---

2. Buttler, 226.
3. Markus, "Saint Augustine's Views," 3–4.
4. Augustine, *City of God*, 176.
5. Markus, 12.
6. Buttler, "U.S. Military Intervention in Crisis," 231.
7. Peach, "Alternative to Pacifism?," 153.

integrity in a corrupted world. Charles Reed supports that view. According to him,

> To argue that nonviolent resistance is morally more acceptable than war and that it offers the best chance of securing harmonious relationships between parties can lead to a prohibition of war under any circumstance. In some instances, war can be preferable to surrender or living with the consequences of a tyrannical oppressor.[8]

The just war theory has been challenged by many theologians, apart from those advocating for nonviolence, in the place of war. "A few feminist scholars have found the just war inadequate, yet their counterproposals are also deficient."[9] Peach identifies that their criticisms of the just war theory are clustered around the following concerns:

> Its relation to realism; its failure to insist that all criteria have been satisfied in accordance with rigorous standards, especially in relation to attempting nonviolent alternatives; its tendency to abstraction and dichotomize reality in accordance with gendered distinctions; and the priority it accords to the state and to state authority vis-a-vis the individual.[10]

It is curious that these scholars' criticism of the just war theory focuses on the exclusion of women from decision-making and participation in war rather than on the negative impact of war, whether just or unjust, on the women and children.

Similar to feminist scholars' criticisms, which to some extent ignore women's vulnerability, the church in Eastern Congo seems dormant in fighting injustice, ill-treatment and corruption. At the same time, church members are being killed and others raped. It does not have a plan for discipling its members who are called to advocate peace. Milfred Minatrea's questionnaire reveals that a missional Church "encourages its members to participate in 'secular' social groups in the community."[11] This includes political and

---

8. Reed, *Just War?*, 28.
9. Peach, "Alternative to Pacifism?," 152.
10. Peach, 155–56.
11. Minatrea, *Shaped by God's Heart*, 184–95.

social groups, and when "war may be an element necessary to peace, rather than completely separate from it,"[12] it is the role of the church to advise the government for a strict respect of just war criteria for peace agreements and principles.[13] The church should involve its members (including women) to advocate against the impacts of war, which affect women and children, as the government is called to legitimately protect its people and land.

2.2.2 Pacifism theory

Addressing the issue of pacifism, Bainton says "that pacifism characterized the early church is evidenced from general abstention from military service, although the Thundering Legion and individual Christians were found in the imperial armies."[14] This view originated from the "Historic Peace Churches, that is Mennonites, Quakers, Church of the Brethren which has held, for four centuries, that all war is sin."[15] Therefore, pacifists argue that "war is to be rejected under any and all circumstances"[16] to avoid suffering and bloodshed caused by violence and war.

In contrast to the just war theory, this view is not practical in the context of war. Military service is part of a whole range of services that can provide justice to the marginalized. General abstention from such service by the church is trying to be "defensive and withdraw from the world" and finding its refuge in "sanctuaries, places of refuge in hostile environment(s)."[17] During revolutionary times, such as in war, both Christians and non-Christians are candidates for peace, social justice and harmony. Peace is kept by armed forces in war zones, displaced people camps and in secured zones. Therefore, if Christians have the mandate for holistic mission, it is imperative that, apart from advising the government on how to handle an armed conflict, the church points its members to its position on whether they may enroll as individuals in the army and be involved in military service or not. The church should even think of being called to minister holistically to the army and their families.

---

12. Peach, "Alternative to Pacifism?," 153.
13. Buttler, "U.S. Military Intervention," 231.
14. Bainton, quoted in Koenig, "Christian Attitudes toward War," 73.
15. Swartley and Kreider, "Pacifist Christianity," 38.
16. Charles, *Between Pacifism and Jihad*, 19.
17. Nasimiyu-Wasike and Waruta, *Mission in African Christianity*, 12.

In the case of Congo, there is a chaplain for every military brigade who is supposed to minister to the force's members and families. It is the role of the church to support such ministry missions in the context of war and armed conflicts. On the other hand, it becomes complicated for the church to be involved in rebellion and armed groups while encouraging ministry among rebels and militia groups. The church prefers to use pacifism theory in that case. The gospel that is used to witness to armed groups may have little, if any, value for the church in a war zone such as in Eastern Congo.

2.2.3 Crusade/Holy War

This is the "militaristic" view of war, sometimes called the "political realist" view, or religious such as the jihadist or crusader-view of war.[18] According to J. Daryl Charles, in a holy war, "no moral restraints beyond political expediency or the 'Command of God' need to be applied."[19] This kind of crusade, often called "holy wars" in the religious arena, started in the ancient Near East where the "ancient civilizations of the Near East from Egypt to Assyria all possessed gods of wars, and their ruling dynasties all claimed their help and authority in the battle."[20] It is true that for this kind of crusade "if people worship gods and fight wars, they expect the former to take interest in the latter."[21] However, it is also clear that in the historical religious wars the Muslim' Jihad has maintained that perspective while the Christian crusades, although they had all elements of war, included missionary conquests.

During the medieval period, the nature of missions took an intermediate state which caused missiological reforms that occurred in the next historical period. Bosch identifies a shift from evangelism to "the text being applied to forced conversion (or at least baptism) of pagans and Jews," the aim of mission being to provide an "assignment of everybody and everything in heaven and on earth a place in the universe, in such a way that the whole constituted a perfect synthesis with no loose ends."[22] In his view, the church shifted from "being oppressed to being the oppressor."[23]

---

18. Charles, *Between Pacifism and Jihad*, 19.
19. Charles, 19.
20. Partner, *God of Battle*, 1.
21. Partner, 1.
22. Bosch, *Transforming Mission*, 236–38.
23. Bosch, 237.

The church in the medieval period, consequently, took the direction of conquest, forcing Jews and others to become members in the absence of any spiritual conversion. This kind of approach is dangerous. It transforms missions from the Great Commission, to disciple the nations, into a political and geographical occupation by Christianity. Following a similar practice, those who transmitted oral history to the researcher's generation revealed that early missionaries in Eastern Congo implemented this approach of geographic occupation to establish the church in new locations. The fact that they were both colonial administrators and missionaries gave them the ability to use the baptism certificate as both an identity card (ID) and a proof of being a member of the body of Christ when they were not. The certificate was provided by the missionary at baptism with the requirement to go to new locations and erect chapels.

Jihads and crusades precipitated current conflicts between Muslims and Christians that have caused instability in many nations, and are one of the primary rationalizations for terrorism. So, responding to the Great Commission by geographic occupation or by any kind of war is unbefitting to the demands of the gospel of Jesus, especially in a context such as that of Eastern Congo where identity conflict is a major issue.

On the other hand, as Jihadists and/or crusaders were responding to any occupation by Muslims, the church may have considered a crusade to be any militant Christian resistance to occupation. For the last two decades, the former Rwandan Republican Forces, formerly called "Interahamwe" and today called "Democratic Forces for the Liberation of Rwanda" (FDRL) has found refuge in the forest of Eastern Congo. Among them are pastors who have guns to defend their groups and consequently contribute to destroying forest and fauna, and cause "prejudice to the rights and obligations of others and the communities."[24]

2.2.4 Nonviolence Theory

According to John Yoder, "Nonviolence is a much younger term, although some of the attitudes and principles it designates are ancient."[25] He uses it to "designate nothing more than the pragmatically rational rejection of violence

---

24. O'Riordan, "Towards a Theology of Peace," 153.
25. Yoder, *War of the Lamb*, 85.

in attitude or action."²⁶ Seán O'Riordan goes further in describing the theology of nonviolence, saying that it "has contributed to the theology of peace."²⁷ According to *Gaudium et Spes*, as quoted by O'Riordan, this contribution is

> ... for those who in vindicating rights renounce violent action and have recourse to means of defence which are, moreover, available to weaker people also -although it adds the qualification, provided this can be done without prejudice to the rights and obligations of others or of the community.²⁸

It is true that a nonviolent approach is accessible for all classes of people, especially the weaker people. Its advantage is that it does protect the lives of the protesters from harm. Its weakness, however, is that nonviolence is exposed to the risk to provide "prejudice to the rights and obligations of others or of the community."²⁹

There could also be a relationship between nonviolence and pacifism. Charles found this correlation in pacifists who "absolutize the distinction between nonviolent and violent resistance."³⁰ He judges it as "a morally absurd position." On the one hand, it seems difficult to disagree with him since the context is to be considered in every case where justice is needed.

On the other hand, however, nonviolence is sometimes "powerless" and may not have much effect on a tyrannical dominion – although some would think it important for change, as in the case of Mahatma Gandhi in India.³¹ It is also possible that the effect may be delayed or unobserved or might be indirect for present and future generations. In Eastern Congo, for example, people suffered quietly under the tyranny of the M23 for a whole year but the nonviolent communities were being killed and raped by rebels on a daily basis. Rebels did not stop doing so because the church in that zone was nonviolent and pacifistic.

---

26. Yoder, 85.
27. O'Riordan, "Towards a Theology of Peace," 153.
28. In O'Riordan, 153.
29. See O'Riordan, 153.
30. Charles, *Between Pacifism and Jihad*, 102.
31. Charles, 102.

2.2.5 The Church Fathers on War

While trying to explain his distinction between *The City of God* in contrast to the city of man, Augustine found that "the city of man, for the most part, is a city of contention with opinions divided by foreign wars and domestic quarrels and by demands for victories which either end in death or are merely momentary respites from further war."[32] Because "the purpose of war is peace," he set three conditions to be met for a war to be called a just war, that is, "a just cause, a legitimate authority, and a right intention."[33] For him, just war is the responsibility of the government to fight against foreign wars and internal quarrels in the country. This view rejects the involvement of rebels and guerrillas in war because they are not legitimate, though some may have a just cause and a right intention. Sheila Harty would further reveal that "the just war tradition begins with the presupposition against the use of force,"[34] which is to say that war should not be in search for peace except by a legal government.

Origen and Clement of Alexandria give a position that pertains to church members' action in war and threats exposing them to death. For Origen, in his letter to Ambrose, confidence should be to the extent of accepting martyrdom and should not compromise with the state.[35] It appears that for Origen, Christians should avoid politics during wartime, and if possible, resist any corrupt offer from the state during wartime. This position may not allow Christians in areas such as Eastern Congo, where some church leaders and Christians have taken sides in prevailing politics, to show their Christian distinctiveness and make a difference for change during wartime. Clement of Alexandria goes further in supporting his view with Heracleon's interpretation of Luke 12:11–12 and says that "confession before the authority is to be made only 'if necessary and if reason demands.'"[36]

Although some scholars argue that some of the early church fathers were opposed to war and killings,[37] general opinion holds that no church father

---

32. Augustine, *City of God*, 327.
33. Augustine, 327.
34. Harty, "Just-War Principles," 2.
35. Oulton and Chadwick, *Alexandrian Christianity*, 389.
36. Oulton and Chadwick, 389.
37. See Morey, *When Is It Right*; Morey, "Early Church and War."

critiqued the just war theory and that none of them argued for pacifism theory that deters Christian involvement in the military.

2.2.6 Protestant Reformers and War

Charles reveals that "the Protestant reformers Luther, Calvin, and Zwingli were unified in the Pauline conviction that the magistrate is ordained by the Almighty to wield the sword of justice" and that "Christians can carry out obedience to God as magistrates or soldiers, even when the spheres of Church and the state remain distinct realms."[38] It is true that they did advocate for integrity in any case and context but they advocated more for those involved in the military for the sake of peace and justice. This idea contradicts Luther's "two kingdom" theories that "subtracted temporal governance from the church, whose mission was only to persuade, preach the Gospel, teach, and counsel the people."[39] But it is in agreement with Calvin's view that "all wars are stirred by [God's] command, and . . . the soldiers armed at His will."[40]

2.2.7 Toward a Theory of Church Survival in the Context of War

Bainton argues that "The pagan authors and the Old Testament revealed three attitudes towards war and peace that were later to reappear in the Christian era: pacifism, the just war and the crusade."[41] Although the nonviolence theory is closer to pacifism theory, our critique is that all these theories are related to the position of the church toward war despite the fact that it is possible to find a biblical foundation for each. The main weakness of the theories is that none of them addresses the issue of the experience of war and the church's survival during wartime. They are all about attitudes and actions to be taken by individuals, government or community such as the church in its search for peace. This study aims to fill this gap in the church's understanding of war.

Antonius Robben and Carolyn Nordstrom who describe the "anthropology and ethnography of violence and sociopolitical conflicts" argue that "violence is a dimension of people's existence, not something external to society

---

38. Charles, "Just-War Moral Reflection," 598.
39. Krey, "Luther in Relation," 38.
40. Miller, *Calvin's Wisdom*, 375.
41. Bainton in Koenig, "Christian Attitudes toward War," 73.

and culture that 'happens' to people."⁴² For them, stories of people experiencing war in every country and context describe or "evoke everyday experiences of violence in its myriad manifestations, ranging from war to popular protest, from rape to the contestations surrounding rumors of violence, from moral discourses concerning conflict to the tragedies of senseless brutality."⁴³

Having researched the eastern Congolese context, which matches the one described above, it is reasonable to agree with them that "we want to focus on the experiential dimension of conflict, on the ways in which people live their lives in contexts marred by inescapable violence."⁴⁴ The survival of the church in such a context deserves attention in light of possible theory building based on its experience of war.

2.3 Church Missions and Wars

2.3.1 Identity Conflicts and the Transmission of the Christian Faith

The transmission of the Christian faith in Africa has faced the issue of identity, thus the construction of missiology affected by African tradition and culture. According to John Mbiti, "the quest for an African theology is rooted in the very process whereby the African Church communicates the Gospel in the context of African existence."⁴⁵ It is difficult to disagree with Mbiti's argument as supported by Kwame Bediako. In his book, Bediako argues that "the development of theological concern and the formulation of theological questions are closely linked as an inevitable by-product of a process of Christian self-definition."⁴⁶

During the Greco-Roman era dominated by the barbarian war/conflict of identity, Christian theology was developed in response to the transmission of the gospel in that context. That context reflects features that prevail in Eastern Congo today. Africa has had its traditions and religions that Mbiti calls "pre-Christian tradition" and qualifies them as "active ingredients . . . in making

---

42. Robben and Nordstrom, "Anthropology and Ethnography of Violence," 2.
43. Robben and Nordstrom, 2.
44. Robben and Nordstrom, 2.
45. Mbiti quoted in Bediako, *Theology and Identity*, 307.
46. Bediako, *Theology and Identity*, xv.

the Christian experience in modern Africa" because it is the "personality" of Africa.[47] It is clear that the "ingredients" together with the modern African context of war require Christian scholars to do a good exegetical interpretation of the gospel message and develop a Christian theology applied to the context of Eastern Congo.

Although in a very pragmatic way, this study develops a theory of missions in the context of war with a focus on the war in Eastern Congo. It is because there is a need to think of an exegetical analysis of the eastern Congolese traditions compared to the Greco-Roman context in order to understand, compare and contrast the survival of the church's missions in Eastern Congo during wartime. As the church fathers did, the church in Africa, particularly in Eastern Congo, seems not to have protected the "process of Christian self-definition,"[48] thus requiring Christian scholars to build a theology that translates the message of the gospel in the current context of war without distorting and promoting the Christian identity as a major characteristic of a united and multicultural church membership.

There is a discontinuity between the African cultural and religious heritage and Christian theology in modern Africa, which is not unrelated to the reasons referred to in the previous paragraph. Bediako argues that "the question of identity constitutes a 'hermeneutical key' which . . . leads to a deeper understanding of the modern situation in particular, and shows how modern context manifests features which are identifiable elsewhere in Christian history."[49] Again, it is difficult to disagree with that argument. Identity is stronger than cultural dynamism and is rooted in the cultural and religious heritage of a people. This idea is confirmed by Gerrie ter Haar who argues that "the definition of identity should result from the process of negotiation in which the people concerned participate . . . , but also that the formation of an ethnic identity is closely associated with the personal security of the individuals concerned."[50]

So, although culture is dynamic, culture and identity have features that determine Christianity in any particular context depending on how the gospel

---

47. Bediako, 333.
48. Bediako, xv.
49. Bediako, 426–27.
50. ter Haar, "Who Defines African Identity?," 269.

was or is bridged through that particular context. The context of war does not escape this reality. Therefore, a consistent and valid biblical study of the gospel message in the Graeco-Roman culture and context, although "closely linked to modern African context,"[51] is not sufficient to transmit the Christian faith. It is crucial that a serious study of the context be done prior to its transmission because the church has to bear in mind "the great principle of translatability which lies at the heart of Christian faith and is demonstrated both in the incarnation and in the Scriptures."[52] There is no incarnational ministry if there is no serious understanding of the context in which ministry is being done to communicate faith, which was first communicated through the Graeco-Roman culture and context that has to be translated to reach out to Africans in their particular cultures and contexts. It is the "quality of the response that matters"[53] rather than the focus on practice.

Vincent Mulago uses the term *Ntu* related to specific Bantu traits. His description reveals that in the Great Lakes region there is "the unity and indivisibility of the founding ancestor's blood."[54] To a certain extent, this is what features in wars in Eastern Congo where identity is connected to the "aspect of land tenure among the Africans" which respected "the role of the custodian of the family land,"[55] thus creating land conflicts in the region.

In much of African culture and particularly in Eastern Congo, identity is exclusively associated with the fact that the religion of a traditional tribal group cannot be transmitted to another tribal group. The reason is that "Traditional religions have no missionaries to propagate them, and one individual does not preach his religion to another."[56] Moreover, with the religion's priesthood and political power being held by the same ethnic leadership within a kingdom, no transfer of identity was possible, and if it did come about, these are the conflicts of land, power and occupation being dealt with today, which have even become political conflicts. Above all, "the demand

---

51. Bediako, *Theology and Identity*, xv.
52. Walls, *Missionary Movement*, 25.
53. Walls, 25.
54. Bujo, "Vincent Mulago," 19.
55. Ndung'u, "Land as the Source," 60.
56. Mugambi, *African Christian Theology*, 5.

for and resistance to autonomy"[57] have been one of the causes of ethnic wars or clashes in Eastern Congo.

With an emphasis on translation in the history of mission, Lamin Sanneh developed a deep analysis of the history that demonstrates a relationship between the culture of the mission field, the bridge of the gospel through culture and the cultural response to the gospel.[58] That relationship between the gospel and culture is a fruit of gospel "translatability" as it was first written from Jesus's spoken Aramaic to the written Greek translation. Therefore, the gospel started from its Hebrew tradition and was progressively translated to the Antiochian perspective, the Ephesian perspective and the Roman perspective. It gained progressive translation across cultures.

Lamin Sanneh attributes the development of missions in the early Christian century to the Jewish-Gentile frontier.[59] The effort to spread the gospel among the Hellenistic Gentiles came about not because it was a priority for the Jewish Christians, due to the Jews' egocentrism, but by God's sovereignty in sharing the gospel to many cultures through Pentecost. It is clear from Acts 2 that the Gentiles, Greek speakers, positively received the gospel of Jesus in their vernacular. This shift of identity from Judaism to pure Christianity was important for Jewish Christians and the Gentiles as well. The church in urban areas (Goma/DRC) does not escape the fact that the gospel was propagated within a Western culture that took place since the arrival of Western missionaries in the nineteenth century. A serious conflict exists regarding the nature of the gospel. To a certain extent, people attempt to present the gospel as in the time of the Western missionaries and ignore that the war has brought about a totally new context. Some people think that it should continue being presented the same way as it was a century ago and others believe that the gospel is not relevant to today's context of war that has affected the cities and rural areas. Therefore, the gospel needs to be contextualized so that it will be understood in the current context of war by people in the city, the rural areas and in war zones.

While Bediako compares the Greco-Roman context with modern Africa, he argues that "the development of theological concern and the formulation

---

57. Ghai, *Autonomy and Ethnicity*, 1.
58. Sanneh, *Translating the Message*.
59. Sanneh, 9–10.

of theological questions are closely linked as an inevitable by-product of a process of Christian self-definition."⁶⁰ He motivated this study to interrogate the missionary translatability of the gospel and thus the transmission of the Christian faith in the African context and verify whether missionaries bridged the gospel message well through African culture and religious heritage to build a contemporary African Christian theology.

Looking at the early church, with an eye on the Greco-Roman context as asserted by Bediako, it is possible that from the great commission in Acts 1:8 through the missionary movement of the early church, Christian theology faced a problem with identity, and the identity in Christ appears to be the resolution to the issue that was dividing Jewish Christians and Gentile Christians. In Philippians 2:5–11, Paul determines a new identity in Christ that he also advocates in Romans 1–11 and 1 Corinthians 12–14 where lack of unity between Gentiles and Jews was a highly problematic issue.

Africa, during the arrival of early African missionaries, was mostly characterized by an isolated identity. Curiously, today Christianity in Africa is still facing the same issue. In a war/conflict zone such as Eastern Congo, it is hard to convince a Christian from the indigenous ethnic group that a Tutsi is a genuine Christian due to the identity crisis between the two ethnicities and vice versa. One has to agree that there are features of eastern Congolese history of migration and identity conflicts that mirrored the understanding of early Christianity by the first believers in Eastern Congo. Today it is also clear that early Christianity and theology should be explained to the eastern Congolese church and that scholarship is needed for a clear development of an African theology with a focus on the context of war in Eastern Congo. It is an easy exercise due to the fact that the two contexts are similar. This is what confirms that the "African context has to do with the possibility of a genuine theology which seeks a synthesis between Christian religious commitment and cultural continuity."⁶¹

The early African missionaries from the West seem to have not taken good care of the transition between African theology (traditional and cultural legacy) and African Christian legacy in the process of the transmission of the faith to Africans. Mbiti says that the modern African "church is trying to exist

---

60. Bediako, *Theology and Identity*, xv.
61. Bediako, 432.

without a theology" because "the missionaries who began this modern phase of Christian expansion in Africa, together with their African helpers, . . . were not theologians."[62] Consequently, these "devout, sincere and dedicated men and women, were more concerned with practical evangelism, education, and medical care, than with any academic or theological issues that might arise from the presence of Christianity in Africa."

This study concurs with Mbiti that "Christianity was not from the start prepared to face a serious encounter with either the traditional religions and worldviews or the modern changes taking place in Africa."[63] In fact, African Christian converts were taught that anything related to traditional religion was heathen and therefore deserved to be abolished. They had no clue of taking care of the theological transition between tradition and cultural heritage and Christianity. Their theology featured liberation in their missions and Mugambi aruges that "theologies of liberation have been very important in the history of Africa."[64] Missionaries seemed to be representing the church in the West while at the same time and, to some extent, resist African cultural features. They seldom included the process of "learning and adapting to the culture around [them] while remaining biblically sound"[65] but rather came with the idea to "develop" Africans, which really means to Westernize them. The main thing most missionaries learned from Africa was the language/vernacular to enable them to communicate the message of salvation.

In Eastern Congo, though, having the message in the vernacular was a tremendous work allowing the translatability of the message; missionaries did translate the scriptures into the language of the most prominent ethnic groups. In the North Kivu province, for example, the Conservative Baptist Foreign Baptist Mission Society (CBFMS) established mission stations mainly in rural areas. Missionaries learned and spoke "'Kinande' fluently and translated, 'with the help of Africans,' the Bible in Kinande, beginning with the gospel of John in 1932 followed by Acts (in 1934), Matthew (1935) and Epistles in 1937."[66] It is obvious that the church became dominantly linked with the

---

62. Mbiti quoted in Bediako, 307.
63. Mbiti quoted in Bediako, 307.
64. Mugambi, "Theology of Reconstruction," 25.
65. Stetzer, *Planting Missional Churches*, 19.
66. Cf. Hurlburt, *Engulu Yowene*; Hurlburt and Mutotoya, *Emibiri Yabakwenda*; Hurlburt, *Esiobarua*.

Nande ethnic group. Another major mission station was in Rwanguba and its surrounding areas where the Hutu ethnic group is the majority population and where the Nande speak the Hutu language and the Hutu speak the Nande language. It has been observed that many pastors from the Hutu ethnic groups who serve under the church, or even Community of Baptist Churches of Eastern Congo (CBCE), speak Kinande because even Rwanguba seems to have embraced the Kinande vernacular, which was the main language the first missionaries used to communicate in the area. It is clear that when the schism within the mission occurred around 1955, although it resembled a tribal division, as it split into the two groups and church denominations – today the CBCA and the CBCE, which are mostly for the Nande and the Hutu, respectively[67] – a minority of the Nande people remained with the majority Hutu within CEBCE and the minority of Hutu joined the CBCA.

Between 1989 and 1990, when the "Kanyarwanda" (MAGRIVI) war broke in Bambo/Bwito, the Nande were being fought by the Hutu. This happened in an area covered by the Baptist district of Bambo (CBCA), which seemed to be thriving, and most of the Nande population migrated out of their comfort zone that the Hutu claimed to belong traditionally to them. In the researcher's view, vernacularization by the mission did contribute to a resolution of the identity conflicts by enhancing coexistence. Therefore, the conflicts' increase with new discrimination, lending importance to one local language over another should be attributed to the political turmoil of the last three decades that came to shutter that peaceful cohabitation of the ethnic groups.

As the church needs to respond to that context of war it is, therefore, difficult to disagree that "African theology has now overturned virtually every negative verdict passed on African tradition by the ethnocentrism of the Western missionary enterprise . . . but African theology is called to engage . . . in developing African intellectual opinion which interprets African reality differently."[68] The issue is not to fear to appear as a heretic, but African scholars are called upon to identify with the Greco-Roman scholars who aimed to defend the transmission of the Christian faith in the midst of cultural confusion. That is why Tatian's work is an "effort of a Christian advocate to establish the ground of self-identity of his co-religionists" in promoting the

---

67. Kighoma, "From an Ethnic Church."
68. Bediako, *Theology and Identity*, 439.

intrinsic value of Christianity, and Tertullian was "more concerned to protect the truth from being adulterated by the world than to validate the relevance of the truth to the world."[69] Though it sounds contradictory, their scholarship made the truth able to be transmitted to many generations that came after them. They understood their context well and the protected truth became relevant to their readers during the barbarian era.

During the war era in Eastern Congo, no one could protect the truth if they ignored the context. The western missionaries built churches that reached out to particular ethnic groups in Eastern Congo, but made sure the church extended reaching out to other villages, that is, at the living place of a specific ethnic group using the first converts from the village where they first started the mission work. The use of one or another vernacular in communicating the gospel message made its transmission easier and closer to local ethnic groups. Our current reality is that migrations due to wars have forced the existence of multiethnic communities exposed to conflicts and war. How Christian scholars interpret that context matters a lot to the church as it has to translate the gospel to "all nations" of Eastern Congo. There is, therefore, a great need to develop a theory of missions suitable for the context of war such as that of Eastern Congo.

The clans' issues around land tenure were ignored by the missionaries; they were teaching a gospel that enabled people to "access" heaven. The "missionary mandate" from the colonizer country (Belgium) was "to make every effort so that the blacks never become rich. To do this, [they should] make them sing every day that 'it is impossible for a rich man to enter the kingdom of God' and teach Congolese that they will be rewarded in Heaven."[70] It is clear that earthly possessions were not a concern for missionaries who were interested in teaching African believers. So, no believer could have been accepted to be involved in traditional priesthood responsibilities and still be allowed church membership because the missionaries were not able to transfer the meaning from a traditional meaning to a kingdom-oriented purpose. Consequently, heads of clans remained attached to their traditional segregationist-oriented

---

69. Tatian quoted in Bediako, 88.

70. Arnaut, "Letter from King Leopold," 1. This quotation is from a letter from King Leopold to missionaries to the Congo. The authenticity of the letter is debated by scholars.

beliefs while the church was ministering to individuals to become Christians with an ethnic identity.

Furthermore, missionaries did not understand the need to present a cross-cultural gospel as the response to the identity conflicts that already existed in traditional Eastern Congo in order to prevent ethnic clashes and wars. One is tempted to think that, some of these workers who "were not theologians . . . but were only concerned with the practical evangelism, education and medical care than with any academic or theological issue that might arise"[71] were moved to go to the heathen whom they thought were in the inland areas. They then used various missionary strategies to evangelize Eastern Congo from upcountry locations to move to the city, a process that was less strategic as far as ethnicity was concerned. The dynamic of traditional Africa was that ethnic groups did not mix themselves to preserve their founding ancestral blood, and therefore rural areas were geographically distributed according to ethnic groups. From the researcher's view, starting mission work in the city would have favored intercultural cohesion. The outcome is that the church in Eastern Congo is an ethnic one because it came to town with its ethnic character and so the church was consequently not able to play a relevant role in ethnic clashes. The researcher is aware that some Africans, may it be in the city or in the rural areas, are driven by ethnic inclination and that sincere believers are free from negative ethnicity. However, knowing that any missionary movement is carried out by mission-minded authentic believers who live their lives out on mission, evangelistic efforts from the inland to the city had less impact on reaching out to people from other ethnic groups since evangelists' effort were hindered by cultural barriers. Any cross-cultural workers or missionaries from the city would easily reach out to people from their own ethnic group together with others ethnic groups in the city. Thus, evangelism is given room to start intercultural communities of faith in the city.

Finally, the fact that missionaries "were only concerned with the practical evangelism, education and medical care, [rather] than with any academic or theological issues that might arise from the presence of Christianity in Africa"[72] resulted in their failure to foster mission strategies to the churches they planted. Since strategy flows from theological reflection and social

---

71. Bediako, *Theology and Identity*, 307.
72. Bediako, 307.

sciences in missiology, these missionaries were not interested in missiological research, be it ethnographic or social research, because they thought the gospel was urgently needed by the heathens of the Eastern Congo. As a result, eighty-five years later church denominations, such as the CBCA, planted from 1927, still manage church missions without any mission strategy and are highly in need of one.[73] In short, the church has not been able to respond to the outcomes of war, such as migrations, social justice needs of the communities, and so on, because it has no biblical or theoretical framework on which to build a clear response.

Charles Nyamiti wrote a volume titled *Jesus Christ the Ancestor of Humankind* and it was used as a "basis for ancestral theologies on Jesus Christ, church and grace."[74] In it he resists an African theology of liberation while advocating enculturation, the "theological insertion of the Christian message into cultural contexts" in the transmission of the Christian message. In the methodological approach of enculturation, Nyamiti introduces the idea of "Christ's ancestral status" that is to be easily understood by Africans who belong to ancestral kinship. This is what is missing in the contextualization approach that the first missionaries adopted in Eastern Congo.[75] In Eastern Congo identity is understood as rooted in both the individual and collective identity of ancestral blood. The transmission of a Christian faith that presented the believer's identity in Christ, the ancestor of all who believe in God, would have impacted identity issues resulting in more unity, cohesion, justice, and harmony.

In his writings, Paul emphasizes the believers' unity with Christ (e.g. Eph 2:11–18). This was indeed a message that helped him to transmit to church members the message of their new identity in Christ. The church in Ephesus had a minority of circumcised people (the Jews) who believed they deserved the identity of Christ for their ancestral identity in Abraham and a majority of Gentiles who were from the Hellenistic cultures and bonds. Paul tells the believers that the body of Christ provides a new identity, just as Judaism has given identity to Jews through circumcision, an inherited practice from their founding ancestor Abraham. So, contrary to what Paul did in the Roman

---

73. Ngayihembako and Midiburo, "Communauté Baptiste," 10.
74. Nyamiti, *Jesus Christ, the Ancestor*, 147.
75. Nyamiti.

church, some among missionaries in Eastern Congo, to some extent, ignored that "'God's people are multiethnic' and that Christian teaching and preaching should be geared toward realities faced."[76] They failed to present to the African believers a new identity in Christ as an inclusive identity of all who believe in him, irrespective of their traditional bonds. Doing so would have changed the church members' understanding of a Christian family, therefore breaking down the ethnic barriers of identity for the benefit of peaceful cohabitation.

Therefore, the dominant mission strategies contributed to strengthening the discontinuity between African theology and African Christian missions, while features of ethnic identity conflicts in Eastern Congo were rooted in the identity of the ethnic ancestral blood and showered by land tenure and marriage bonds. From the rural areas that were the strongholds of ethnic identity, missionary work might have been affected and become weak in presenting the message of the gospel to a cross-cultural audience in the city when war and migration brought people from various groups and nations together.

Hiebert argues that "if the behavioral change was the focus of the mission movement in the nineteenth century, and changed beliefs its focus in the twentieth century, then transforming worldviews must be its central task in the twenty-first century."[77] This researcher agrees with him that conversion must encompass three levels: behavior, beliefs and worldview. It is only by this kind of change that we can speak of a holistic Christianity. This identity issue is what has to change in the Christian worldview in Eastern Congo. People identify themselves by their ancestral blood and at the same time belong to a community of believers where everyone feels that belonging to one's ancestral blood is more important than identifying with the community of faith in Christ.

We agree with Hiebert that there is a "need to turn to the biblical view of transformation, which is both a point and a process" because "we cannot divorce evangelism from nurture or conversion from the church."[78] If we go about evangelism and mission in a digital-set approach, we limit the gospel to only educated people who have to read and learn about Christianity after conversion. If the intrinsic set approach to mission is considered then we are

---

76. Ngaruiya, "Multifaceted Genesis," 89.
77. Hiebert, *Transforming Worldviews*, 12.
78. Hiebert, 310, 312.

likely to take salvation as a process that involves every person encountering the gospel. Hiebert instead introduces the idea of salvation as "a turning point" and a Hebraic approach to change: conversion, a journeying process of discipleship and growth in the community of faith.[79] It is through that journey that mission contributes to transforming a believer's worldview from the former to a biblical worldview in the convert's context. It is this that the church mission in Eastern Congo needs, as people have come to the church but are still tied to their cultural identity and worldview. In a word, because there is little change in worldview, traditional ties to the ancestral blood are stronger than Christian identity and the church remains ethnic even in multicultural settings such as the city and other migrant agglomerations.

2.3.2 Church Growth during Wartime

While "successive governments in Khartoum had hopes of establishing national unity on the basis of the programs of Islamization and Arabization"[80] the church in Sudan, in the war period between 1983 and 1996, "has been described as the fastest growing church in Africa and the Episcopal Church of the Sudan (ECS) in particular has been described as the fastest growing Church of the Anglican Communion."[81] Andrew Wheeler attributes this growth to "an indigenous process without significant input or participation from outside."[82]

On the one hand, one can agree with Wheeler that the "journeys of individuals and communities to faith and the purpose of God was discovered through suffering the people struggled with," because the community in South Sudan encouraged themselves "in hymns and music, in prayers, and in the community internal dialogue."[83] It is plausible to think that mixing prayer and worship with community dialogue in the church life might have built the trust of the suffering community of South Sudan toward the church. Although this was an "African encounter with the Bible and with the Christian faith,"[84] it was also a serious struggle of the church with the context and the gospel.

---

79. Hiebert, 311.
80. Wheeler, "Church Growth in Southern Sudan," 36.
81. Wheeler, 11.
82. Wheeler, 37.
83. Wheeler, 37.
84. Wheeler, 37.

In the process of contextualizing the gospel in the Sudanese context of war, the church translated the gospel message in the vernacular of the suffering people. It is possible that this is what has caused this Nubian church to be unable to reach the Arabs and therefore made a division that led to the split of the Republic of Sudan into two countries. Furthering this, it is plausible to think that even though the vernacularization of the gospel to the Nubian was helpful to its own church, it might have isolated Arab people from being reached by the Nubian church, with which they shared Arabic as a national language. Furthermore,

> The role of the Gospel and vernacular scriptures has a negative underside. In many areas the rapidly growing churches have a distinct ethnocentric character, in some measure because of their isolation, but also because in the Christian message they find a specific message of hope for and an affirmation of them as a people.[85]

The Congolese church was exposed to the same challenge as that of South Sudan. It is likely that the war, having roots in features of ethnicity in Eastern Congo, had an effect on the church in that the church became a growing ethnic church at the expense of an intercultural mission. Or, to put it differently, unity, love, peace and harmony are exercised within an ethnocentric church. It is time that, as missiologists, we encourage the eastern Congolese church leadership to carefully contextualize the gospel during war and promote an intercultural church that ministers to a united country and people. For this reason, one is likely to point out and question ethnicity as a factor responsible for the survival of the church during war.

On the other hand, we do not agree that the growth of the church in South Sudan was a thoroughly indigenous effort. Oliver Duku contradicts Wheeler's view when he points to guaranteed financial backing as one of the factors that contributed to the growth of the Catholic Mayo congregations in Sudan. He reveals that "a large percentage of this comes from external sources, from friends and relatives of the expatriate priest."[86]

---

85. Wheeler, 37.
86. Duku, "Development and Growth," 42.

The fact is that Nubian communities fled into the neighboring countries (Kenya, Uganda, DRC and the Central African Republic) as a result of the war. The church in these countries has influenced the faith of Sudanese refugees in one way or another by a vibrant Christianity. The present writer recalls attending Commission 2004, a Focus-Kenya Mission Conference held at Kabarak University in December 2004. A young Sudanese delegate told him that he was excited to be in a setting where he could enjoy free Christian fellowship for his spiritual growth. It became clear that the input of the church outside the war zone, both from the West and Africa, has resulted in planned and implemented strategies and missions to help the Sudanese church survive during that hard times. For example, many Christian missionaries have worked through the UN and NGOs in Kakuma and in Sudan with the purpose of reaching out to the Sudanese.

The growth of the church in Sudan seems to have been insignificant before the war. There were six Christian denominations working in the Moyo Community before the war period of 1983–1996. According to Duku, "some like the Catholic Church has been in Moyo since 1972."[87] He identifies the following as factors that significantly contributed to the growth of both the Catholic church and the Episcopal church in Moyo /South Sudan:

1. Migration from troubled areas in the southern and western parts of Sudan and the Nuba Mountains.
2. Active evangelization through house churches and home visits.
3. Social services like schools, adult education classes, health services and water supply.
4. Relief supplies.

Duku also identifies positive and negative growth caused by relief supplies. The growth of the Roman Catholic church, for example, became more stable due to some factors that other denominations lacked. These factors were:

1. Discipline and unity which were guaranteed by a rationalized and strict leadership.
2. A well-organized distribution system of the aid.
3. A definite financial sustenance from outside the country.

---

87. Duku, 55.

Furthermore, what helped the Episcopal church, and to a lesser extent the evangelical church, in Mayo to grow was aggressive evangelism through home visits and educational and income-generating projects. Consequently, other denominations that did not invest in education and income-generated activities experienced little growth.[88] It appears from the above that evangelism is not enough to keep individuals faithful to God; it requires a holistic gospel that promotes Christianity and fights poverty at the individual, family and community level.

The war in Congo has negatively affected the population at the age when they become productive through, among other things, frequent movement and sexual and gender violence. These factors caused food scarcity and famine, malnutrition, the death of children under the age of five and a high illiteracy rate among children and women. The rural area is affected and internally displaced people's (IDPs) camps are established both in the cities and in the rural areas. Families are being supported by the NGOs' emergency and relief projects but the church seems to be absent even in the emergency scene. It became clear that good schools in Eastern Congo belong to both the Catholic and evangelical churches. But these schools do not yet have programs that fit the context of the mobile communities called internally displaced people. The church needs to be aware that education and livelihood programs will improve discipleship and benefit church growth. So, it is up to the church to plan and implement programs for the livelihood of the people.

2.3.3 African Wars Framework: Ethnic Clashes and Wars in Eastern Congo

In trying to understand "why . . . ethnic clashes/wars increased worldwide," Andreas Wimmer argues that

> during the political thaw that the end of the Cold War and the new hegemony of democratic state ideals have brought, the last multicultural empires dissolved. They were transformed into nation-states before strong civil societies could take root. In the newly nationalizing states, politics was quickly transformed into an arena of ethno-nationalistic competition.[89]

---

88. See Duku, 55–56.
89. Wimmer, *Nationalist Exclusion*, 113.

In Africa, in particular, these kinds of empires were managed by dictators. The DRC, for example, experienced thirty-two years of President Mobutu's reign. His reign favored a particular category of people. The collapse of his government brought a multi-party system into existence and inaugurated the idea of ethnic autonomy and freedom. Empires, rather than promoting multicultural interactions, seem to have endorsed a planned idea of an ethnic search for autonomy. Burnett Rubin supports this view. He comments that in "the Great Lakes region of Africa conflicts have been organized around cultural identities . . . They have linked groups within a state to trans-border networks and warfare, as elements of regional conflict formations."[90] In the case of Congo, for example, "the polarized violent conflicts between Hutu and Tutsi-led movements in Rwanda and Burundi have triggered and escalated others, including the more amorphous conflicts that developed in Zaïre (Congo)."[91]

It is true that when "mechanisms for mediating conflicts break down" most of the ethnic wars occur. The mediator fails to reconcile the groups involved in the conflicts when undermined by "economic conditions, loss of legitimacy, or outside intervention."[92] This happens due to the fact that conflict destroys interpersonal or inter-group relationships and collapses exchanges of any kind to the expense of families' well-being and social stability. The mediation process is expected to produce a balanced win-win agreement. When it fails, the result is a clash or war.

Although "ethnicity is not an immutable fact that inevitably leads to war" because "symbols, myths, and memories can be altered over time," the case of Eastern Congo falls into a different category.[93] The ex-CNDP Movement and the recent M23 movements claimed that the "Tutsi ethnic group" is marginalized and needed to share power with other groups. When a group or movement starts a dissident rebellion, other ethnic groups form their ethnic militia for self-defense against the danger (i.e. the rebels) and therefore try to face the rebel group and resist its oppression.

---

90. Rubin, "Central Asia and Central Africa," 5.
91. Rubin, 9.
92. Nye, *Understanding International Conflicts*, 158.
93. Nye, 158.

2.3.4 Direct Results of War

Migrations of thousands of families from the war zone to the cities and the deterioration of livelihoods at the family and community level, as well as in the war zone and with a displacement of a host of whole communities, are the direct results of ethnic clashes and wars.

Jehu Hanciles reveals the complexity of the African experience of migrations. He argues that

> Undeniably, untold millions involuntarily abandon homes and livelihoods in response to brutal violence, persecution, and ecological disaster. Yet, for masses of people, the irrepressible urge to "move" can also stem a reduction of life expectancy, a sense of hopelessness about the future, the widespread disempowerment that accompanies failed political leadership, desperation born of misfortune and poverty, or even the inability to provide basic necessities to the family.[94]

We partially agree with him because in most cases, in Eastern Congo, the population movement is unpredictable. Citizens do have a belief that God gave them one of the best places to live with very fertile soil across the region, good grazing for livestock and, above all, the ethnic organization of societies in the region, which makes every citizen feel that they belong fully to their community. Therefore, during clashes, they hope to come back and resettle in their homes. However, it became clear that the long-suffering to which populations have been exposed and the mistrust of the political system, which families think may take a long time to handle the war, make some people reluctant to go back to their villages even when peace appears to be real.

John Oucho presents consequences of the conflict at the societal level and at the internally displaced peoples' level as well.[95] According to him, "conflict has important economic, political and social consequences." He explains:

> Economic consequences include disruption of agricultural and non-agricultural activities as well as loss of income-generating activities. Political consequences include the zonation of the country into strongholds of political parties, government's

---

94. Hanciles, *Beyond Christendom*, 221.
95. Oucho, *Undercurrents of Ethnic Conflict*, 174.

biased allocation of the national cake . . . in terms of projects . . . and administrative units along ethnic lines. Social consequences have to do with the dismemberment of families (as family members flee for their lives) and inter-ethnic tensions, disturbances among different ethnic groups and the disruption of children's education and socialization.[96]

The consequences described above are what Tom Steffen and Lois McKinney Douglas call "a hurting world."[97] For them the "hurting world is characterized by poverty, global concerns such as environmental problems, water problems, children suffering, and girls and women victimized, natural disasters, pandemics, and violence."[98] This affirms that wars transform and have transformed, in the case of Eastern Congo, the conflict area into a "hurting world" where the livelihoods of the families and community are critical and their security and cohabitation distorted by events.

The second consequence that Oucho points to is that conflict affects the IDPs in "politicizing demographic accounting undertaken in censuses and surveys, disturbing fertility and increasing morbidity and mortality; and generating a colony of IDPs who remain thus indefinitely."[99] This study agrees with this; the conditions in which IDPs live in camps expose them to diseases and death. With the instability in regions, some IDPs have borne their IDP status indefinitely. For example, when the M23 attacked Kibumba and Rutshuru, most of the population moved and camped in Kibati. In October 2013, the same M23 attacked Goma and destroyed the IDP camp that then had to resettle beyond Goma toward Sake. IDPs who found conditions of their displacement better than their home kept their IDP status and refused to return.

During an interaction with the researcher in December 2013, one IDP, a woman in the Mugunga camp who had been receiving a food kit every month for more than a year, informed the writer that she was not ready to return home. She asked, "how will I start that hard life of a farmer, and yet here I am used to receiving food to live?" This serves as proof that some people may

---

96. Oucho, 174.
97. Steffen and Douglas, *Encountering Missionary Life*, 296.
98. Steffen and Douglas, 296–306.
99. Oucho, *Undercurrents of Ethnic Conflict*, 179.

use migrations to access areas where they believe life is better compared to their home village. In the case of Eastern Congo, migration has made the population of the city of Goma increase at a very high speed. People prefer remaining in Goma due to its multicultural and multiethnic aspects, which provide safety and security to everyone.

2.4 Views on Migration and Mission

Migration is a major issue that missiology is facing today. In 2003, Samuel Escobar came up with the "migration model" of mission which he said, "is also an avenue for mission in our days." According to that model, "Migrants from poor countries who travel in search of economic survival carry the Christian message and missionary initiative with them."[100] Hanciles supports this model and argues that "attentiveness to the nature and composition of human migration is crucial for understanding the possibilities and potential of Christian missionary endeavor," and that "the future of global Christianity is intricately bound up with the emerging nonwestern missionary."[101] This study agrees with the fact that the center of evangelization has moved to the Majority World. But we have to understand that everywhere in the world is a missionary center from which we can send missionaries, even from a refugee camp, irrespective of whether from poor countries or from the West.

The model of the believers from poor counties who witness to Westerners is not practical in terms of the approaches used. Although the communication of the gospel is not a one-way action, integrating migrants into Western social local communities and life is a challenging process that might take time to favor the sharing of the gospel message. African refugees in the West are, to some extent, simply able to minister to people from their countries who also migrated to the West unless they are absorbed in the Western system and worldview. In many cases, we have transplanted pastors in the West and can only reach out to their fellow Africans or other nationalities from the Majority World. There are also wars between rich countries, like the war between China and Japan in the year 1941, that have certainly forced populations to move. In this case, the migration model of war may work a

---

100. Escobar, *Time for Mission*, 66; see also Hanciles, "Migration and Mission," 118.
101. Hanciles, "Migration and Mission," 129.

hundred percent effectively. However, this is not to reject the view of Tite Tienou that "the evangelistic activities of the Africans in the diaspora, together with their other ministries, had added another dimension to the missionary involvement of African evangelicals beyond the continent by the end of the twentieth century."[102]

Another factor affecting the African witness in Western cultures is the lack of worldview transformation. While "conversion changes the fundamental ways in which we configure our view of reality,"[103] some African migrant churches in the West use their culture and worldview as a component of the gospel message and would like Westerners to replace their old set of beliefs and practices with African ones.[104] The African migrant churches should be involved in a process of transforming their African worldview into a biblical worldview and then converting their Western friends from Western culture. For example, the researcher notices that some African migrant preachers who are from oral tradition cultures unsuccessfully attempt to assimilate into literate cultures with a very low reliance on oral communication. Furthermore, it is good to note that "in the century after A.D. 1500 European explorers became aware of the wide differences among the world's peoples in technology and political organization, they assumed that those differences arose from difference inmate ability."[105] Today, as Africans migrate to the West such an assumption might hinder Westerners to embrace the message of the gospel from African migrants.

On the other hand, while the migration model has been tried in the West, it is applicable in Africa. For example, in 2012 the situation report of the United Nations Office for Coordination of Humanitarian Affairs estimated that "over 900,000 people were living as displaced in North Kivu province."[106] Due to wars in Africa, especially in Eastern Congo, populations have moved from rural areas to the cities, from the cities to rural and from Eastern Congo to other countries. Some are living in IDP camps or refugee camps and others are living with host families. There is no connection between the church in

---

102. Tienou, "Great Commission in Africa," 173.
103. Hiebert, *Transforming Worldviews*, 319.
104. Hiebert, 319.
105. Diamond, *Guns, Germs, and Steel*, 19.
106. OCHA 2012, 1.

the city and the believers in camps who sometimes have moved with their pastors. There is a need to use IDPs and refugees and host families in mission. The priority is a mission theory/model that will lead to developing mission strategies that would fit the needs of the Congolese church to do missions through the use of migration as an opportunity for missions.

Bevans also supports the migration model of mission. He suggests two ways in which mission may be carried out in the context of migration:

> On the one hand, the church's mission is to migrants – that is, migrants should be the objects of the church's pastoral care. On the other hand, however, the church's mission is of migrants – that is, the migrants in our midst are the subjects of mission. They both call the local church to a new way of being church, and they themselves need to be active within the church serving the church within and outside of their communities and serving the wider world as well.[107]

This view seems to emphasize the impact of migrants' missional practices on the church. While migrants are reaching out to people in their context, the host of churches are to use their presence as an opportunity to exercise missional practices. In this regard, the church in Goma can embark on such missional practices and learn from the migrants' church in the city and IDP camps while joining it to serve the world in crisis.

2.5 War – an Avenue for Church Missions

Tom Steffen and Lois McKinney Douglas call for the missionary mandate of the church in the "hurt world" because "Jesus is the answer to the hurts of our world. He uses us as his messengers of love and compassion in the midst of poverty, disaster, diseases, and conflicts that are tearing it apart."[108] Bosch argues that "the church has lost its position of privilege."[109] He reveals that the church itself is being tested. Therefore, his thesis is that "a paradigm

---

107. Bevans, "Themes and Questions," 13.
108. Steffen and Douglas, *Encountering Missionary Life*, 296.
109. Bosch, *Transforming Mission*, 363.

shift always means both continuity and change, both faithfulness to the past and boldness to engage the future . . . both tradition and transformation."

In a time of testing, the church is likely to be ineffective to fulfill its mission if it holds onto its traditions and is unwilling to adjust itself to the current context until it realizes that the "Christian faith gives articulation to this mystery by saying that whenever the world suffers God is suffering too, with the world."[110] This study, therefore, disagrees with C. M. Mwikamba that scientific and industrial "revolutions forced the churches to become defensive and withdraw from the world."[111] The African church was not forced to withdraw from the world but the church did not understand its mission to present a holistic gospel to a corrupt world. It refused to be in the world without being "of the world" (John 17:16). Therefore, the church found so much comfort in becoming "sanctuaries, places of refuge in hostile environment(s)"[112] that it became unable to address mission outside its comfort zones.

The same is happening in the DRC where the wars and migrations have become sensitive issues and even difficult to address. The wars, having a political and ethnic character, should be addressed by the church, which should provide social justice and defend human rights, to resist lawlessness, poverty, food scarcity and famine, injustice, violence, rape and kidnapping in war zones. This church has instead kept silent and stood firm in being faithful to its regular church celebrations in church buildings. In war zones, while many people continued to be victims of these churches, the faithful ones have not closed their doors. This is why Bosch concludes that "both the centrifugal and centripetal forces in the emerging paradigm . . . will have to be taken into account throughout" and he says, therefore, that "it is only within the force field of apparent opposites that we shall begin to approximate a way of theologizing for our own time in a meaningful way."[113]

Consequently, although wartime is a time of testing for the church, the church remains the carrier of its mandate of translating the holistic message of the gospel to the people. The church has to face "the challenge of making

---

110. Bosch, 354.
111. Mwikamba, "Shift in Mission," 12.
112. Mwikamba, 12.
113. Bosch, *Transforming Mission*, 367.

the missions of the church relevant to the contemporary African context"[114] of wars. Ann Nasimiyu-Wasike and her colleagues, in colloquium papers, advocate two obvious approaches: "Inculturation and innovational mission of the church and liberative and prophetic mission of the church."[115] It is the role of the church to identify contemporary issues that are being faced by the church's mission and provide a proper church response to the issues.

Rather than being considered either as a social being or a spiritual being,[116] man was created in Eden as a holistic being.[117] This is what the church in Eastern Congo has to understand. The researcher conducted a Livelihoods Needs Assessment in the four localities formerly under the control of the M23 movements and found that the church is not in the community to promote social justice as a business as advocated for by NGOs and other village help groups. Two percent of the assessment respondents earn their income from selling firewood or charcoal from the national park. These are members of the church and other faiths. The church should, therefore, involve social justice and be able to educate the world on being stewards of the creation. Along this way, the church is fulfilling its cultural mandate.

Aiming at models of biblical and global missiology, African evangelical missiologists during the Iguassu consultation "sought missions which were true to scripture, sensitive to the world's cultures, and relevant for the entire family of God in mission."[118] Tokunboh Adeyemo identifies the decline of Christianity in the West, religious plurality and global hostility as the "three global realities facing Christian missions."[119] This researcher agrees with him because while the West has become "to a great extent, an evangelized continent, there is a rapid spread of Islam in Europe and America today."[120] At the same time, Muslims and other religions and cults are using global strategies to reach out to Christian countries. The peacekeeping mission in the DRC called MONUSCO is said to be the biggest UN mission in the world.[121] It does have,

---

114. Nasimiyu-Waisike and Waruta, *Mission in African Christianity*, 3.
115. Nasimiyu-Waisike and Waruta, 3.
116. Erickson, *Christian Theology*, 493.
117. Grudem, *Systematic Theology*, 445.
118. Taylor, *Global Missiology*, 257.
119. Adeyemo, "Profiling," 266–67.
120. Adeyemo, 266–67.
121. "DR Congo Peacekeeping."

in Eastern Congo, representatives from countries such as Pakistan, Uruguay, Bangladesh and India. Apart from Tanzania and South Africa, most of the UN Peacekeeping Forces are from Muslim countries. These Muslims utilize the UN policy of freedom of religions and have influenced many people to join their faith in the region. The researcher is personally familiar with two mosques in Lubero and in Nyanzale, both in the rural areas of the region, that were built by UN soldiers (i.e. Peacekeepers). He has watched the UN soldiers do the manual construction of the mosque in Nyanzale in 2010. Thus, the church should use the war as an opportunity to reach out to people from different nations around the world, as they are their neighbors.

2.6 Church Mission: Advocating for Peace, Justice and Harmony

Necati Polat opposes the political view of peace.[122] This view, with its roots in political philosophy, defines peace as the absence of war. According to him, peace is primary and indigenous, and concludes that "peace is war."[123] This researcher agrees. Peace is an entity, a condition that has to be created and fought for by indigenous people as their primary need. However, peace must be advocated for and requires the involvement of both individuals and communities at every level, from indigenous to international, and reaching as far as the ends of the global world. The church needs to be part of that advocacy for peace, justice and harmony for and from the citizens, let alone the participation and support of other stakeholders.

2.6.1 The Church and War

The church can use its credibility to advocate for peace by calling the actors involved in war and other stakeholders to stop the war. For example, when the Rwandese church was surprised by the sudden events of cruel hostilities and bloodshed that resulted from four years of political instability, between 1990 and 1994, the church from outside its borders was the first to call upon the Rwandese church to remain faithful to its mission during the cruel time. It appears that the church was deeply involved in genocide from

---

122. Polat, "Peace as War," 318.
123. Polat, 317.

the beginning of the atrocities. The Roman Catholic church, four days after President Habyarimana was killed, called for an urgent synod where the theme was "You shall be my witnesses" (Acts 1:8 NASB). In his address to the bishops at the synod in Rome, the Pope appealed to the Rwandese church and said: "I wish to recall in particular the people and the church of Rwanda who these days are being tried by an overwhelming tragedy . . . I raise my voice to tell all of you: Stop these acts of violence. Stop these fratricidal massacres."[124] Rather than promoting unity and justice during its time of trial, the church leadership failed "to listen to the Pope's cry of suffering for people of Rwanda"[125] and the Catholic church and the Protestant church were decimated.

The church, rather than promoting the renewal of the believers' mind (Romans 12:1–2) and presenting the church as the new and united community where everyone has an identity in Christ, promoted culture and gospel. Contextualizing the gospel in a community so divided by ethnic identity was an opportunity the church missed in its task of making of disciples. Thus, it could not resist the shock and waves of genocide and, therefore, joined the militia that depended on tribal alliances formed two and a half centuries ago. This study agrees with DeLame who said:

> Instead of working to remove such distortions, so as to reinforce the many factors promoting unity, an imperative of the Christian message, the church, both Catholic and Protestant, co-operated in modeling society in the interest of the imperial power, and were thus incapable of offering an alternative to forced labour, to fatigue, to compulsory conversions.[126]

2.6.2 War and Social Development

Bosch, in his lecture on the vulnerability of mission, recalls the *kenosis*, the "self-emptying" of Christ, to demonstrate that "it is only in the way of giving up himself that Jesus came to us"[127]; he therefore had to accept to be crucified among sinners. Accordingly, "in Christ, God does not necessarily save us from suffering, but in and through it." This study agrees with him because Jesus

---

124. McCullum, *Angels Have Left Us*, 63.
125. McCullum, 64.
126. Gatwa, *Churches and Ethnic Ideology*, 26.
127. Bosch, *Transforming Mission*, 356.

accomplished his mandate and "when the resurrected Jesus appeared to his disciples, his scars were proof of his identity." It is "at this point that the missionary significance of the cross emerges" and that "the affliction missionaries endure is intimately bound up with their mission."[128] The church in Eastern Congo cannot make its suffering people disciples of Christ if the church does not identify with the people's pain. One of the best things that the church can ever do for peace, justice and harmony, in its zone of ministry to unreached groups in the area, the government and other stakeholders, is to demonstrate its scars from the war and identify with the eastern Congolese world.

2.7 Summary and Gaps in Existing Literature

The study of related literature on the topic of missions and the church's encounter with war and violence, aimed at knowledge from earlier Christian views, can be applied to the contemporary context of war. Bosch, addressing the issue of suffering, says that "the affliction missionaries endure is intimately bound up with their mission."[129] This is also true in the context of war for the church's mission is also bound to the experience of war.

However, to synthesize the experience of Christian leaders involved in missions in the context of war, it was noted that different theories have been developed in response to how Christians should view war: the just war theory, the pacifism theory, the crusade/holy war, and the nonviolence theory. None of these theories addresses the issue of the experience of war and the church's survival during wartime. They are all about actions to be taken by individuals, government, or communities such as the church in its search for peace. This study is an attempt to fill this gap.

To identify the nature of mission from the biblical experience(s) of war is undertaken by identifying that nature through a biblical exegesis of the Greco-Roman context in which the scripture was translated. Bediako, dealing with the issue of identity, argues that a proper biblical exegesis of the gospel message in the Greco-Roman culture and context, although "closely linked to modern African context," is not sufficient in the transmission of the

---

128. Bosch, "Vulnerability of Mission," 207–8.
129. Bosch, *Transforming Mission*, 356.

Christian faith.[130] It is crucial that a serious analysis of culture be conducted prior to the transmission of the Christian faith. In a context of war such as the one in Eastern Congo, "the great principle of translatability lies at the heart of Christian faith and is demonstrated both in the incarnation and in the Scriptures."[131]

Many scholars have taken interest in the transmission of the Christian faith. Some of them have emphasized contextualization in the process of translating the gospel's message.[132] According to Scott Moreau, "Contextualization is at the 'mixing point' of the gospel and culture."[133] This work agrees with them because "the relationship between the gospel and culture is a fruit of gospel 'translatability.'"[134] However, some scholars have developed views that support Donald McGavran's theory of the homogeneous unit principle.[135] In the Great Lakes region in general, and in Eastern Congo in particular, identity is rooted in "the unity and indivisibility of the founding ancestor's blood."[136] The ever-changing context of war, in an area marked by ethnicity and migrations, has not been dealt with in terms of the transmission of the Christian faith in the experience of war. It is clear that the message of the gospel continues to be spread in a homogeneous approach in multicultural contexts such as cities and migrants' settings.

In relation to a biblical view of missions, this chapter has identified that the focus for missions from both the Old and New Testaments is "all nations." Curiously Israel, the missionary people in the OT, responded to that mandate by being involved in conquests and wars against other nations.[137] Israel was in the pursuit of God's promise to give Abraham a land, posterity and a mission of blessing (Gen 12:1–3). The New Testament presents the church mandate

---

130. Bediako, *Theology and Identity*, xv.

131. Walls, *Missionary Movement*, 25.

132. Bediako, *Theology and Identity*; Hiebert, *Transforming Worldviews*; Ngaruiya, "Multifaceted Genesis"; Sanneh, *Translating the Message*.

133. Moreau, *Contextualization in World Missions*, 19.

134. Sanneh, *Translating the Message*, 9–10.

135. McGavran, *Homogenous Unit*, 71–292; cf. Stetzer, *Planting Missional Churches*, 150.

136. Bujo, "Vincent Mulago," 19.

137. Glasser, Gilliland and Redford, *Announcing the Kingdom*, 105.

to "all nations" with a single description by different scholars[138] and identified with the oral proclamation of the gospel message, the discipling of the nations, teaching disciples to love the poor and promoting love, peace and unity. It is noted that the biblical view of missions lacks a holistic understanding of missions in earlier scholarship. The experience of World Wars I and II brought about a shift in the understanding of the church's missions as the idea of a geographic conquest beginning in the twentieth century through church planting in order to become a global (holistic) endeavor in scope.[139] However, the effects of wars have also affected the concept of missions and caused the replacement of words related to a geographic occupation such as "heathens" and the like. This has consequently led the users of the concept of missions to borrow military words such as "target," "unreached," and the like.[140]

The interaction with different scholars in grappling with the research question has therefore enabled the researcher to identify the following gaps in existing knowledge:

1. Throughout the Old and New Testaments, the Great Commission is presented by a specific description of the nature of mission. Therefore, the understanding of the nature of mission may differ at the church level due to the existing gap of knowledge. Churches may be lacking a holistic understanding of mission from the OT to NT as both the oral proclamation of the gospel message, discipling the nations, teaching the disciples to love the poor, disciples practicing love to the poor and promoting love, peace and unity.
2. Contextualization is thought of in terms of preaching, teaching and sometimes the transmission of the Christian faith in translating the scripture. The ever-changing context of war, ethnicity, and migrations does not interest many scholars in the transmission of the Christian faith.

---

138. Bosch, *Transforming the Message*; Lewis and Demarest, *Integrative Theology*; Glasser, Gilliland and Redford, *Announcing the Kingdom*; Peters, *Biblical Theology of Missions*; Wright, *Mission of God's People*, etc.

139. See Moreau, Corwin, and McGee, *Introducing World Mission*, 142; Barnett, "Global Century," 303.

140. Barnett, "Global Century," 288

3. It has been noted that the different theories of war aim at either the advocating or fighting for peace and justice. It appears that there is no theological theory on the survival of the church and communities' experiences related to war even as the church and government struggle for peace.

CHAPTER 3

Church, Mission, and War – Biblical Perspectives

3.1 Introduction

This chapter presents what can be learned from the Bible regarding a Christian's response to church, violence and war. Because the responses are in action (ministry and mission) and in the theology that underlies that action, the aim is to assess biblical teaching on Christian responses to the church, violence and war, and then to summarize the teaching. Prior to, and in support of that assessment, the researcher presents the biblical view of church missions (in connection with the context of war). The experience of, and response to, war and conflicts are explored by studying three New Testament passages, namely, Matthew 5:38–45, Acts 18:1–4 and Hebrews 10:32–34. The first provides an insight into Jesus's attitude to conflict. The second highlights the response of the apostles to the challenges of survival in a hostile world. This is understood within the context of the misuse of power in the Roman Empire. The final passage deals with the suffering of the early Christians.

The development of a comprehensive theology of mission in the context of war is beyond the scope of the present study. It had to limit its focus to a small number of passages that are relevant to the theme of mission in the context of war in Eastern Congo. The expectation is that a preliminary exegetical analysis of these passages will provide a biblical perspective on mission in the context of war. The assessment involves an exegesis of each of the three passages and a critical analysis of different views on each, together with consideration of political, social, missiological and diplomatic dimensions of the war. This is done with reference to relevant Old Testament texts related to war such as Joshua 6 (Israel in war against other nations), 2 Samuel 3 (war between the house of Saul and that of David) and 2 Chronicles 20. The researcher is, however, not addressing war from the holistic perspective: men and the kingdom of darkness waged war against God from the garden forward (see Genesis 3). The initial enmity serves as the prelude to every other conflict.

3.2 Biblical View of Missions

3.2.1 Missions and War in the Old Testament

The images of Genesis 1–3 give a biblical perspective on the war, the insurrection led by the serpent and willfully joined by the first family. Every war since then is simply an outbreak and related skirmish that has been going on since the enmity that began in the garden. Arthur Glasser, who explored "the emergence and development of the Kingdom of God motif within both the Old and the New Testaments taken as a whole, in order to understand God's mission through God's people in God's world,"[1] argues "with confidence that the central theme of the Old Testament is the revelation of the redemptive activity of God in and through his Son, Israel."[2]

It is agreed that "all aspects of the Old Testament, particularly those concerning Israel, should be seen as related to God's worldwide, redemptive purpose."[3] It is also curious that mission, being "in the heart of God"[4] and the Great Commission that did not begin with the early Christian mission but is, instead, seen as the mainstream mandate of God in the history of mankind, having embraced a nature of conquests and wars: God's promise to give Abraham a land, posterity and a mission of blessing (Gen 12:1–3). It is a promise later repeated to the patriarchs, an insistence of God's efficient will executed with God's pleasure.[5]

---

1. Glasser, *Announcing the Kingdom*, 12.
2. Knight, *Christian Theology*, 9.
3. Glasser, *Announcing the Kingdom*, 17.
4. Terry and Smith, *Missiology*, 97.
5. Lewis and Demarest, *Integrative Theology*, 300.

The focus for the mission of blessing is "all nations" of the earth. God chose and used one nation to be a blessing to all nations; Christopher Wright concludes that the "Abrahamic covenant is one of the key unifying threads in the whole Bible" and says that "what could be more 'gospel' – in the light of Genesis 3–11 is that God has committed himself to bless all people of the earth."[6]

It appears as contradictory that God chose Israel as a missionary people in the process of fulfilling his redemptive plan and proclaiming his kingdom to all nations of the earth and that this nation started with conquests and wars against different nations of the Middle East. Glasser, Gilliland and Redford show that

> During the conquest, Yahweh used his covenant people to wage war against the Canaanite people. This pattern was completely reversed during the period of the judges and will continue during the monarchy. Increasingly, during the monarchy, the prophets would predict that foreign peoples would be used by Yahweh to chasten his people when they disobey him.[7]

It is clear that in Genesis God's mission did require the judgment of nations and the conquests of God's people. The Abrahamic covenant was connected with Canaanite land tenure which needed to be implemented from Jericho because the mission of God required Israel's "active response and moral responsibility"[8] to access the blessings and to be a channel of God's blessing to the nations (Gen 12:1–3). This is the first proclamation of the gospel (Gal 3:8), and is God's declaration of bringing an end to the enmity for all peoples, his plan for peace with God through his sacrifice. This appears to be a strategy fitting in the Middle Eastern context of the Abrahamic era.

However, during the period of the Judges and the monarchy, Israel was a nation that faced wars and invasions that were simply an indicator of the increase of the rule of that kingdom. Israel possessed the land and then needed to witness to other nations and, by so doing, establish the kingdom of God in accordance with God's divine plans. In other words, wars and conquests

---

6. Wright, *Mission of God's People*, 71.
7. Glasser, Gilliland and Redford, *Announcing the Kingdom*, 105.
8. Lewis and Demarest, *Integrative Theology*, 300.

were part of the context in which Israel was to remain a covenant people for the benefit of the nations that were not friendly to Israel.

Very similar to Israel, Eastern Congo has experienced wars from other nations around it as well as internal ethnic wars. Although the wars in the DRC have a very different nature compared to the wars in ancient Israel, the eastern Congolese church had to be established in geographical locations and is today facing such a context of war in which it has to fulfill its mandate to make disciples of all the nations or ethnic groups in Eastern Congo. With the cross being "God's victory over whatever opposes and oppresses,"[9] it is clear that this church's first mandate is to establish God's rule and kingdom rule in the region through the proclamation of the gospel message and then to develop survival mechanism as it experiences war.

If, as Kaiser argues, "mission points to a central action: the act of being sent with a commission to carry out the will of a superior"[10] even in the midst of war, then this study would agree that "it is God who commissions and God who sends."[11] He called Abraham (Gen 12:1–3), Moses (Exod 3), Joshua (Josh 1:1–9), judges and prophets with specific missions to accomplish his will and to make Israel into a big nation through which all nations were to be blessed.

However, with Israel's experience of war and conquests, this study disagrees with him that in the Old Testament, "the association with God's mission is the office of the prophet."[12] In the whole of the Old Testament, the redemptive plan of God is clearly stated through covenants and prophets were not the only channel to fulfill God's missions but were fully part of the collective channel, namely, Israel. Because one has to agree that Genesis 12:1–3 is seen to be a "divine program to glorify himself by bringing salvation to all on planet earth," the strategy, theology and the mission of the Old Testament are, therefore, dominated by this Abrahamic covenant.[13] It is because "the most recognizable symbol of Christianity is the Cross. Its significance is found in the work of Christ"[14] who appears as the fulfillment of both the Abrahamic covenant and the Davidic covenant in the Old Testament (Gen 12:1–3; 2 Sam

---

9. Wright, *Mission of God's People*, 103.
10. Kaiser, *Mission in the Old Testament*, 11.
11. Kaiser, 11.
12. Kaiser, 12.
13. Kaiser, 12.
14. Erickson, *Christian Theology*, 798.

7:1–17). God used, among others, kings, prophets and priests as channels to help Israel to fulfill her mission. The word "prophet," in Hebrew הַנָּבִיא (meaning "a spokesman" or "a speaker") and in Greek προφῆτης ("a messenger"; cf. Acts 13:1; Rev 16:13) or εὐαγγελιστοῦ ("the messenger"; cf. 2 Tim 4:5 and Acts 21:8), preachers of the gospel should not carry the burden for mission alone, but should instead allow every member of the body of Christ, the church, to be and feel part of it.

James Chukulwa Okoye identifies four faces of mission in the Old Testament[15]: the aspect of universality (universality of salvation and universality of righteousness), community-in-missions, the "centripetal mission" in Isaiah 2:2–5 and the "centrifugal mission" in Isaiah 56:1–8. It is true that "God is not limited to or contained by any racial or cultural boundaries,"[16] but Israel was given the Torah to illuminate not only themselves but other nations also. The church in the DRC resembles in this respect Israel whom the Bible referred to as a nation. God gave the commandments to Israel as a community in Exodus 20:1–21. It is that community that was to be a light to other nations. The church in Eastern Congo identified itself as the body of Christ, which holds the mandate of winning the nations for Christ. No member should be isolated due to any reason from that mission in the context of war and ethnicity. That is why the mission needs a centrifugal aspect in building the church up through discipleship and a centripetal aspect by discipling the nations in a holistic approach.

3.2.2 Church Missions in the Gospels

Written with a critical factor in dating as per how the gospel stands in the horrors of the Jewish War of AD 66–70,[17] the Gospel of Matthew presents mission as disciple making. We agree with Bosch that "Matthew is not only describing Jesus' life" but also that he provided "guidance to the community of believers which needed to understand the church's calling and mission."[18] To his audience in the midst of, or having experienced, that war Matthew reveals Israel's disobedience to God and presents Jesus as the fulfillment of the

---

15. Okoye, *Israel and the Nations*, 10–12.
16. Okoye, 11.
17. Stacey, *Groundwork of Biblical Studies*, 351.
18. Bosch, *Transforming Mission*, 57.

Mosaic covenant (Matt 5:17). Craig Ott and his colleagues support the view of Bosch by arguing that "Matthew's formulation of the Great Commission, which concludes his Gospel, must be understood together with the opening of his Gospel which begins with the genealogy of Jesus with Abraham and David."[19]

It is agreed that Matthew shows that "the particularistic work of redemption completed by Christ makes possible the fulfillment of the universal intention that the good news is brought to the nations."[20] God's plan to bless the nations of the earth through Abraham and his descendants in Genesis 12:1–3, which was shaped through the Davidic covenant in 2 Samuel 7:12–17, was fulfilled by Jesus Christ. So, the nations are the concern of the gospel. That is why the commission uses the imperative "go" to emphasize the urgency of reaching every nation in its context and does not leave room for any other way.

In Matthew chapters 8 and 15, the author presents to his readers Jesus's acceptance and admiration of two Gentile persons' faith, namely, that of the centurion in Capernaum and that of the Canaanite women. This revolutionary message affirms the shift in mission. However, Bosch presents this Gentiles' mission as the one to become effective after the resurrection of the Messiah.[21] In the time of the post-2011 election crisis in Eastern Congo, while many are losing hope for Congo, it is a very wonderful time for the church and missionaries to commission the believers to fulfill the Great Commission which is a holistic and inclusive mission. Only that commission can help the nation see the riches hidden in accepting all people, even foreigners, as part of the change.

Bosch emphasizes that "according to Matthew's 'Great Commission,' it is not possible to make disciples without telling them to practice God's call of justice for the poor"[22] as well. This is remarkably evident in Matthew 5:3, 11:5–6, 25:31–46 and especially Matthew 19:21. The poor must have included those affected by the outcomes of the conflicts that made their livelihoods and social stability vulnerable in different ways.

---

19. Ott, Strauss and Tennent, *Encountering Theology of Mission*, 36.
20. Ott, Strauss and Tennent, 36.
21. Bosch, *Transforming Mission*, 64.
22. Bosch, 81.

According to George Peters, Mark reports the church's mandate to preach the gospel sometime during the forty-day period preceding his ascension (Mark 16:15).[23] According to him, the method of missions in Mark is preaching while the mission field is the world and the message the gospel. Mark's gospel, "from a Jewish hand intended for Gentile Christians around 65 AD,"[24] does not integrate the context of the Jewish war which happened between AD 66–70. On the one hand, this study partially agrees with Peters that Mark is talking about "the oral proclamation of the Gospel of Jesus Christ"[25] because "all nations" of the world have to hear the message. Believers in every context including those from "the Jewish war context and those in Rome where the Gospel of Mark was first given,"[26] therefore, were subjected to the task of proclamation. Matthew 28:18–20 also emphasizes the need to witness by teaching the new disciples "all that Christ taught" the first disciples. This is a skill transfer of Christ's teachings and life and means that discipleship is key to Christianity.

On the other hand, Mark speaks of "going into all the world and preach the gospel to all creatures" (Mark 16:15), which is to preach the redemption of the restoration of the image of God that was distorted in Eden from the beginning of the enmity that has inaugurated war (Gen 3, Rom 8:20). It is clear that Mark is telling his readers that preaching the gospel involves doing justice to the creation in which individuals and communities from different nations across the world live. During wartime there is the destruction of the creation, as is being observed in Eastern Congo: illicit exploitation of mineral resources, destruction of the forest and the flora by the militia, and even by the community. It is the role of the church, during this time of war, to promote the preaching of Christ to the community and to all creatures. The redemptive nature of our mission includes our responsibility as stewards of the natural resources that war manifestly destroys. Ott, Strauss and Tennent, however, articulate that "Mark emphasizes proclamation accompanied by confirming signs."[27] These may be understood as the church becoming the

---

23. Peters, *Biblical Theology of Missions*, 190.
24. Stacey, *Groundwork of Biblical Studies*, 349.
25. Peters, *Biblical Theology of Missions*, 190.
26. Stacey, *Groundwork of Biblical Studies*, 349.
27. Ott, Strauss and Tennent, *Encountering Theology of Mission*, 37.

center for change and holistic transformation of a world "characterized by ill health, limited access to clean water and hygienic sanitation, poor quality housing, hunger, illiteracy and premature death."[28]

In the Gospel of Luke and Acts, mission is presented as practicing forgiveness and solidarity with the poor (see for example Luke 4:8, 7:22; Acts 9:36, 10:4, 24:17). Bosch tries to reveal how Luke takes interest in mission. Different to Matthew, Luke quotes an Old Testament text (Isa 61) while explaining the "Great Commission." Luke is addressing his message to the Gentile Christians who were confronting an identity problem after the crisis caused by the Zealots, which had a negative impact on Judaism and even caused the destruction of the temple of Jerusalem.[29] The Gentile Christians needed to know whether they related to Judaism and if Christianity was just a continuation of the faith of the Old Testament or a new religion.

To this generation, Luke presents the account of Jesus which, according to Conzelmann, is the "salvation story" in three different epochs: the epoch of Israel up to John the Baptist, the epoch of Jesus's ministry and the epoch of the church, which started with Pentecost.[30] In his writing, Luke also emphasizes Jesus's message of repentance and forgiveness, love and acceptance of enemies, justice, and human inter-relationships and presents the poor as the beneficiaries of salvation (Luke 4:18).

Ford argued that "the books of Luke and Acts show that the Samaritan mission was the beginning of the Gentile mission and was part of God's plan."[31] As far as Israel needed to be restored as one nation and healed from idolatry before the gospel reaches the very end of the world (i.e. the Gentiles), it needed to reach Jerusalem and Samaria the divided parts of one nation first.

This situation is applicable to the church in Africa in general and in particular the church in the DRC where the war and armed group conflicts have destroyed the young generation's confidence and trust in Christianity. In 2015, there were some groups in the forest, for example, the FDLR – the ex-Rwandan army that has spent twenty years in the forest – and every group of them have pastors who preach the gospel and at the same time have guns

---

28. Clarke, "Introduction," 2.
29. Bosch, *Transforming Mission*, 85.
30. Conzelmann in Bosch, 86.
31. Ford in Bosch, 89.

to fight for the group. This kind of situation puts the young generation into confusion and they ask "What is Christianity?." In Eastern Congo where "over 200,000 rapes have been reported since war started . . ., where 8,000 cases of sexual violence took place yearly in 2009 and 2010 and 5,485 cases were counted in North Kivu province last year,"[32] all these cases perpetrated by some other armed tribes/groups' members, hatred has taken place to the extent that some young people may join either the army or a militia out of revenge. A pastor told one of the Christian Union students,

> gentleman, it is good for me to contribute to your mission conference of December 2010, but as you said it will deal with peace and reconciliation. Let me tell you that reconciliation with Congolese and Rwandese will be solved in heaven.

Such church leaders' responses may not help the new generation of leaders respond in a Christian way to war and violence.

The church's mandate in the Gospel of John is found in John 20:19–23. Prior to the church mandate, John (cf. John 12:20–27) presents Andrew and Philip bringing Greeks who sought an audience with Jesus, and the cloaked response Jesus makes. This served as the prelude to "all nations." According to Moreau, Corwin and McGee, "Jesus sends his disciples into the world as he was sent . . . to make God known to the world in the same way Jesus did, glorifying God and telling the world what they learned through the one who sent them."[33] This confirms the idea that discipleship involves a skill transfer to new believers. It is curious to notice that John emphasizes the time of the event as he says the commission was given in the same evening (John 20:19) when the disciples were assembled. Luke and John are therefore reporting the same scene. It is also clear that John reports one experience of his interest while Luke observes another experience of the same event.

John seems to be much aware of the lack of peace in the midst of disciples who were "hiding" in the same room because of the fear of the ruling government's sword. That is why he mentions the formula of greetings as "Peace be with you" (John 20:21). It is only when they have been assured of God's support for peace that he gave them the physical proofs of his resurrection

---

32. Burrow, *Violence against Women*, 26.
33. Moreau, Corwin and McGee, *Introducing World Mission*, 49.

and therefore restored their joy, then commissioning them for their most comprehensive ministry. The lesson for the church in Eastern Congo is that they too must work for peace and reconciliation in order to prepare the nation for discipleship in their "world filled with pain."[34]

3.2.3 Church Mission in Pauline Writings

Many scholars have failed to understand Paul's writing due to the perspective they hold on Paul's writings. Donald Senior and Carol Stuhlmueller identify the foundation of Paul's mission theology in his conviction that "God exercises his sovereignty over all creation and through Christ both Jews and Gentiles are all chosen."[35]

In the same line of thought, Bosch identifies the following six characteristics of Paul's missionary paradigm[36]:

1. *The church as New Community*: Unity in the divided first-century church was needed.
2. *Mission to Jews*: Christians should be aware of their new identity in Christ and therefore all nations including the Jews are subject to hear the gospel.
3. *Mission in the Context of God's Imminent Triumph*: This gives to his message the priority of the gospel above all other church activities in service of the kingdom rule of Christ.
4. *Mission and the Transformation of the Society*: Although advocating a gospel of a soon returning Christ, Paul rebukes Christian non-involvement in society. At the same time, Paul is clearly hesitant about stressing too much participation in the world.
5. *Mission in Weakness*: Paul encourages his readers to serve God.
6. *The Aim of Missions*: This is that Christians "set apart for the gospel of God" by Jesus Christ "through him we received grace and apostleship to call all the Gentiles to the obedience that comes from faith for his name's sake" (Rom 1:1, 5).

---

34. Moreau, Corwin and McGee, 49.
35. Stuhlmueller and Senior, *Biblical Foundations*, 171.
36. Bosch, *Transforming Mission*, 171–78.

Thus, it can be said that Paul's writings emphasize the new identity in Christ, which is expressed in the unity of the church even though each of its members still holds their ethnic identity. Therefore, the church is called to reach out to all nations and share their faith in Christ in the world full of pain.

Caroline Hodge uses Galatians 2:7–9 as the foundational parameters for Paul and his Judean colleagues to spread the gospel as "all agreed that 'we should go to the Gentiles, and they to the circumcised' (Gal 2:9; NIV)."[37] Hodge's idea is not complete without being connected to the fact that Paul refers to Genesis 12:3 as he reminds his readers that, "Scripture foresaw that God would justify the Gentiles by faith, and announced the gospel in advance to Abraham: 'All nations will be blessed through you'" (Gal 3:8). However, the researcher agrees with her that "ethnicity determined the organization of the mission and Paul was responsible for the ethnic and religious 'other.'"[38] It brings a new dynamic to the church's missions task that "involves the crossing of ethnic boundaries"[39] while others concentrate on reaching out to people of their ethnic identity. In a time of crisis and war that, to an extent, is linked to ethnicity, the church in Eastern Congo needs to do its missions by investing in tasks that allow both individuals and itself an exercise of crossing ethnic boundaries and building a multiethnic community of believers.

Paul leaves room for his Judean colleagues who felt called to their own people to do missions among them. It is as if the survival of the church in that context of ethnicity in the first century AD needed the church to consider the nature of missions as both crossing the ethnic boundaries to reach out to other nations and doing missions with interest in the missionary's own people. Although this may look contradictory, Paul's idea behind it is that the survival of a church may depend on the ethnic character of the church in an ethnic setting but in a multicultural setting there is a great need for the church to concentrate on planting multiethnic churches. In recording the experiences of pastors who pastored churches during the wars between 1990 and 2011, this work verifies whether the survival of some local churches was not connected to their ethnic character or if, to some extent, ethnicity did not contribute to their survival.

---

37. Hodge, "Apostle to the Gentiles," 288.
38. Hodge, 288.
39. Hodge, 288.

3.2.4 Conclusion

The focus on mission in both the Old Testament and the New Testament is "all nations."[40] Thomas R. Schreiner reveals that "Paul concludes Romans 3 with the truth that all people, both Jews and Gentiles, are righteous by faith."[41] The fact that "Paul introduces Abraham in chapter four, the forefather of Jewish people" supports "the truth that the universal blessing is received by faith."[42] Thus, Romans 4 presents Israel not according to the flesh, but by faith. It is curious that Israel, the missionary people in the OT, is involved in conquests and wars against nations.[43] In the New Testament, Matthew presents mission as disciple making. Bosch says that "according to Matthew's 'Great Commission,' it is not possible to make disciples without telling them to practice God's call to justice for the poor."[44] George Peters identifies Mark's concept of the Great Commission as "preaching the Gospel to the entire world and to all creatures."[45] In Luke and Acts mission is presented as practicing forgiveness and solidarity with the poor and the great commission takes interest in nations (Gentiles).[46] In John 20:19–23, "Jesus sends his disciples to the world as he was sent"[47] after imparting his peace to them.

Every synoptic Gospel presents the church's mandate with a single description of the nature of missions as given by different scholars.[48] The same thing occurs in the OT. God commissioned particular people to fulfill his plan and purpose beginning with Abraham whom "God promised to give a land, a prosperity, and a mission of blessing (Gen 12:1–3), a promise later repeated to the patriarchs."[49] There is a gap in the lack of a holistic understanding of missions as comprising oral proclamation of the gospel, discipling the nations,

---

40. Wright, *Mission of God's People*, 71.
41. Schreiner, "Interpreting Romans," 6.
42. Schreiner, 5.
43. Glasser, Van Engen, Gilliland and Redford, *Announcing the Kingdom*, 105.
44. Bosch, *Transforming Mission*, 81.
45. Peters, *Biblical Theology of Missions*, 190.
46. Bosch, *Transforming Mission*, 85.
47. Moreau, Corwin and McGee, *Introducing World Mission*, 49.
48. Bosch, *Transforming Mission*; Lewis and Demarest, *Integrative Theology*; Glasser, Van Engen, Gilliland and Redford, *Announcing the Kingdom*; Peters, *Biblical Theology of Missions*; Wright, *Mission of God's People*, etc.
49. Lewis and Demarest, *Integrative Theology*, 300.

teaching the disciples to care for the poor, practical demonstration of love to all and promoting love, peace and unity.

At the beginning of the twentieth century,

> missions still denoted the idea of geographical expansion. From the Missionary conference called Edinburgh 1910, the nature of missions took the character of unity for the conquest of the so-called "heathens" with the Gospel and establish "the kingdom of God on earth."[50]

This was to be done by planting the church, which became the church's purpose. By questioning the source of the word "missions" in relation to the World Wars I and II in preparation for this study, it was discovered that before these wars the word missions referred to the work of the Western church to evangelize the "heathens" and plant churches in the Majority World. Not until well after World Wars I and II did its meaning shift to "the whole Gospel to the whole world"[51] with Ralph Winter at the Lausanne Conference in the 1970s advocating for "God's mission among all peoples."[52] This meant that, "missions and the range of its participants became global (holistic) in scope."[53]

While trying to reveal the effect of the two world wars on the understanding of church missions, Mike Barnett says, "the world in the mid-1900 witnessed a series of dizzying and interrelated social, political, economic, technological, and religious changes that thoroughly impacted the mission of God."[54] One of the effects is that the use of words such as "heathen" and "un-evangelized" was abandoned as missions borrowed military words such as "target (-evangelism)" and "unreached (people groups)."

---

50. Moreau, Corwin, and McGee, *Introducing World Mission*, 142.
51. Barnett, "Global Century," 303.
52. Ralph Winter in Barnett, 303–4.
53. Barnett, 304.
54. Barnett, 288.

3.3 Matthew 5:38–45: Not War but Peace as the Christian Response to War

3.3.1 Introduction

Matthew 5:38–44 is a passage in which Matthew contrasts "patterns of conducts: the first based on the strict justice of the Old Testament's code, the second based on a new set of priorities wherein disciples sacrifices their rights for the benefits of others," and the third based on "love from the Old Testament tradition" forming a Christian response toward mistreatment or an injury caused by the enemy.[55] Using Jesus's Sermon on the Mount, the author is not directly addressing the issues like war, but the context of the first readers of Matthew indicates that of a "church settled in Syria after the failure of mission in Israel and the Jewish war,"[56] which makes the book also a theological inspiration for the church in the context of war such as that in Eastern Congo. Because the enemy's offences and crimes could be seen as justification for retaliation, this text also fits the context of war and Christian attitudes toward war or armed conflict to which a Christian is exposed.

3.3.2 Structure

The passage can be divided into two parts and be given the following titles: retaliation and nonviolence (5:38–42) and love of the enemy (5:43–48).

3.3.3 Context of Matthew 5:38–45

The immediate context of this passage is Jesus telling his disciples to let their "yes" be "yes" and their "no" be "no" in order to avoid partaking in evil by evil decisions (Matt 5:38) and his command that his disciples should not only love those who love them, but show their distinctiveness in loving their enemies (Matt 5:46–48).

The wider context of these verses is Jesus's Sermon on the Mount as he taught his disciples to go the second mile, which is something that goes beyond the Mosaic law and, therefore, to love their enemies. It appears at the beginning of his ministry, which ends with his arrest, death and resurrection, prior to his giving of the Great Commission to his disciples and forty days after the resurrection when he commissioned them to witness his

---

55. Hagner, *Matthew 1–13*, 130.
56. Luz, *Studies in Matthew*, 7.

gospel to all nations (Matt 28:18–20). Matthew translated Jesus's message to "a Jewish Christian community which was at a turning point; a time after the destruction of Jerusalem in the Jewish war,"[57] a time when this Jewish community experienced a doctrinal or theological crisis and took a new direction and determination in their affairs because of their experience of the Jerusalem war and their determination "to carry its proclamation to the Gentiles."[58] It is to this Christian community, facing opposition and war, that Matthew presents Jesus's instruction to Peter not to use the sword against the enemy (Matt 26:50–54) and his response of silence when interrogated by Pilate (Matt 27:13–14).

3.3.4 Historical Background and Authorship

The historical background of this passage is Matthew aiming "to strengthen and inform a large number of followers"[59] by meeting their many needs:

1. To instruct and perhaps to catechize.
2. To provide apologetic and evangelical material, especially in winning Jews for Jesus.
3. To encourage believers in their witness before and to a hostile world.
4. To inspire deeper faith in Jesus the Messiah along with a maturing understanding of his person, work and unique place in the unfolding history of redemption.[60]

The church, therefore, had to prepare itself to face opposition to Jesus's message in a hostile context as well as being important for the author to establish the identity of the church as the true people of God, whose unity in service despises racial, class and religious barriers. The author of the Gospel captures for his audience the warnings and predictions of Jesus to the twelve that they would face opposition at every level, be taken before rulers and even die for his name (cf. Matt 10; 24:9–13). While most scholars take Antioch as the place of composition during Bishop Ignatius's days, Carson argues that Matthew "wrote to meet the need of his own center and that of other centers during his

---

57. Luz, *Matthew 1–7*, 84.
58. Luz, 28.
59. Carson, "Matthew," 24.
60. Carson, 25.

time as he was more itinerant."[61] The audience in Antioch churches included both Jewish and Gentile Christians (cf. Acts 11:19–26; 13:1–3).

The author of the book, a former tax collector under King Herod, reflects his knowledge of the Mosaic law toward evil and also mentions in the immediate context the tax collectors' good deeds, which were not righteous people because they were not morally changed by the law. He also mentions the absence of the crowd to this teaching which seems to be proper to the church, a group consisting of Jesus's disciples at the Mount. Therefore, in contrast to what Grudem supports, "the idea of a violent attack to bodily harm or even murder[ing] someone"[62] is also in view in this text.

Jesus is advocating for peace in opposition to war. Carson says that "the OT prescription (Exod 21:24; Lev 24:19–20; Deut 19:21) was not given to foster vengeance . . . rather, . . . to provide the nation's judicial system with a ready formula of punishment, not least because it would precisely terminate vendettas."[63] Jesus is teaching his disciples that they must not be revengeful (v. 39). In the text, he calls for consistency of retaliation and love for the sake of peace.

This situation closely resembles the context in Eastern Congo where the church has been acting in the context of war and ethnic conflicts during the last two decades. In the middle of the two decades of war, that is the year 2000, 97 per cent of the Congolese population was said to be Christians.[64] The groups involved in causing the war are ethnic militia, rebel groups like M23 and the FDLR, which is the former Rwandan defense forces hidden in the forest in Eastern Congo since the Rwandan genocide. All these groups, to a certain extent fight against the Congolese defense forces, and among themselves, and/or against specific ethnic communities. The church is located in every area where these groups have operated or are operating and therefore has been victimized in many ways, such as the rape of Christians and other abuses, the burning down of a whole village, killings of people and repeated looting of property. Some Christians and church leaders have been found to be involved with or collaborated with war scenarios. For example, Laurent

---

61. Carson, 25.
62. Grudem, *Politics According to the Bible*, 202.
63. Carson, "Matthew," 155.
64. Barrett, *World Christianity Encyclopedia*, 758.

Nkunda, the Founder of the CNDP, used to be a preacher of the gospel and the M23 Movement was first led by Bishop Runiga, a top leader of JSS church in Congo.

3.3.5 Retaliation and Nonviolence (5:38–43)

Verse 38, which states "You have heard that it was said, 'Eye for eye, and tooth for tooth,'" presents the retaliation in its essence. Bernard Jackson reveals that "even if the 'meaning' of 'an eye for an eye' in the Hebrew Bible refers to a literal retaliation,"[65] which Davies assumes without argument to be an exclusively judicial measure, it assuredly originates in institutions of self-help.[66] In the ancient Hammurabi code and the biblical law in Exodus, "talion is assumed to mean the mandatory application of like physical retaliation for bodily injuries interpreted 'literally.'"[67] It seems clear that "there was a common assumption what an 'eye for an eye' should be, and that this meant that physical retaliation was a mandatory sanction to be imposed by the courts."[68] However, the retaliation law seems to have been in practice also in the community as a measure of retributive justice because

> ... the association with the victim's suffering, in turn, associates vengeful desert with the feelings of revenge and hatred that we commonly see in victims. Thus, punishment under this conception of desert is sometimes seen as essentially an institutionalization of victim revenge; it is "injury inflicted on a wrongdoer that satisfies the retributive hatred felt by that wrongdoer's victim and that is justified because of that satisfaction."[69]

Therefore, in the desert community, "Physical equality was particularly palpable in the reciprocity sought in punishment, 'Eye for eye, tooth for tooth, hand for hand, foot for foot' (Exodus 21:24)" to the extent that Aristotle "defined justice as retaliation."[70]

---

65. Jackson, "Lex Talionis," 201–2.
66. Jackson, 201–2.
67. Jackson, "Models in Legal History," 17.
68. Jackson, 7.
69. Robinson, "Competing Conceptions," 147.
70. Noonan, "Metaphors of Morals," 35.

Matthew 5:38–42 reveals the presence of the words δὲ and ἀλλ', the two translated as "but" in English (v. 39). The first one has a dual meaning and it can be analyzed as a disjunctive conjunction of "but" or a conjunction of coordination "and." In this case, δὲ takes the meaning "and" while ἀλλ' means "but." In this case "but" (ἀλλ') is stronger in force than "and" as it emphasizes the contrast between tradition and the teaching of Jesus. So, the conjunction δὲ connects with verse 38 to mean "You heard it was said 'eye for eye' *and* 'tooth for tooth'" summarizing the law that states "eye for eye, tooth for tooth, hand for hand, foot for foot, burning for burning, wound for wound, stripe for stripe" in Exodus 21:24 and Leviticus 24:20 by Moses. However, ἀλλ' introduces a firm opposition of what has been said, that is, the retaliation law encouraging war in response to war. In fact, Donald Hagner uses the word "but" in verse 39 and refers to it as "the command of Jesus, again introduced with the introductive 'but I say to you.'"[71]

Why did Jesus hold that position and teach this kind of passivity to his disciples in a special discipleship meeting (Matt 5:1)? The answer seems to be that Jesus was setting a new direction for his disciples whom he said were in the world without being of the world (John 17). In the world are "wars and rumors of wars" that must happen as "nation will rise against nations" which is also "the beginning of [the] birth pains" of the church (Mark 13:7–8). Therefore, the use of this "shocking contrast to the principle of justice defended by the OT test" is a call to an opposite direction toward not "resisting evil at all meaning, do not render evil for evil."[72] Fighting appears to involve the church as a stakeholder of war and not of peace and may not allow the church to reach out to all stakeholders involved in war and conflict. So, for him, war appears to be a greater contributor to the planting of Christianity. The church then will have to face the same challenges. Fortunately, the church survived and grew through the pains of persecutions and suffering due to different causes, starting with identity conflicts.

In the Sermon on the Mount, Jesus advocates for nonviolence as a Christian response toward violence and war. The use of the verb "to resist" or "to oppose" in its infinitive active aorist form (ἀντιστῆναι) brings the idea of an ongoing act of violence or war to which Christians are to respond with

---

71. Hagner, *Matthew 1–13*, 130.
72. Hagner, 130.

a nonviolent attitude. Jesus warned his audience not to fight back against the enemy and not to respond to ongoing war with war.

The interpretation of verse 39 appears to bear misinterpretation of the meaning of the disjunctive conjunction used by Jesus. According to Warren Carter,

> Jesus' authoritative interpretation (But I say to you) is Do not violently resist an evildoer forbids self-protection and invites the same submissive approach to tyrants which the vassal king Herod Agrippa urges the crowds to adopt, rather than rebel against Rome (Josephus, JW 2.345–401).[73]

Although he brings out the real context from Josephus, the researcher does not agree with him that "It suggests that God legitimizes evil and requires disciples to capitulate to and collude with, not oppose, evil action."[74] Matthew is writing in the context following the Jerusalem war that caused the Christian community to be displaced and to live in fear of persecution. In this case, the ruling power is the oppressor. If God legitimizes evil then Jesus would not have contradicted "the code of Hammurabi which was a provision for justice with room for preventing much more damage for a wrong done as one had to revenge."[75] In the case of the Matthean first audience, it can be agreed that "verse 39 offers scenes of resisting oppressive power"[76] but without bearing in mind that that power refers to "the devil which Jesus resisted in Matt. 5:3–6."[77] Hagner contradicts such an interpretation and says that "the articular $τῷ$ $πονηρῷ$ here clearly does not mean 'the evil one,' that is, Satan (as in v37; cf. 6:13)."[78] On the other hand, to support Foulkes' view that verse 39 is saying that the church can align with the ruling power but not call it to change by resisting its wrongdoing is to hinder it from advocating for justice.

Reading verses 40 to 42 of Matthew 5 in light of verse 39, one may feel that Jesus asks his followers to act naively during violence caused by an offender, an enemy, a rebel and the like, especially in a war context. During the war, abuses such as rape, kidnapping and killing are perpetrated by community

---

73. Carter, *Matthew and the Margins*, 151.
74. Carter, 151.
75. Foulkes, *Guide to St Matthew's Gospel*, 46.
76. Foulkes, 151.
77. Foulkes, 151.
78. Hagner, *Matthew 1–13*, 130.

members, including Christians. Currie observes that the words κριθῆναι in Mathew 5:40 and *anarare* in Luke 6:30 indicate legal action.[79] He opposes Lohmeyer who wants to understand the use of the Syriac root *qûm* to mean "adopt an attitude of defense," or, more colloquially, "square off," and says that "*qûm* can be used precisely to mean 'stand up' and testify against."[80] It is acceptable to him because this is "resisting the oppressing power"[81] through being a voice to fight for justice. In a context where an individual disciple would be subjected to violence, the church would need to stand up and testify against the various abuses of the enemy, even when the oppressor would have been the ruling government, by speaking out and denouncement.

From the above analysis, one may argue with Glen Stassen that retaliation versus initiatives of peacemaking in Matthew 5:38–42 means that "Jesus' teaching arises from the recognition that the injuries under which human community suffers cannot be healed or rebuilt anew by way of the right of retaliation."[82] In reaction to war, the church takes a nonviolent attitude and moves toward "the liberation action that breaks the vicious cycle of retaliation and group exclusiveness, and creates a new community among people through forgiveness, reconciliation, and peacemaking."[83] This is a deeper significance of "if anyone wants to sue you and take your shirt, hand over your coat as well. If anyone forces you to go one mile, go with them two miles" (Matt 5:40–41). The church, in the context of violence, is called to advocate and act for reconciliation and plant churches; this includes the creation of healing communities of believers from all nations. In the context of ethnicity, the church is called to react to war with building communities of faith promoting forgiveness, reconciliation and peacemaking.

Richard Harries "attempts to show how there has been a tension through Christian history between two strands"; according to him, "Jesus told his disciples not to resist those who wrong them . . . (Matt 5:9). Yet this is not the only strand that relates to violence in the New Testament, let alone the Bible as a whole."[84] We do not totally agree with him that there is a tension; on the

---

79. Currie, "Matthew," 141.
80. Lohmeyer in Currie, 141.
81. See Carter, *Matthew and the Margins*, 151.
82. Stassen, "Fourteen Triads," 306.
83. Stassen, 306.
84. Harries, "Non-Retaliation," 1.

contrary, there is clarity from Jesus. Using the example of John the Baptist, which Harries states as "having accepted military life as legitimate vocation,"[85] it is clear that Jesus was telling his disciples that not to take revenge is not rejecting the legitimacy of the power of correction believers are to accept in the process of providing peace to the people. On the other hand, it can be agreed that the "both Jesus' teaching on non-retaliation and this positive attitude to secular authority have to be seen against the background of the imminent arrival of the Kingdom, which Jesus proclaimed and ushered in."[86]

But even so, both governments in Christian countries and the church have struggled with the extent to which retaliation has to apply, the death penalty being at the center of the debate, for example, which the church has rejected. In political arenas some scholars have argued against it and rather recommended (or advocated for) life sentence, saying that "the overwhelming evidence of injustice of death sentences could not sway popular support for capital punishment, but evidence that switching to life sentences could save millions of dollars is swaying many pro-penalty voters and legislators."[87] At the same time, the church has wrestled to try to influence politics and scholarship on that issue. For example, while "American Catholics and Pope John Paul II confluence over the issue of death penalty,"[88] Derrida "accepts the widespread view of Jesus' death as one propounding forgiveness and grace."[89] Using the death penalty as an example, it appears that the interpretation of the scriptures by various scholars can change the non-retaliation command of Jesus to pacifism for some and to nonviolence for others. It is agreeable that the church is called to promote forgiveness and preach the gospel of grace, but this view is limited by not giving the government any new way of dealing with matters of criminality, and this gives room to advocate for life sentence rather than forgiveness. From the researcher's own experience in the war zone, a simple escape of a criminal from prison or mismanagement of a militia team by the government has always caused not only new massacres but also possibilities for new clashes.

---

85. Harries, 1.
86. Harries, 13.
87. Gudorf, "Christianity and Opposition," 109.
88. Mulligan, "Pope John Paul."
89. Taylor, "Derrida, the Death Penalty," 100.

On the other hand, war has brought church leaders and scholars to advocate for peace and justice and also to re-evaluate the church's position on war. The Catholic church has the just war as a part of the Catholic's rich theology. During the Iraq war, it changed its teachings on peace and war to include: "the defense of human rights, the right to integral human development, support for international law and global institutions as well as the relatively new teaching on nonviolence and forgiveness."[90] This was done with a specific stand on

> situations of conflicts, a constant commitment to strive for justice through nonviolent means, when attempts at nonviolent action to protect innocent against injustice, then legitimate political authorities are permitted as a last resort to employ limited force to rescue the innocent and establish justice.[91]

Reading through the church's attempts to respond to war, it also appears that some churches fully supported the just war position. For example, Joseph Fiorenza, former US Conference of Catholic Bishops president, presents views of several religious leaders around the world regarding US military operations in Afghanistan and argues that "military action is always regrettable, but it may be necessary to protect the innocent or to defend the common good"; while other leaders like Cardinal Edward Egan of New York was advocating for prayer "for safety of the armed forces of the US and its allies and for a speedy and decisive victory."[92] Although the United States has wrestled with how Christians ought to retaliate when foreigners attack, a theology of war is still lacking to interpret the legitimacy of the attack. But sometimes this debate leaves out of consideration the believers living in the war zones to whom Matthew 5:39 is also addressed. The debate should take into account Jesus telling his disciples to protectively take a purse, a bag and a sword in a particular context (cf. Luke 22:35–38).

3.3.6 Love of the Enemy (5:43–45)

In verse 43, Jesus quotes from the Mosaic law in Leviticus 19:18, which called upon the Jewish people to love their neighbor. However, the second part of

---

90. Christiansen, "Wither the 'Just War'?" 6.
91. Christiansen, 6.
92. Fiorenza, Onaiyekan and Sabah, "Other Catholic Views," 16.

that quote is absent in Leviticus 19:18. Rather than the biblical Hebrew law that speaks of "You shall hate your enemies" it calls upon love for the enemy. According to L. B. Paton, "Lev 19 follows its analogy by beginning with a law, 'Thou shalt not hate thy brother in thy heart' and following this up with a set of laws against sinful inward dispositions."[93] Furthermore, the sentence "You shall love your neighbor" (ESV) appears in Leviticus 19:18, which starts with "Do not take revenge or bear a grudge against members of your community" (HCSB). This highlights the idea of nonviolence in the Hebrew law.

Andrew Galloway quotes Cox who insists that "You shall love your neighbor and hate your enemy" "is not Leviticus 19:18, but a case of early 'supersession.'"[94] He rejects Cox's view saying "yet, Leviticus 26:7–8 does recommend hating and persecuting your enemies; to ignore that is special pleading."[95] We may agree with Galloway because this is one of the passages that explains Israel going to war with its enemies. Israel needed to work for its peace, which required them to overcome their fear. In the case of Israel, "the two sources of fear that are specified in Leviticus 26:6–8 are war and wild animals."[96]

On the other hand, when reading the first paragraph of the Code of Hammurabi it appears that its mandate was "to bring about the rule of righteousness in the land, to destroy the wicked and the evildoers so that the strong should not harm the weak."[97] It seems that revenge against the enemy was part of the justice provision and legal in the Middle East under the influence of the Hammurabi Code and was strengthened in Israel by the recommendation in Leviticus 26:7–8. That is why Jesus, who, in Matthew 5:43, knew that the tradition that was said and practiced was to love the neighbor and hate the enemy, introduced an authoritative opposite direction for his disciples to govern their law of love. Just as in Matthew 5:39, in verse 44 Jesus introduces the sentence with the word δὲ, meaning "but" to oppose what the disciples knew. The disciples knew that "you shall love the neighbor and hate the enemy" as in the early "supersessionism" approach or culture or the misunderstanding of the Torah; Jesus now brought to them the opposite

---

93. Paton, "Original Form," 63.
94. Galloway, "Judaic Other," 401.
95. Galloway, 401.
96. Gorman, *Divine Presence*, 143.
97. "Code of Hammurabi," 1.

principle, which is a principle of love for enemies. This principle of love does not assume that loving your enemy means to allow them to act at will. Neither is it in contradiction with Jesus telling his disciples how to handle the issue of your brother or sister in sin (cf. Matt 18:15–16) nor with the discipline of a child (cf. Proverbs 22:6).

Jesus's law of love is actually not in opposition to Leviticus 19:18 but a completion of it as he "did not . . . come to abolish the law and the prophets, . . . but to fulfill them" (Matt 5:17). Matthew reveals how the Middle Eastern culture and custom affected the message, the law of love, and presents to his audience the original meaning of that law of love, which Jesus comes to restore and proclaim as inclusive, targeting both the neighbor and the enemy in every context. Harrington presents Matthew 5:43–48 "not as a law code but as a general principle of love of the enemies"[98] and states that "the sermon makes no sharp distinction between law and love. Rather, they work together, due to Jesus's claim that he came 'not to abolish but to fulfil.'"[99]

Verse 45 emphasizes more the issue of love in comparing what the disciples have heard (verse 38 and 43) with the character of God, their Father in Heaven, whose love is beyond the human character of love. Jesus is opposing the wrong practice of hating the enemies and confirms the Hebrew law of love to both the neighbor and the enemy as he said, "Ye have heard it, too, as God's law: 'Thou shalt love thy neighbor and hate thine enemy.' But I tell you, love your worst enemies, and plead even for your persecutors, that you may become in spirit like your heavenly Father."[100] In his article entitled "Christians – What does Christ teach you concerning war?," M. G. T. interprets Matthew 5:43–45 as Jesus's address to Jews and uses verse 43 as what they have heard and tells them:

> This is what is still said, and we send armies and navies to kill and destroy our enemies. But this is an error and a sin which Jesus most positively and plainly rebukes and corrects, saying . . . love your enemies, bless them that curse you . . . do good to them that hate you.[101]

---

98. Harrington, "Sermon on the Mount," 7.
99. Harrington, 6.
100. Burtt, "Free Translation," 340.
101. M.G.T., "Christians," 259.

Therefore, it is clear that during war enemies are to be loved by the community of believers to whom Jesus is addressing the message of love as not only a biblical principle but also as a Christian precedent.

It seems like one cannot speak about love for the enemies without forgiveness of the enemies in the process of advocating peace. Thomas Upham presents the view that:

> The doctrine of forgiveness and love, carried to the extent of embracing our enemies, is addressed to Christians, to those who are supposed to understand the precepts and to process the spirit of Christ; to those who are developed under the leadings of the Holy Spirit from the self-hood to what may be called perhaps universal-hood or that of mind which loves our neighbor as ourselves.[102]

The church should respond to violence and war by encouraging believers not to avenge themselves, rather to exercise forgiveness and love their enemies to the extent of embracing and praying for them.

According to Richard Horsley, "Many scholarly and semi-popular treatments of Jesus' teaching understand 'enemies' in Matthew 5:44 and Luke 6:27 to refer to foreign or national enemies or to include national as well as personal enemies."[103] This study agrees with all his assertions. First, that "the natural assumption is that a political, usually foreign, enemy is meant, such as the Romans for Jesus and his Jewish contemporaries national as well as personal enemies."[104] This is because the war, especially in Eastern Congo, involves both foreign powers and nationals while both communities and individuals may be stakeholders and victims. Therefore second, "the saying there can be understood as referring to the foreign or political enemy,"[105] which include the militia, rebel groups, the national army and the like in the context of war. And third, Jesus's "teachings" also "interpreted directly over against 'the zealots,' since the zealots were supposedly an organized, religiously motivated movement of national liberation by force from their

---

102. Upham, "Forgiveness," 278.
103. Horsley, "Ethics and Exegesis," 7.
104. Horsley, 7.
105. Horsley, 8.

Roman overloads,"[106] under "the leadership of a military leader"[107] and "were busy advocating for a violent war called a messianic holy war."[108] One has to note that this brings the idea of an identity conflict/war with which first believers were confronted after the crises of the Zealots. These crises caused the destruction of the temple, created confusion for Gentile Christians who did not know whether Christian faith was the continuation of Judaism or a new religion[109] due to the attitude of Jewish Christians.

This research agrees with Horsley that "This understanding of 'enemies' persists and is prominent"[110] and with Ferguson who even refers to Jesus's "embracing the Romans within the community of love (Matt 5:38–48)."[111] In the first century, the divided church members needed to understand "the church as the new Community"[112] of faith, which is identified by Bosch as Paul's missionary paradigm. That is why Jesus, in Matthew 5:38–42, calls for an attitude not to fight back or take revenge during the war but to respond to war by breaking the cycle of retaliation and group exclusiveness and plant churches that work towards creating healing communities of faith through love for both the neighbors and the enemies. These communities would be created as the church, being kingdom oriented, in its commitment to fulfilling the Great Commission, sought to share love and to promote forgiveness by loving the enemies who are rebels, militia and so on. Loving the enemy, therefore, also means denouncing the abuses and promoting the message of love, which is the gospel message propagated in the process of the ministry of presence in the war context as far as the church's actions go together with the activities of war. Jesus used the Aramaic that disciples/authors recorded in Greek active ἀντιστῆναι meaning "to resist" asking the disciples not to respond with resistance but with love to the enemies and praying for them.

Rudolf Bultmann, as quoted by Kirk, however, challenges the so-called golden rule in Luke 6:27–35 and judges the "love your enemy" command as

---

106. Horsley, 8.
107. Foulkes, *Guide to St Matthew's Gospel*, 23.
108. Horsley, *Jesus and the Spiral*, 149.
109. Bosch, *Transforming Mission*, 85.
110. Horsley, "Ethics and Exegesis," 8.
111. Ferguson, *Politics of Love*, 86.
112. Bosch, *Transforming Mission*, 171–78.

expressing "naïve egoism."[113] Yet other interpreters have opposed the way of "viewing that command to love the enemies in terms of reciprocity, feeling that, its unmistakable recourse to the logic of reciprocity ethics renders it morally inferior to the altruistic, unilateral stance of 'love your enemies.'"[114] This study may also disagree with Bultmann because even beyond the fact that loving the enemy requires sacrifice from the oppressed, the enemy may be either not aware of being the oppressor or the oppressed may develop the fear of the oppressor before being oppressed and therefore look for means to defend themselves from possible attack. In the two cases, the reciprocity in the exercise to love the enemy does not exist to judge the command as naïve and egoistic. In the context of the Jerusalem war, for example, which the Matthean first audience experienced,[115] the oppressor appears to be the ruling power by the fact that it was not conscious of the Christian community being oppressed. It may have been mistakenly considered as part of the messianic groups (the Zealots) and be persecuted as a violent resistance group in the same way the Zealots were subjected to violence during the Jerusalem war and to displacement as the direct effect of that war which led the community to Antioch.

The command to love the enemy that Matthew and Luke use, in Mathew 5:43–48 and Luke 6:27–28 respectively, are not "naïve egoism" as Bultmann sees it[116] but a real command that Jesus himself demonstrated through the sacrifice of the cross as he prayed for the enemies saying "Father, forgive them, for they do not know what they are doing" (Luke 23:34).

According to Jonathan Pennington,

> the theme in Matthew is to undergird the radical nature of the ethics and teachings of Jesus which have a clear ring about them challenge, urgency, and world-overturning realities . . . because of which disciples must love and pray for their enemies.[117]

The researcher does not agree that Matthew is asking his readers to love their enemies because "the world is depicted as dipartite-heaven and earth

---

113. Kirk, "Love Your Enemies," 667.
114. Kirk, 667.
115. See Luz, Matthew 1–7, 84.
116. Kirk, "Love Your Enemies," 667.
117. Pennington, Heaven and Earth, 346.

and Jesus' disciples are the true people of God aligned with heaven, as opposed to the rulers (Romans and Jewish) on earth."[118] Matthew is writing to a community in a particular context and has to refer to the teaching of Jesus on matters related to that context. Jesus himself is addressing a context and uses the Middle East context of the Mosaic law of justice and love. What is known is that the law was given to Israel as a nation that had to face war against other nations (Josh 6). That nation was then ruled by kings such as David who also fought wars with foreign kings and with Israelites (1 Chr 20:1–8). For example, during the wars between the house of David and Saul, the Scriptures (2 Sam 3:1, 6) present David as sparing Saul's life because the latter was anointed by God. The Sermon on the Mount, the researcher can rightly infer, was not only heaven oriented, otherwise the gospel message would not exist; there would be no message of love for all nations, which includes the neighbors and the enemies as the object of church missions. Therefore, in a context of hostility or violence, loving both the neighbor and the enemy may also mean sharing God's love with both neighbors and to the enemy camp, which requires sacrifice, especially in the context of war. These are the multitude from every nation, tribe, people and language that need the witness that will get them before the throne (Rev 9, 15, 21, 22). It is clear that such an outcome will result from the church overcoming their trials by "the blood of the Lamb and by the word of their testimony" (Rev 12:11) in the midst of war, which is also experienced by neighbors and their enemies.

3.3.7 Conclusion and Theological Meaning of Matthew 5:38–45

The Gospel of Matthew, which many say was written "some sixty years after Jesus' death . . . is a Jewish wisdom instruction."[119] Rather than being a law code made from the Hammurabi code and the law of Moses, this passage is a new law that gives "general principles such as love of enemies"[120] to help the disciples to survive violence and wars while being able to plant communities of faith in the midst of that context. While reminding his readers not to fight back physically and not to respond with violence or revenge, he calls them to

---

118. Pennington, 348.
119. Harrington, "Sermon on the Mount," 7.
120. Harrington, 7.

an attitude of nonviolence and to a practice of love. That love is experienced as the disciples take an attitude of forgiveness and build a community of faith that practice love for the enemy instead of revenge. However, when the ruling power is the oppressor, the church's attitude of nonviolence should not be the hindrance for it to fight for just practices, for example, through advocacy and denunciation. Its response is a war for peace[121] that calls the ruling power to serve the just cause[122] and ensure peace for its citizens.

3.4 Acts 18:1–4: Power, Identity Conflict and Migration and Missions

3.4.1 Introduction

Acts 18:1–4 narrates how Paul dealt with a couple that was a victim of ethnicity in the Roman Empire (with reference to the fact that they were persecuted as Jews)[123] and the impact of the victim integration to build the church and the host of societies.

3.4.2 Context of Acts 18:1–4

The immediate context of this passage is Paul presenting his message (the gospel) to the council of Athens at the Areopagus where some notable people accepted it and the council requesting further explanations (Acts 17:16–33). Paul decided to devote his ministry to the Gentiles after he unfruitfully preached the gospel to the Corinthians (Acts 18:5–6).

The wider context of Acts 18:1–4 introduces the beginning of the ministry of Aquila and his wife Priscilla in Asia. Their introduction and induction were done by Paul because they played a role in the church of Corinth such as discipling Apollos and commissioning him to a preaching ministry (Acts 18:28). There was also a church in their house in Corinth (Acts 18:1; Cor 16:19).

3.4.3 Historical Background of Acts 18:1–4

The text fits into the historical background of the book of Acts which "seems to have been written in Rome between AD 59–61 when Paul was a prisoner

---

121. Cf. Polat, "Peace as War," 317.
122. Cf. Buttler, "U.S. Military Intervention in Crisis," 231.
123. Cf. Gaebelein, *John–Acts*, 481.

there."[124] This was before the burning of Rome and the first persecution of the church and the destruction of the temple of Jerusalem (70 AD).[125] For some African scholars the reason why Luke wrote the book of Acts was to defend the Christian faith to the Roman authorities or to make an effort of mediation between Judaism and Christianity in order to reveal the reason why Jews were continuing to reject the gospel, which had gone beyond the Jewish boundaries to the ends of the Roman world. Luke tries to remind Christians of the priority of the gospel, which is to live for Christ and serve him wherever they are without considering the geographic and ethnic boundaries and live their faith in the particular critical and challenging period of persecution.

According to F. F. Bruce, Corinth was a strategic city connecting the Peloponnese with northern and central Asia, and, with its commerce, the junction between Asia and the west; and from 27 BC it was the seat of administration of the Roman province of Achaia.[126] Apart from its strategic position in commerce, the city had also "acquired a reputation for sexual license remarkable even in classical antiquity"[127] and "was also the center for the worship of the goddess Aphrodite, whose temple . . . boasted of thousand sacred prostitutes and crowned the Acrocorinth."[128]

Bruce reveals that the leather worker trade "was closely connected with the principal product of Paul's native province, a cloth of goats' hair called *cilicium* used for cloaks, curtains" and that "in Judaism, it was not considered proper for a scribe or rabbi to receive payment for his teaching and so many of them practiced a trade in addition to their study and teaching of the law."[129] That is why Paul "on his missionary journeys earned his living in this occupation."[130] This brings home the custom of the Jews to bring up their people in some trade. It explains why Paul and Aquila and Priscilla, who were intellectuals, knew how to make tents. They made use of that knowledge for their subsistence and ministry in a migration context in Corinth.

---

124. Kisau, "Acts of the Apostles," 1297.
125. Kisau, 1297.
126. Bruce, *Book of Acts*, 345–46.
127. Bruce, 346.
128. Longenecker, "Acts," 479.
129. Bruce, *Book of Acts*, 346.
130. Longenecker, "Acts," 479.

3.4.4 Analysis and Comment

An exegesis of Acts 18:1–4 reveals that the Roman power and abuse of the imperial government of Claudius led to decisions that resulted in the migration of a group of Jewish people. The Roman church members, such as Priscilla and Aquila, became refugees in Corinth, far from Pontus (the native home of Aquila), and here they connected with Paul, a Jew, who also had Roman citizenship, and together, they did mission work. This became the beginning of the couple's ministry in Corinth. The survival of the church during the war and ethnic conflicts, therefore, demands the fellowship of the church with the migrant church, working in unison to fulfill the Great Commission and joining their efforts for their livelihoods.

Verse 1

Μετὰ ταῦτα ("after this") introduces an action or activity that was initiated after a special event. For Martin Culy and Mikeal Parsons, "the use of this prepositional phrase (lit. 'after these things'), with no conjunction, indicates that 'there is no connection between the events which follow and those that precede.'"[131] In this case, then, the phrase presents a brutal change of focus. Paul has spoken about resurrection to the intellectual "cream" of Athens in Greece, and then he traveled to Corinth, the capital of Achaia, a Roman province. In Athens, the center of Greek civilization, Paul has just presented the message concerning the "resurrection of the dead which required a complete change of outlook, only possible if hungry and submissive souls turned to the Lord for light and salvation."[132] His message was not accepted except by a few people. It is possible that Paul, who was asked to continue speaking the following day, might have sensed that reaction as an opposition. So, he decided to go to "one of Athens' ancient rivals,"[133] Corinth, which was "the cultural capital of Greece – as also of the Hellenistic civilization"[134] and a "business and immoral town"[135] and announce the gospel there. This reveals that even for Paul, Corinth is a city of refuge to a certain extent, for Corinth

---

131. Culy and Parsons, *Acts*, 343.
132. Howley and Bruce, *New Testament Commentary*, 223.
133. Keener, *IVP Background Commentary*, 375.
134. Howley and Bruce, *New Testament Commentary*, 223.
135. Keener, *IVP Background Commentary*, 375.

received all the people who belonged to the Hellenistic world. So, he might have felt his message was not understood in the prestigious, idolatrous and intellectual city of Athens so that he went to Corinth where everyone from the former empire was accepted.

Verse 2

Verse 2 starts with the use of εὑρών (aorist active masculine nominative singular εὑρισκω) meaning "attendant circumstance or temporal,"[136] meaning that Priscilla and Aquila were in Corinth as temporary residents without any plan to stay permanently there. Paul and Aquila and Priscilla did not know each other, it just so happened they met due to common circumstances. The search for peace and temporary shelter led this couple to meet Paul with whom they worked in the area of ministry and business and started the church in Corinth.

Aquila was a native of Pontus, "in the northeastern region of Asia Minor."[137] Pontus was situated far away from the Jewish territory. By pondering Acts 2:7–9, one realizes that Pontus may have received the gospel from people who attended the Pentecost event in Acts 2. If so, then Aquila was a Jew from the diaspora who was born in Pontus. Paul, on the contrary, was also a Jew from the diaspora but from Tarsus (Acts 22:3), which was near Cilicia and far from Jerusalem. Yet Paul was also a Roman citizen (Acts 21:39) by nature of his birth (Acts 22:28–30).

Verse 2 reveals a geographic movement of Aquila and Priscilla and the reason for the movement occurred at the time of the event being narrated. Although from Pontus the couple lived in Italy. Luke uses two Greek words to emphasize the movement: the first word is the adverb προσφάτως meaning "recently" to show that Paul met the couple in Corinth when they had freshly arrived there too. The second word is διά, which is a preposition accusative meaning "because of, on account of."[138] The proposition introduces the phrase "Claudius had ordered all Jews to leave Rome" to mean that the couple's recent movement occurred because of the edict of Claudius for all Jews to leave Rome. This is, therefore, a forced movement from Rome that led the couple to Corinth as refugees.

---

136. Culy and Parson, *Acts*, 344.
137. Barker and Burdick, *NIV Study Bible*, 1687.
138. Wallace, *Greek Grammar*, 369.

It is useful to clarify that there were Jews in Rome before Christianity spread to Rome. The Jewish population had "started to grow in 62 BC when Pompey brought many Jewish captives to use as slaves and these Jewish people were participants in the civil war in support to Julius Caesar against Pompey."[139] An old and reliable source reveals that "in 41 BC, Claudius accessed to power" came "after the assassination of Caligula."[140] Scholars like Josephus mention active proselytizing by two Jews during the same period but also mention unrests within the Jewish community about Christianity.[141] It may be that the assassination of the emperor and the ethnic war/conflicts mixed with the fact that Jews had a rich history in a guerilla involvement. It may also be argued that the Claudian edict was written in the context of war, which led Priscilla and Aquilla's displacement and taking refuge in Corinth.

Craig Keener explains that "Claudius' expulsion of all Jews from Rome was the second to happen after the one done by the early Emperor Tiberius."[142] According to Richard Longenecker, this "expulsion order was proclaimed during the ninth year of Emperor Claudius's reign (i.e., 25 January 49 and 24 January 50) and directed against the Jews in Rome to put down the riots arising within the Jewish community there."[143] The edict argues that "as the Jews were indulging in constant riots at the instigation of *Chrestus*, he (Emperor Claudius) banished them from Rome."[144] This was an excess and misuse of power rather than building peace with the Jewish community in Rome. The ruling emperors contributed to an increase of hate by banishing the Jews from the city. Priscilla and Aquila, victims of the edicts, "were Christians before they left Rome, and founder-members, perhaps, of the Roman church."[145] When Paul reached Corinth he realized that there was a certain Jewish Christian Aquila and his wife Priscilla who had just arrived from Rome (Italy), who were victims of Claudius and the emperor's decree that Jews are to leave Rome.

---

139. Evans and Porter, *Dictionary of New Testament*, 1014.
140. Feldman, "Scholarship of Philo," 284.
141. Cf. Evans and Porter, *Dictionary of New Testament*, 1014.
142. Keener, *IVP Background Commentary*, 375.
143. Gaebelein, *John-Acts*, 481.
144. Gaebelein, 481.
145. Bruce, *Book of Acts*, 347.

The refugee couple arrived in Corinth shortly before Paul arrived, and upon Paul's arrival, "he went to see them." He went to see them means that the Roman citizen, Paul, wanted to show compassion to these Jewish refugees of Roman ethnic/racial hate. The fact that Paul left Athens before attending the next day's meeting leads us to think that he was discouraged by the reaction of Athens' citizens to his message, but "comforted by meeting Aquila and Priscilla, lately expelled from Rome by the Claudian edict against the Jews."[146]

Verse 3

Paul and the couple, although from the educated Jewish diaspora, knew how to make tents due to "the Jewish custom to teach boy children some trade due to the Jews high respect for trade in all its forms."[147] In other words, they survive through their trade of tentmaking. Furthermore, Bruce reinforces that by revealing that it is the "Jewish law that directed that young theological students be taught a trade"[148] and argues that "on his missionary journeys Paul earned his living as a tentmaker and leather worker."[149] Paul, having gone through the same Jewish schooling process learned the trade in Cilicia, the area in which he spent his youth. It is said that "The Cilicia of Paul's youth was known for its leather goods as well as its cloth."[150] This then explains why "The New Testament pictures Paul as a roving evangelist – the Apostle to the Gentiles."[151] The ministry to the gentiles required a nomadic lifestyle, which might have been easy with Paul's career of an artisan. Furthermore, Paul's Roman citizenship gave him the ability to move around in the Roman Empire especially due to the fact that "He was both Roman citizen and an ordinary artisan."[152] It is also clear that the trade of Paul's hosts probably influenced his decision as to where he would set up base in Corinth since this would be an easy entrance into the business community.

In a larger context, which includes the context of war such as that in Eastern Congo, the church should teach its young leaders how to hold two

---

146. Bruce, *New International Bible Commentary*, 1299.
147. Schaff, *Lange's Commentary*, 835.
148. Gaebelein, *John-Acts*, 480.
149. Gaebelein, 480.
150. Priest, "Holding Down Two Jobs," 144.
151. Priest, 145.
152. Priest, 145.

jobs, that pertaining to making disciples of all nations and that of being able to cater for their livelihoods through an income-generating activity. Including this in the mission strategy will have value both for the preparation of church leaders in seminaries and for disciple making at the local church level. The pastors who do not have a source of income outside the pastoral work may be exposed to failure to survive the war.

On the other hand, Paul may have understood the context in the Roman Empire, especially the danger Jews were facing and maybe the stereotype that they would face, with consideration to their history as slaves who once fought against a ruling king.[153] The Claudian edict did not apply to Jews who had Roman citizenship. Paul was a Roman citizen and therefore enjoyed the associated rights and privileges[154] for his security while he had the specific means to access livelihoods for his gospel to survive in this context with self-support through "his manual work, which put him in a Hellenistic social setting"[155] and therefore facilitated his missionary task.

Like Paul, church leaders in the context of war in Eastern Congo are to be strategic for the survival of their church and their own survival, which requires access to sources of survival such as crafting, farming, small business, and the like. Therefore, advocating for church survival is advocating for church members and leaders being able to afford livelihoods for their survival in a particular context.

Despite his dual citizenship, Paul did not get involved in politics. It is a strategic position that in this context works for the good of the gospel. In a context of war such as that of Eastern Congo political involvement of a church leader, though it may enable them to work in a war zone, may also endanger their life if the opposite camp takes over the control of the zone where the church is located. The neutrality of church leadership in the context of war gives the church the ability to reach out to both rebel groups and government groups. One bishop joined the M23 group; his position affected his church denomination and their church buildings were burnt down in Butembo and Bunia, places located far from the occupied zone by the M23.

---

153. Cf. Evans and Porter, *Dictionary of New Testament*, 1014.
154. Bruce, *Acts of the Apostles*, 437, 461.
155. Bruce, 392.

Verse 4

Because Paul had access to accommodation where his basic needs were met, he was able to διελέγομαι (meaning to argue, to discuss) with people who were coming into the synagogue, by giving evidence of the Christian truth and exhorting them, reasoning with them about the gospel and "persuade Jews and Greeks." It is curious that at that time Greeks were still meeting with Jews in the synagogue. These were two different ethnic or racial and cultural groups. People attended the synagogue as belonging to their social groups. This is supported by David Williams, who argues that Paul first met Aquila and Priscilla in the synagogue and then found lodging and worked with them, explaining that "arrangements in the synagogue at Corinth have been like those of Alexandria, where the various trades sat together."[156]

It is curious that Paul reasoned with Jews and Greeks in the synagogue and tried to persuade them about Jesus every Sabbath day. Bruce uses the Greek of verse 4 and points to the additional καὶ ἐντιθεὶς which, he suggests, "implies that, as the scriptures were read, Paul explained them by inserting the name of the Lord Jesus where appropriate; cf. the Targumic insertion of 'Messiah' after 'My servant' in Isa.42:1; 52:13."[157] It is clear that the ministry of Paul and his colleagues in Corinth followed the routine of the existing Jewish synagogue, which met every Sabbath, and used it as an opportunity for missions to their community of Jews and Greeks. By implication, they did not have to arrange for an evangelistic outreach. The fact that they have been involved in their trade as a means to earn their livelihoods during the week leads to the logical inference that they must have been seen as dependable people in the then community of Jews and Greeks.

According to Gerd Ludermann, "the expression τη κάτω'οἴκων αυτών εκκλησία (1Cor 19:19) denotes the house community which gathers around Aquila and Priscilla."[158] However, rather than using that expression and say that "It gives a first indication of the couple's prosperity,"[159] it is better to say that this was the starting point of the couple's involvement in the planting of churches among gentiles, as stated in Romans 16:4. Their meeting with

---

156. Williams, *New International Biblical Commentary*, 314.
157. Bruce, *Acts of the Apostles*, 392.
158. Ludermann, *Early Christianity*, 201.
159. Ludermann, 202.

Paul in Corinth created for them to an opportunity for ministry in a refugee context, which might have led to their ministry journeys and "the stages Rome-Corinth-Ephesus-Rome which can be reconstructed by Paul's letters."[160] In many cases, including Eastern Congo, a context of war extends to a context of displacement and/or refuge. The oppressed and families run away from the insecure zone to seek for safety and refuge. Displacement allows them to have moved beyond an active war zone to an IDP and/or a refugee zone, which is supposed to be under the supervision of the government and other peacekeeping groups such as the UN and NGOs.

From the above discussion we conclude that Priscilla and Aquila left Rome because of the edict of Claudius, but then settled in Corinth where there was peace (v. 2). Although Corinth was far from Rome, it still was within the Roman Empire. The researcher notes that the oppressed did not challenge the edict or fight back as they were evicted from their homes. The misuse of power by the ruling emperor forcing the couple to move is far from the ethnic ultimatum issued by ethnic militia fed by the leadership crisis in Eastern Congo that has forced individual believers, families and churches to be displaced inside their own country or to become refugees in neighboring countries. It is useful to clarify that in the case of Eastern Congo, families move from less secure zones (under the militia control) to towns or other parts of the region are also not fully peaceful and may even be under the rule of a guerrilla force such as M23. That slight difference does not affect the application of Acts 18:1–4 to the context of displacement and refuge which the church frequently experienced, and survived.

Migration and refugees (IDPs) are very common in Eastern Congo. IDP camps and host families are common features in the regions. In the Roman ethnic and identity conflicts that led to the expulsion of the marginalized Jewish elite class from Rome, the migrants were able to connect with both the church and the world in Corinth and therefore contributed to the planting of churches in the region. They also contributed to building the socio-economic capital of the Corinthian community. In other words, migration and refuge are not only opportunities to strengthen believers' faith but also a strategic opportunity to equip and build the mission force for the church to spread the gospel among the host families and a safe training arena to prepare for

---

160. Ludermann, 202.

the growth of the home church when the migrants return home. This can catalyze church leaders in war countries and zones such as Eastern Congo to encourage associations such as "Paul's association with Priscilla and Aquila in referring to their shared craft."[161]

3.4.5 Conclusion and Theological Meaning of Acts 18:1–4

Poor leadership and the misuse of power in a multiethnic context affects the stability of some groups and therefore causes migration and forced refuge of people, church leaders and members. While both Paul and Priscilla and Aquila needed hope, their shared craft became a platform to both survive in their host community and to partner in spreading the gospel. Shared craft is vital for the association of church leaders from various backgrounds for their survival and for missions to the host communities and even beyond. Theological institutions should, therefore, put entrepreneurship into the training curriculum to prepare church leaders for missions in particular contexts.

A refugee/IDP camp and the host community provide an opportunity for church leaders' preparation to make disciples of all nations, beginning with host communities. It is also an opportunity to prepare the church to face the challenges of church missions in their home church once they return.

In a context of war that highlights realities such as migration and refuge, there are issues that demand attention and are consequently given priority over church service/meetings. Therefore, church meetings become a secondary activity that, while being important, remain subordinate to missions of the church. Also, it is important to note that Aquila and Priscilla were the hosts who benefited Paul and at the same time were missionaries in their host country. That means that other refugees in the camps should not feel that they are helpless and wait only for their host country to provide training among others for the incoming IDPs and/or refugees. This will make "migration and missions to be closely connected"[162] in the context of war in Eastern Congo as it was the case in the first century during which "migration was a key factor in the expansion of the church in the New Testament times."[163]

---

161. Ludermann, 202.
162. Nguyen, "Migrants as Missionaries," 194.
163. Nguyen, 205.

With this understanding of missions in the migration context, the experience of missions by both Paul and the couple in Acts 18:1–4 then completes the so-called migration model of mission suggested by Escobar with an emphasis on the "Christian migrant traveling from poor countries in search of economic survival."[164] The context of migration in a war zone that is missing in the "migration model" is a very complex one, with repeated displacement movements and the existence of IDPs/refugees in camps or in host families. In such contexts, the author of Acts 18:1–4 is also "calling the church to new ways of being church,"[165] looking at missions as a reciprocal business. On the one hand, migrants are to "be an object of pastoral care," and on the other hand, the host church or individuals allow "migrants in their midst, that is, in camps and in host families be subjects of mission."[166] Diamond, for example, states that population movements affect food productivity of the host communities as food producers share their experience with their hosts.[167] In the context of war in Eastern Congo, migrants can be part of a holistic transformation that is needed in their host communities.

3.5 Hebrews 10:32–34: The Experience of War Provides Guidance for a Suffering Church and Discipleship

3.5.1 Introduction

In this text of Hebrews 10:32–34, the author is addressing Hebrew Christian church members and advises them to stand firm and remain in the faith. These Christians "have been abused for their faith and have reacted well to the plundering of their property."[168] In this address, the author uses their experience of persecution, suffering and conflicts to call for their perseverance. This text fits this study dealing with missions of the church and the experience of war. Both individual believers and Christian leaders and their families experience suffering in such contexts, whether in the war zone or

---

164. Hanciles, "Migration and Mission," 118.
165. Bevans, "Themes and Questions," 15.
166. Bevans, 15.
167. Diamond, *Guns, Germs, and Steel*, 351.
168. Guthrie, *Hebrews*, 23.

during displacement, which needs to be addressed with a theological response of the church.

3.5.2 Context of Hebrews 10:32–34

The immediate context of this passage is that vengeance and retribution belong to God through his judgment (Heb 10:31), how terrible it is to fall into God's hand for judgment (Heb 10:30–32) and the call to Christian confidence and endurance in the faith (Heb 10:35). The wider context is the author's exhortation to the church members to stand firm in their faith in suffering, persecution and the like and continue the ministry received through the high priest. The readers needed to draw themselves near to God in enduring faith as they reflect on their former experiences. He presents to them the bigger picture of the church of Christ and its character in times of hardship. It is founded on the high priesthood of Christ and is built as a community of priests, adopted sons of God (Heb 1) ministering the gospel in the context of trials (Heb 13:23). The new covenant people are called to survive the challenge because it belongs to a new order of eternal priests under Melchizedek (Heb 7).

Written probably between AD 60–100, with "the preponderance of evidence favoring a date before 70,"[169] and although it is controversial who its author is, Hebrews is an address to "Greek-speaking Jewish Christians not to renege on their existing Christian commitment,"[170] thus supporting an old source that says that the book was addressed to "a group of Jewish Christians, tempted to relapse into Judaism."[171] The context was that in which "the religion of the Jews was recognized by the Romans while Christianity was not."[172] And so, Jewish Christians "were in danger of focusing on novel teachings at the expense of the apostolic Gospel."[173] Mitchell goes further in his description of the context of Hebrews; he writes that "the book itself has a few clues which demonstrate that the audience is the second generation of Christians

---

169. Carson, Moo and Morris, *Introduction to the New Testament*, 400.
170. Isaacs, *Reading Hebrews*, 8.
171. Morris, *Understanding the New Testament*, 35.
172. Carson, Moo and Morris, *Introduction to the New Testament*, 404.
173. Carson, Moo and Morris, 404.

(2:3–4;13:7) that has suffered in the past (10:32–34) and is undergoing another form of persecution."[174]

3.5.3 Historical Background of Hebrews 10

The first century was characterized by the persecution of Christians. Their meetings were seen as a danger to the political rule and therefore made kings and emperors opposed to Christianity. James Jeffers recalls the complaints written by Pliny the Younger to Trajan. He said,

> The sum total of their guilt and error amounted to no more than this: they had met regularly before dawn on fixed days to chant verses . . . in honor of Christ . . . If people assemble for common purpose, whatever name we give them . . . they soon turn into a political club.[175]

In addition, in attempts to bring believers back to life in line with Greco-Roman virtues such as "expressions of civic loyalty through cult," the Greco-Roman society reacted against the Christian communities "often by insulting, reproaching, abusing and harassing the Christians (Heb 12:32–34,1 Pet 2:11–12; 4:1–4)" and at the same time they had "similar pressures from their Jews by the synagogue."[176]

Donald Guthrie notes that "the features of the Hebrews particularly align with a Jewish background."[177] It seems that Jewish Christians would easily understand the author wanting to reveal "the thought of superiority of Christ both as priest and as a sacrifice"[178] due to the fact that they were not new to the religious context of Jewish people. The Christian message had to be translated into a Jewish context, which they were very much familiar with. The author, therefore, had to use the Jewish religious symbols to translate their Christian meaning. Different scholars[179] have presented indications that

---

174. Mitchell, *Hebrews*, 11.
175. Jeffers, *Greco-Roman World*, 71.
176. Evans and Porter, *Dictionary of New Testament*, 521.
177. Guthrie, *Hebrews*, 38.
178. Guthrie, 39.
179. Carson, Moo and Morris, *Introduction to the New Testament*, 400; Montefiore, *Commentary*, 3.

"the Epistle was written early in the Christian era"[180] particularly before the destruction of the temple of Jerusalem in AD 70. That is why "The writer has a splendid indifference to the actual circumstances of Jewish sacrifice in the Temple, and to the actual characters of historical high priests."[181] In fact, his readers understood the structure of the first temple and were, therefore, able to understand, in their own context, the writer's "abstract argument of this epistle demonstrating the superiority of the new covenant with its heavenly sanctuary over the old covenant with its earthly Tent of Meeting."[182] This particular context, therefore, points to Jewish Christians who lived "in the fifties, before the mutterings of the Jewish revolt, and before the imminent threat of destruction to the Herodian Temple."[183]

Most scholars in search of the identity of the author point to a Jewish Christian writer "who had engaged with Hellenistic culture established in the fourth century BC."[184] Because of his knowledge of the world of his time he addressed his Jewish Christian readers, both Jewish and those in the Hellenistic world, who might have been facing persecution and suffering in the context of a world exposed to Jewish traditions if not also the realities of Platonism or Gnosticism. Depending on where they were located, and having in mind that these were house churches, Hebrews gives no indication as to the location or situation of its recipients.[185] This research agrees with Kiwoong Son "that Hebrews is a simple theological treatise and not a collection of topics from various traditions"[186] because the epistle interprets scripture using the Old Testament references and presents the superiority of Jesus. The author is trying to present his message to his audience in response to current philosophical schools of thought. This rejects also the view that "the world of thought found in Hebrews is a complex one, sharing many traditions contemporary to it: aspects of its thought were probably held in common with (various) Jewish traditions, with Alexandrian Platonist circles and even with Gnostic

---

180. Montefiore, *Commentary*, 3.
181. Montefiore, 3.
182. Montefiore, 3.
183. Montefiore, 3.
184. Mason and McGruden, *Reading the Epistle*, 15.
185. Isaacs, *Reading Hebrews*, 8.
186. Son, *Zion Symbolism*, 14.

groups."[187] On the contrary, these schools of thought were part of the pressure which believers experienced from their opponents.

3.5.4 Christians and Vengeance

The context of the text recalls Deuteronomy 32:35–36 which was also quoted by Paul in Romans 12:19. According to Chineque and Ngewa, "In the original context, God's vengeance was directed against Israel's enemies, who reaped what they had sown."[188] This supports "Paul's point that Christians ought to live at peace with all others and should not seek revenge."[189] It is true that "governments may sometimes punish wrongdoing (Rom 13:4)" and that "no individual should assume he or she is entitled to revenge,"[190] but in a context such as war-torn Eastern Congo where sometimes the government and the rebels are causing personal and communal suffering, this warning not to revenge oneself definitely is a nonviolence attitude towards war, knowing that "Vindication of God's people goes hand in hand with the judgement of his enemies."[191]

On the other side, in Joshua 6, when Israel was at war with other nations, God appeared as "a man with a sword" in Jericho to fight on behalf of Israel. Although God commanded this war to eliminate the people of the land, whereas the war in the Eastern Congo was between different factions, the idea of God with his people during war is common to the two. The idea of "The battle belongs to the Lord"[192] gives to Deuteronomy 32:35–36 the role of a God who avenges his people in a physical battle. However, in Hebrews 10:32, vengeance goes together with judgment. This means that the writer is telling his readers that their hope for God's reward should go together with perseverance during hardship in times of war. In different words, he writes to them about a paradigm of the biblical portrait of "God as warrior who slays Israel's enemies, brings victory or defeat, and gives orders to attack and slaughter the Canaanite population (Exodus 15, Deuteronomy 20, Joshua)," with "the conception of God as Warrior who neither justifies nor sanctifies

---

187. Punt, "Hebrews," 152.
188. Chianeque and Ngewa, "Deuteronomy," 252.
189. Chianeque and Ngewa, 252.
190. Chianeque and Ngewa, 252.
191. Guthrie, *Hebrews*, 220.
192. Chianeque and Ngewa, "Deuteronomy," 270.

war, but it does provide hope for his abiding presence and participation in an evil world," a God, who, "in the incarnation, becomes the crucified God, a recipient of violence."[193]

Moore goes further. He connects Hebrews with the idea of the Jubilee in Leviticus and the Qumran perspective. He quotes a view of Contra Weisenberg that has not been followed, saying that, "the Sinai revelation takes place forty years before the entry into Canaan and will occur . . . at the culmination of the fiftieth 49-year jubilee-the jubilee of jubilees"[194] and notices that "such range of chronology revitalizes Israel's failures while locating her success as part of God's overarching plan for the world."[195] Consequently, he argues that "in Hebrews heavenly and earthly worship is conjoined; as in the jubilee; however, the sacrificial and atoning aspect of such worship is ongoing."[196] The conquest of the land happening between the Sinai revelation and the entry of Israel into Canaan is not enough to compare the suffering in these wars with "little eschatological indication in Hebrews."[197] These will be true when it is Israel that is defeated, but it is clear that Jubilee also benefits slaves who were captured from the enemy's side when Israel was defeating other indigenous nations. This will then mean that rather than building the readers' hope linked to eschatology, the author of Hebrews refers to Leviticus to assure the people of the presence of the incarnated God in the midst of suffering and violence which his readers, who were probably slaves.[198]

3.5.5 The Value of Church's Past Experience in Context (Hebrews 10:32-34)

The original text begins with "but remember those early days" (Ἀναμιμνῄσκεσθε δὲ τὰς πρότερον ἡμέρας). This is a request to recall those early days. Curiously, the author is telling them to recall the toughest period of their Christian experience and life. In his paper titled *Pilgrim Motives in the Book of Hebrews*, William Johnsson says, "Pilgrimage involves hardship. Physical difficulties

---

193. Perdue, "*Problem of War*," 446.
194. Moore, *Repetition in Hebrews*, 43.
195. Moore, 43.
196. Moore, 46.
197. Moore, 43.
198. Cf. Evans and Porter, *Dictionary of New Testament*, 1014; it is also an idea supported by Perdue, "*Problem of War*," 446.

and religious trials make the threat of failure a grim possibility."[199] This means that while Christians are called to leave revenge to God, they needed to accept that hardship and trials are part of their Christian journey to which they had to respond with forgiveness.

On the other hand, the conjunction δὲ in the phrase Ἀναμιμνῄσκεσθε δὲ τὰς πρότερον ἡμέρας was translated as a coordinate conjunction and therefore kept silent because the translation assumed it links independent sentences, that is, verse 31 is independent to the beginning of verse 32.[200] However, in this indicated context, the conjunction δὲ is "a contrastive conjunction which suggests a contrast or opposing thought to the idea to which it is connected"[201] and means "but" or "rather." The writer is telling the Jewish Christians that, in their context of persecution and suffering, they should not avenge themselves; rather, as they are exposed to unjust suffering, they have to recall their toughest times of suffering and learn from their own experience to strengthen their faith and for their church to stand firm and survive the current hardship. This view is supported by Guthrie who says that "the word *recall (anaminmesko)* used here denotes some efforts in calling to mind."[202] According to him, "The process of recollection is sometimes a fruitful pursuit when it calls to mind former lessons, even if those lessons have been learned in a hard school."[203] The contexts that prevail during wartime in Eastern Congo exposes the church to suffering and hardship to the extent that church members are exhausted, having been victims of abuses and homeless beyond measure. In such contexts, the writer of Hebrews calls his readers to use their previous experience of hardship and therefore gain confidence and hope from it to survive the current hardship. Thus, recalling for the church its own experience in a particular context is a secret for its survival during suffering.

3.5.6 Church Survival during Hardship

"[You] endured a great fight of afflictions" (Heb 10:32 KJV). This sentence refers to what the church had to endure when it was younger than the date at

---

199. Johnsson, "Pilgrim Motives," 244.
200. Wallace, *Greek Grammar*, 667.
201. Wallace, 671.
202. Guthrie, *Hebrews*, 221.
203. Guthrie, 221.

which the letter to of Hebrews was addressed to them. The author reminded his readers that they "endured much"[204] and they "withstood public persecution in the past."[205] The church stood with people who were suffering, even those put in jail during times of conflict. So, this church's experience of pain and suffering not only made the church grow but also provided inspiration for the future nature and work of the church. Christians accepted being put in jail and their possessions being confiscated because of their hope for eternal life. So, Christians needed to remember that "being Christians in those days meant no token pain, but 'a hard struggle with suffering.' It meant public abuse and meant being linked to others so abused. It meant forfeiture of goods."[206] They needed to remember "they have been 'washed' (6:2; 10:22); they were 'enlightened' (6:4); they endured a 'hard struggle' after joining the community (10:32)."[207]

However, if they had to do so because "their journeyings are not aimless: they have their eyes fixed on 'the city which has foundations, whose builder and maker is God' (11:10),"[208] then believers are called to use their previous experience to gain strength to persevere journeying toward "the real city . . . which is to come (11:16; 13:14)."[209] The community of believers, therefore, survives as a unity of believers nourishing their eschatological hope. These two verses seem to contradict the view of God's incarnation reality during suffering which is supported by Perdue[210] and favors Nicholas Moore's idea of "conjoined earthly and heavenly worship."[211] Cockerill says, Hebrews 10:32–39 "makes a smooth transition from the priesthood's description and the description of the heroes of faith (11:1–40) and urges the readers to draw near and persevere through the privileges now theirs in Christ (vv19–25)."[212] This research agrees with him that "the author is urging them to maintain their identity with faithful people whose style and promised destiny he will

---

204. Keener, *IVP Background Commentary*, 672.
205. Kassa, "Hebrews," 1504.
206. Morris, *Understanding the New Testament*, 65
207. Johnsson, "Pilgrim Motives," 245.
208. Johnsson, 245.
209. Johnsson, 245.
210. Perdue, "*Problem of War*," 446.
211. Moore, *Repetition in Hebrews*, 46.
212. Cockerill, *Epistle to the Hebrews*, 496.

describe in Hebrews 11:1-40."²¹³ The heroes cited in Hebrews 11:1-40 are a few of the Jews who persevered in the midst of suffering and trusted in the hope according to the promise of God of a better and perfect life (Heb 11:40). But "no human prior to Jesus has experienced this eschatological blessing; the heroes of faith in Hebrews are still awaiting."²¹⁴ Matthew Easter, therefore, argues that "the eschatological hope in Hebrews is one of the enduring life in the God-building heavenly homeland."²¹⁵ This research agrees because, in its struggle to endure, the church gains strength from the victory of Christ who first reached the fullness of heroism and the hope. Therefore, both Moore and Perdue agree, except for the statement that "the sacrificial and atoning aspect of the earthly and heavenly worship is ongoing."²¹⁶ This is dangerous because, in the context of persecution, which he had also addressed, believers will expose themselves to sacrifice and suffering as part of their atonement and worship while Jesus has already completed the atonement for humankind. Instead, worship or "church attendance is important for the fellowship of believers during such contexts for a mutual encouragement to steadfast in the Lord."²¹⁷

This situation is also similar to that of war in Eastern Congo, where people have suffered and the church, despite the length of the war, survived. Chapter 5 will describe in detail how this survival can be in part be explained by the fact that Christians believed in the end of time that would end their suffering, and thus remained committed to attending church meetings or gatherings. As stated earlier, church members suffered abuse during the war. In such a context, if believers use their experience to endure out of the fear of judgment, then there is a possibility to question discipleship in that context because "judgement is the most frightening prospect regarding the future for those who are apart from Christ but for those in Christ it is something to look at for it will vindicate their lives."²¹⁸ On the contrary, rather than attending churches and praying out of fear for what is to come (Heb 10:32 and 11:1-40), believers are assured of the permanent presence of the incarnated

---

213. Cockerill, 496.
214. Easter, *Faith and the Faithfulness*, 103.
215. Easter, 103.
216. Moore, *Repetition in Hebrews*, 47.
217. Chianeque and Ngewa, "Deuteronomy," 1504.
218. Erickson, *Christian Theology*, 1207.

God if they will continue to exercise their faith as they experience war and suffering together with perseverance in the hope of the blessings to come.

Verse 33 expresses a kind of conjunctive syllogism. If, "Sometimes you were publicly exposed to insult and persecution; at other times you stood side by side with those who were so treated" (Heb 10:33), then they were always publicly exposed to insult and persecution or stood side to side with those who were so treated. This is a constant state of exposure to suffering. According to Donald Guthrie, "the kind of suffering that the readers had endured is described as being publicly exposed to abuse which shows how they had had a personal involvement in the suffering of Christ."[219] Although Montefiore states that in this verse "there's no reference to such persecutions as Nero's burning of Christians in the public gardens and Rome (Tacitus, *Annals*, 1 5.44) or to a personal appearance in an arena (cf. I Cor15:32),"[220] he favors Guthrie's (2007:221–222) view saying, "both the verb and the noun derive their force from a theatrical spectacle, the idea being that the Christians had been made a target for public abuse." He also argues that "the suffering was partly the result of their enemies' insulting and contemptuous attitude (taunts) and partly due to actual bodily assaults (afflictions)."[221]

Hebrews 10:33b says, "you stood side by side with those who were so treated." This sentence uses the noun nominative plural κοινωνοί which means "partners" or "sharers." This is a nominative of appellation "used because of the special character of the individuals described."[222] This means that individual Christians had attitudes and behaviors of genuine partners from the members of their community church whenever they were being exposed to suffering and threats. Montefiore says, "they have made clear, by their witness and practical help, their kinship with those who bore the brunt of these misfortunes."[223] This understanding of verse 33 emphasizes the idea of the church as not only a community of believers but also a new family of believers. The church is "one of the few visible forms of a corporate relationship among believers."[224] That is why, for Guthrie, "the writer reminding the

---

219. Guthrie, *Hebrews*, 221.
220. Montefiore, *Commentary*, 181.
221. Montefiore, 181.
222. Wallace, *Greek Grammar*, 61.
223. Montefiore, *Commentary*, 182.
224. Erickson, *Christian Theology*, 949.

readers that they were partners (κοινωνοί) recalls the familiar New Testament concept of fellowship or participation."²²⁵ When believers' fellowship is tied with participation it ceases to be perceived as merely attending church meetings or gatherings. In the case of Hebrews 10:34, "The believers had found it as a privilege to 'share' each other's sufferings" and it is agreeable that "this is fellowship on the deepest level."²²⁶

The writer is encouraging them, however, that "they need to continue to meet to 'encourage one another'"²²⁷ which requires participating in members' sufferings and not merely attending meetings. When the church members are exposed to public insult and suffering in contexts such as that of war in Eastern Congo, it is possible that even church attendance will be affected due to the isolation of the particular believers who were exposed to mistreatment. For example, in Eastern Congo when a believers' family lose a militia child on the battlefield during a fight between the national army and the Mai-Mai militia, the other church members are likely not to share that shame and pain resulting from the loss and stand by its side with one another. In most cases where families are mourning their relatives, they do not enjoy the benefits of having the church community helping in arranging funerals or attending celebration meetings. Instead, such people are subjected to stereotyping and the questioning of their faith. What about a Christian woman who experiences rape? She may not be protected by the community of believers; sometimes even her husband betrays her. In some cases, marriages break apart after such an incident. The woman is blamed by both her husband and some members and accused of being responsible for her condition, rather than the church protecting her and her family.

Verse 34 is a continuation of verse 33 and the writer "enlarges on the believers exemplary behaviors under persecution."²²⁸ It recalls more particular experiences that Christians had during that particular time as an expression of their hardship and suffering. During that time, they experienced prison and had their properties confiscated. While some scholars think that the writer

---

225. Guthrie, *Hebrews*, 222.
226. Guthrie, 222.
227. Chianeque and Ngewa, "Deuteronomy," 1504.
228. Montefiore, *Commentary*, 182.

"was speaking concerning himself and the rest who were in prison,"[229] some African scholars, however, avoid the discussion and focus on the meaning of the verse and say that the readers "had stood by those who were publicly humiliated, had sympathized with those in prison and had accepted material loss."[230] Guthrie considers the particular cited experiences as representative of an active and passive approach of "standing side by side with those who were so treated" (Heb 10:33b), meaning that "these Christians' compassion consists of their ability to 'suffer with' those who suffer, they identified themselves in their minds with prisoners" and "they joyfully accepted the plundering of their property with a more positive attitude than resignation."[231] In most cases of looting of goods and other properties in the context of war in Eastern Congo, it is hard to identify with that positive attitude of their acceptance. Christians accept the looting of their property with an attitude of resignation and this explains the fact that no church has planned to go and reach out to FDLR and other militiamen in their camps because Christians hate them and have suffered unjustly from their looting expeditions and many other mistreatments such as rape, beatings, killings and the like.

It is curious to notice that the last sentence of the verse recalls the eschatological hope of the readers, which was emphasized in verse 30. The readers joyfully accepted the confiscation of their property "because you knew that you yourselves had better and lasting possessions" (Heb 10:34). This means that because they look forward to the last judgment for their eternal peace and their life at the expense of the enemies of peace who will be subjected to God's revenge (Heb 10:30), these believers accepted the plundering of their property with a positive attitude. They did not desire the loss of their property to access heaven but accepted to forfeit it knowing that "their treasure was in heaven (Matt 6:20), a city that lasts (Heb 8:14), the heavenly Jerusalem (Heb 12:22)."[232] On the other hand, the readers with their Jewish background know God throughout Israel's history as a God of war who fights for his people. The Old Testament is full of "the metaphors of God as a warrior . . . ,

---

229. Oden, *Ancient Christian Commentary*, 169.
230. Kassa, "Hebrews," 1504.
231. Guthrie, *Hebrews*, 222.
232. Montefiore, *Commentary*, 182.

predominantly from the perspective of Israel vs. ancient Nearest Eastern warfare."[233] Therefore, the readers accepted joyfully the confiscations of their property knowing that God will avenge them one day.

3.5.7 Conclusion and Theological Meaning of Hebrews 10:32–34

The author's writing of Hebrews 10:32–34 is an exhortation for Jewish Christians to persevere and to have fellowship with other believers in times of sufferings and hardship. When the church members are publicly being afflicted and ill-treated, the author reminds his readers that the God of Israel is known as "Warrior and God of heaven" in the history of Israel.[234] Therefore, Christians ought to leave vengeance to him, as scripture recommends, and build their strength in the incarnated God, a God who is present in their suffering, and persevere in the hope of the last judgment of God.

Survival of Christianity in contexts such as that portrayed by the writer is rooted in remembering past experiences in similar contexts and drawing from that experience secrets to endure and act accordingly. Enduring afflictions requires that the church members stand as one body side by side with those being subjected to sufferings through genuine fellowship and participation in members' sufferings. This is an exhortation that extends beyond church meetings because it calls for actions out of compassion and an attitude of sympathy towards members in trouble as a true way of partnership in sufferings.

Being victims of suffering and trials is not a sign of holiness and the believers' condition is not a guarantee that they are nearing the eschatological blessing. On the contrary, believers are encouraged to attend church meetings or to worship God because it is there where encouragement to persevere occurs. Church meetings and fellowship will, therefore, help individual believers to joyfully persevere during mistreatment for the sake of their hope in eternal reward and also because they are experiencing God's presence in their suffering.

---

233. Klingbeil, *Yahweh Fighting*, 1.
234. Klingbeil, 309.

3.6 Summary

In relation to what can be learned from the Bible regarding the Christian responses to church, violence and war, Jesus gives a new law and introduces a nonviolence command to the community of faith in the context of war (Matt 5:38–45). Hebrews 10 recalls the historical character of God who is a "God of war fighting for his people from heaven"[235] to whom Christians should leave the right to avenge all afflictions to which church members are publicly exposed, such as insult and ill-treatment. Vengeance and judgment belong to him (Deut 32:35–36). The researcher takes into account the fact that, in acts of aggression that include war, Jesus told his disciples to protectively take a purse, a money bag and a sword in a particular context (Luke 22:35–38). Jesus also rebuked violent revenge when Peter cut of the ear of Malchus (Matt 26:52).

While Christians are not to revenge, the war is still going on and this context exposes them to migration and refugees, poverty, food scarcity and famine. The texts assessed in the New Testament indicates that the texts are limited to believers who are not in the military. However, many centurions are commended in the NT as Christians, God-fearers and men of good character (e.g. Matt 8:5; Acts 10 and 11). The NT also uses military terminology in a very positive way. It is possible that the author of Hebrews refers to Deuteronomy 32:35–36 and Matthew quoting Leviticus 19:18 and 26:7–8 in order to remind individual believers in the military or in government that they are not excused from the call to persevere as they hope in their eternal reward. Perhaps he reminds the whole church that the God who is called a God of war is also the God of heaven[236] meaning that as the church looks forward to eternal blessing it has to believe in God's presence with them in their context.

Therefore, while Christians are not allowed to take up weapons to defend their cause and revenge themselves in order for the church to survive, one may follow the example of the Jewish context in which Paul and Priscilla and Aquila were raised.[237] Churches in a war context should invest in training people in crafts and other livelihoods skills. When population movement,

---

235. Klingbeil, 309.
236. Cf. Klingbeil, *Yahweh Fighting*, 309.
237. Cf. Acts 18:1–4; Schaff, *Lange's Commentary*, 835.

refuge and the like occur, a shared craft will allow church leaders to obtain their livelihood and establish a believers' platform that will involve the church in missions to the host communities and will also prepare them to be useful for the growth of the church once they return home.

Knowing a craft allows one to obtain one's livelihood and also provides an opportunity to spread the gospel, as the Christians in Asia (Acts 18:1–4). It did not exempt it from suffering and hardship in their contexts. Believers need to use the memories of their experiences of trials and suffering (Heb 10:32a) as a tool to strengthen their hope and perseverance. The church experience of hardship and suffering in contexts such as war helps to provide direction for the church's survival during similar challenging times even when it is worse than the previous one. That survival is rooted in the strength that comes when believers partner and share their sufferings in church meetings, and develop attitudes and behaviors pertaining to a true fellowship and participation in one another's suffering and abuse.

Instead of the law of retaliation, Jesus calls his disciples in Matthew 5:38–45 to a nonviolent attitude and towards the search for peace, which is to be demonstrated by their exercise of love beyond boundaries for the benefit of a community in which forgiveness, reconciliation and peace prevail. The church's practice of the "general principles like loving the enemy"[238] is key for the church's outreach to people and disciple making in their context of war and, therefore, the establishment of communities of believers who will also show love in response to abuse instead of revenge. Hebrews 10:32–34, however, emphasizes the need for the disciples to practice a true fellowship that encourages one another to accept with joy even the plundering of their property because members participate actively through their acts of compassion looking forward to "the last judgement when justice will be at their side."[239] In these conditions, the church will survive hardship and will be able to make disciples in their context of war.

Therefore, in the context of war, from a biblical perspective, missions are tied to the church's attitude toward war and the world around it, which calls for nonviolence and the love for enemies such as rebels/militia. Missions in the context of war may be channeled and expressed by the church's associations

---

238. Harrington, "Sermon on the Mount," 7.
239. Erickson, *Christian Theology*, 1207.

(according to shared business such as craft for survival and livelihoods and the like) and the accepted norms of Christian faith that allow the church to disciple its world. As the church is doing so in a war context and with the diverse backgrounds brought together by its members, it has to confront and overcome the challenges to its mission from the experience of war and suffering. The way to do it is for the church to use its experience to strengthen attitudes and practices pertaining to developing a suffering Christian community (or church) that is called to make disciples whatever the context.

On the other hand, like "the early church [that] faced the problem of war and military service in a pagan world,"[240] so did the first readers of Matthew 5:38–45. It is true today in various contexts. It is to be noted that the highest virtue recommended is "neither courage nor honor nor even justice, but love, and love that demands compassion for one's enemies of which courage and honor and justice know little."[241] Jesus's non-retaliation command in Matthew 5:38–45 leaves room for pacifism or for nonviolence depending on the perspective which scholars take when interpreting it. However, it is clear that a gap in knowledge has been identified when referred to in a war context where stakeholders are the government (which is sometimes the oppressor), militia and guerilla and the church controlled by either the government or by occupying rebels or the militia.

---

240. Holmes, *War and Christian Ethic*, 35.
241. Holmes, 35.

CHAPTER 4

Historical and Ethnical Context of Eastern Congo from 1990 to 2011

4.1 Introduction

In this chapter, the aim is to retrace the historical and ethnic context of Eastern Congo in order to address the relationships that exist between the ethnic wars and clashes and the rebel movements' war during the period 1990 to 2011. It portrays and describes the context of war in which the church has been undertaking missions during the study period. It will be argued that the war was a complex event caused by a combination of factors dominated by an identity crisis expressing itself in different conflicts and wars and having multiple results. An identity crisis had always fed political agendas of warlords and their supporting countries, international involvement and the Congolese minerals as a target that sustained the war at the expense of the Congolese.

In order to gain and analyze the relevant information, the four steps of historical research mentioned by Deiros were used: the "heuristic step," "critic step," "synthesis step" and "exposition step."[1] This chapter is, therefore, a description of events that constitute the written presentation of the result obtained through the historical research. The following wars are discussed: ethnic wars in the early 1990s (1990–1994); the ethnic war in Eastern Congo (1994–1996); the First Congo War (1996–1997); the Second Congo War (1998–2002); the war in Eastern Congo during the transition (2003–2006);

---

1. Deiros, "Historical Research," 136–40.

and the war in Eastern Congo between 2006 and 2011. A conclusion summarizes the key results and presents the relationships between ethnic clashes and other wars.

4.2 Ethnic Violence and War in Eastern Congo: Root Causes

While the colonial transformation of the Congolese society and the Rwandan immigration and colonial policy are known as precursors of the conflict in Eastern Congo, the "post-independence identity, land, and violence"[2] fueled the ethnic violence and wars in the early 1990s.

The annexation of the Rwanda-Urundi area to the Belgian colony "as the fifth Province of Congo"[3] after World War I seems to have featured in the ethnic wars in Eastern Congo, which were fueled by political ambitions. Identity has driven the conflicts that caused the wars due to the fact that there has been "the predominance of ethno-nationalist language in the politics of DRC and the Great Lakes region, and the near absence of the language of the class."[4] From 1937 to 1956, the Belgian colonial authorities installed around 80,000 displaced people and "the transplanted" Hutu people from the neighbor Rwanda in this region.[5] Mathieu and Tsongo reveal that "since 1945 and 1960, a huge number of Rwandese citizens (especially Hutu farmers) had succeeded in crossing the border separating their country with the Kivu for diverse reasons, especially to run away from the famine or to find lands."[6] This justified the "rapid demographic increase in the meridional part of North Kivu province for half a century beginning in 1933, especially in Masisi" which was the most touched by various population movements from Rwanda to DRC.[7]

---

2. Stearns, *North Kivu*, 21.
3. Authaler and Michels, "Post-War Colonial Administration," 2.
4. Turner, *Congo*, 75.
5. Mathieu and Tsongo, "Guerres paysannes," 385.
6. Mathieu and Tsongo, 385.
7. Mathieu and Tsongo, 385.

According to Jason Stearns, "the Belgians only considered certain groups as 'indigenous' and restricted native authority to those communities."[8] He reveals that

> those that did not qualify, including most Rwandophones who arrived later, had no similar guaranteed access to land, instead of having to rely on good relations with the local chief. This was the material basis for territorialization of identity: a significant legacy of colonial rule in Central Africa and elsewhere.[9]

Stearns reveals further that "some Rwandan historians claim that the Rwandan King Rwabugiri was able to conquer much of the Rutshuru, Masisi, and Walikale" – during an expansionistic conquest "to extend his influence within the present-day Rwanda and into the highlands of the Kivu" – "a claim that has been repeatedly revived and exploited for modern political ends."[10] This view seems to be held mostly for political reasons, to the extent that even the former "Rwandan President Pasteur Bizimungu notoriously repeated it, for example, in front of diplomats on the event of the invasion of Zaire in 1996. But most sources and historians reject the claim."[11] Furthermore, another contradiction appears in the statement that "the areas currently called Bwisha and Nyiragongo, which had been inhabited by the Hutu and Tutsi for several centuries, the [area called] *Petit Nord* was inhabited largely by Hunde, Nyanga, Tembo, Kano, and Pere communities."[12]

It is also known that "lengthy resistance to colonial rule delayed Belgian efforts to organize the region and begin economic exploitation."[13] That "resistance to colonial occupation flared up on several occasions" in the early years of the twentieth century and made the Belgians recruit labor,[14] from Rwanda where there were "events from 1959 . . . also brought many Rwandans to Eastern Congo,"[15] thus that the colonialist administered "a mass immigration

---

8. Stearns, *North Kivu*, 14.
9. Stearns, 14.
10. Stearns, 12.
11. Stearns, 12.
12. Stearns, 11.
13. Turner, *Congo Wars*, 110.
14. Stearns, *North Kivu*, 14.
15. Turner, *Congo Wars*, 116.

of over 150,000 Rwandans between 1928–56 to provide labor for European-owned farms and mines."[16] In fact, the Belgians initiated the creation of "the chiefdom of Gishari with its administrative center in Nyamitaba" to make the immigrants fit into the existing context of Chiefdoms that existed in Eastern Congo. Unfortunately, this initiative and the mass immigration of "the Rwandaphones" (people speaking Kinyarwanda) was considered by the "Hunde" people, who were the indigenous people, as "marking the beginning of Rwandan domination."[17]

Moreover, the colonialists were not the very first people to bring in people speaking Kinyarwanda (Rwandophones) to the area around Goma. History reveals that the indigenous people (autochthones) in Eastern Congo had started using them as servants in their farms and welcomed others to live alongside them as cattle raisers. This explains the presence of both a few Hutu and Tutsi on the Congolese soil before the arrival of the colonialists. That is why Thomas Turner reports the following:

> Some of the current "Rwandophone" areas of North Kivu were not under Rwandan domination in any sense. Dr. R. Kandt, a German resident at the Rwanda court, visited the Mokoto Lakes (present Masisi territory) in 1899. He wrote that "several Watussi" visited him. He found them to be "likable and simple" but "not handsome and elegant" as the Tutsi of Burundi and Rwanda, because these men had to work. They were not the "sovereigns of the country," but lived in isolated villages as cattle raisers, alongside the first residents of the region, who were farmers. This was near "Kischari," i.e. Gishari, where the Rwandophone cheferie would be created in the 1930s. The description of these Tutsi reminds one of the future Banyamulenge of South Kivu, who lived among locals without dominating them.[18]

The immigrant Hutu and Tutsi in Eastern Congo have had in common the "contested citizenship status and thereby also insecurity concerning their right to land, to vote and stand for election."[19] At Independence in 1960, the

---

16. Stearns, *North Kivu*, 15.
17. Stearns, 17.
18. Turner, *Congo Wars*, 108.
19. Boas, "'New' Nationalism," 27.

negotiations in Brussels, known as "table ronde" (roundtable), had one resolution stated that Rwandans and Burundians present in the Congo for more than ten years would have the right to vote.[20] This then brought the "issue of citizenship, and thus the number and weight of the political representation of the *Banyarwanda* at the background of political debate and the source of tensions."[21]

But because this right to vote was not based on true citizenship, the Kanyarwanda war broke out as the Rwandan speakers opposed the indigenous (autochthone) politicians (specifically the Nandes) because of the split of the Kivu into small provinces between1962 and 1965. It started in September 1962 when the Banyarwanda attacked the Hunde and police stations at Kibabi. A dozen people were killed. This violence was followed by a more severe one that was named the "Kanyarwanda war" in May 1965, after the Hunde had been the most successful in legislative and provincial elections. A new revolt in Masisi broke out because of opposition to the Banyarwanda Hutu and the 1963 Tutsi refugees against the autochthones people and the police force. Lootings, arson attacks and killings of civilians were then perpetrated by armed young people from both sides.[22] As a result, the North Kivu provincial assembly voted in October 1965, stating, "the resolution aiming to 'send away all Rwandans for their supposed collusion with rebels' (the Mulele), but the decision, as others, was not executed."[23]

One of the precursors to the wars between 1990 and November 2011 is the unsolved issue of citizenship of the immigrant population speaking Kinyarwanda. Various changes occurred in the law concerning the issue. In 1964, the constitution of Luluabourg recognized

> only one Congolese citizenship . . . attributed, on 30 June 1960, to any person with one ancestor who was or is a member of a tribe or part of a tribe established on the territory of Congo before 15 November 1908.[24]

---

20. Stearns, *North Kivu*, 24.
21. Mathieu and Tsongo, "Guerres paysannes," 293.
22. Mathieu and Tsongo, 393.
23. Mathieu and Tsongo, 394.
24. Stearns, *North Kivu*, 24.

On 26 March 1971, the state of Zaire gave a collective citizenship "to all people originally from Rwanda and Burundi who had come to Congo by 30 June 1960."[25] On 5 January 1972, President Mobutu Sese Seko vulgarized a "law that was passed in the spirit of *authenticité*,"[26] that contradicted the previous law of 1971 as it adjusted the citizenship to any people from Rwanda and Burundi who migrated before 1950. In 1981, a new law "repealed previous legislation, pushing back to 1885 the date by which an ethnic community had to have been established in the Congo. It also canceled the collective attribution of citizenship in previous legislation."[27] Finally, the transitional government of Congo passed the law in 2004 "stating that 'any individual belonging to an ethnic group whose people and territory constituted what became the Congo' have right to citizenship, reintroducing 30 June 1960 as the key date in determining citizenship."[28] It is clear that ambiguity may still be present but at least citizenship is now an individual business and may require an individual to make application to obtain it, as it happens in many other countries.

In summary, the material context of Eastern Congo has been dominated by "a heterogeneous population, forced or imposed cohabitations, and a rapid rareness of available lands"[29] that governed the politics and/or influenced social coexistence in the region since the colonial era.

4.3 Ethnic Wars in the Early 1990s (1990–1994)

The 1980s were marked by "the emergence of the *mutuelles* (ethnic solidarity groups), as well as NGOs that formed the basis for mobilization, patronage and protection."[30] Around Goma, "the main mutuelles were called Magrivi

---

25. Stearns, 24.

26. Stearns, 24. *Authenticité* was introduced for Mobutu's elevation of indigenous culture – Mobutu's bid for the exaltation of indigenous culture (cf. Stearns, 24). The concept *Autenticité*, also known as Zairianization or Zairization was a politically oriented movement initiated by president Mobutu Sese Seko, in the then Republic of Zaire. It covered the period between 1972 to 1978 and consisted in the return to the African authenticity of toponyms and patronymics, hence suppressing everything that could echo European influence. (Cf. Mandjumba, *Chronologie générale*, 105).

27. Stearns, *North Kivu*, 24.

28. Stearns, 24.

29. Mathieu and Tsongo, "Guerres paysannes," 390.

30. Stearns, *North Kivu*, 27.

(representing Hutu), Bushenge Hunde (Hunde), Kyaghanda (Nande), and Umoja (Hutu and Tutsi)."[31] Stearns emphasizes the fact that "the best organized of all these – in particular Magrivi – carried out local development projects in addition to mobilization and lobbying."[32]

Thomas Turner confirms that "the nationality question was muted during the years of the Mobutu Sese Seko dictatorship, but the move toward multi-party competition after 1990 heated up the question of who is Congolese."[33] In April 1990, President Mobutu Sese Seko introduced a policy of democratizations with a multi-party political system and national elections with the perspective of national elections.[34] The Sovereign National Conference (Conference Nationale Souvereine, CNS) of 1991 to 1992 started in August 1991. This conference offered local autochthon leaders from North and South Kivu an opportunity to seize the advantage over their Rwandophone rivals by barring them from participation.[35] During the preparation and the course of the CNS, the Banyarwanda and the autochthons of North Kivu were in opposition and tension for the choice of the North Kivu delegates to the conference.[36] It is important to note that prior to the conference, municipal elections that were implemented in 1989 in the entire country (Zaïre) were postponed in the two provinces, that is North Kivu and South Kivu.

According to Mathieu and Tsongo, for these elections to be effective there was a need "to identify with precision the voters,"[37] consequently, an identification of national citizens planned for 1989 started in North Kivu in June 1991. Due to

> the decision not to censor or identify as Zairians the descendants of "transplanted people," and generally all the Banyarwanda of Kivu, armed Hutu groups attacked the administration offices in Masisi, destroyed the population lists and changed the team in charge of the identification operation.[38]

---

31. Stearns, 27.
32. Stearns, 27.
33. Turner, *Congo*, 77.
34. Mathieu and Tsongo, "Guerres paysannes," 394.
35. Mathieu and Tsongo.
36. Mathieu and Tsongo, 394.
37. Mathieu and Tsongo, 394.
38. Mathieu and Tsongo, 394.

This attack engendered a "serious war between the army force of Zaire and the armed Hutu groups which caused the loss of thirty people and the identification process to fail."[39]

These Hutu groups managed to carry out the operation because MAGRIVI was the best organized of all the ethnic *mutuelles* which carried out "mobilization and lobbying work"[40] with regards to identity issues. It appears that mobilization strengthened the Hutu groups and failure of their lobbying for them to access the right to vote made them choose the armed approach to advocating their rights. It is curious that this armed violence in Masisi in June 1991 did not force the state to include the Banyarwanda to participate in the CNS. Thomas Turner reveals how the MAGRIVI *mutuelle* was more than mutual but a politico-military organization that watered ethnic violence and wars in the area around Goma and was also instrumental in the instability that occurred in the Great Lakes region. In this vein, Turner has this to say:

> In 1989–1990, Hutu of North Kivu formed the Mutuelle Agricole de Virunga (Agricultural Mutual Aid Society of Virunga, MAGRIVI), to defend their interests. Despite its banal title, this was a politico-military organization. About the same time, the predominantly Tutsi Rwanda Patriotic Front (RPF) became active in North Kivu, recruiting fighters and preparing a rear base for its campaign against the Habyarimana government. Between 1990 and 1992, there was localized violence in North Kivu associated with the census or identification des nationaux. In Masisi territory, conflict pitted Hunde against Hutu. In Rutshuru, Tutsi were aligned against Hutu in Jomba (Bwisha) and Kihondo (Bwito). In 1993, a full-blown "Masisi war" broke out. It was not limited to Masisi Territory but included the Wanyanga Collectivity in Walikale Territory and Bwito Collectivity in Rutshuru Territory.[41]

Shortly before 1993, the social cohesion between the autochthons and the Rwandophones disappeared completely due to "social disobedience and

---

39. Mathieu and Tsongo.
40. Stearns, *North Kivu*, 27.
41. Turner, *Congo*, 118.

the appeal for a boycott of any payment of tax by the Banyarwanda, which was spearheaded by the Banyarwanda politicians and the Magrivi."[42] Ethnic groups constituted armed self-defense militias (*millices d'auto-defense armée*) that were established in the area on an ethnic basis. The fact that the members of MAGRIVI were no longer paying land tenure taxes meant they could not benefit from any support from landlords and chiefs of different chiefdoms in Masisi Territory and Bwito collectivity. This paved the way for a serious ethnic war which, from March to September 1993, aimed at an ethnic cleansing of one ethnic group or the other as the militia entitled it "them or us" ("*eux ou nous*")[43] hence consecrating an environment of non-ethnic cohabitation.

On the 20 March 1993, the groups of Hunde, Nyanga and Tembo young people organized by local politicians sparked the first massacres of Hutu people in the market of Ntoto (east of Walikale Territory) and in the neighboring villages. Similar groups, organized by the Hutu in Masisi reacted by attacking the Hunde.[44] This was the beginning of six months of civil war and killing by both parties that claimed at least 7,000 lives and forced more than 20,000 people to flee from these areas to Goma (the Hunde) or Rutshuru (the Hutu).[45]

According to Mortem Boas this "spilled over into interethnic skirmishes that exploded in anti-Banyarwanda violence in 1993 when armed youth groups of Nande, Hunde and Nyanga origin attacked Banyarwanda Communities"[46] in Ntoto. There seems to be no evidence that the Nande had been part of that in Walikale, but it is clear that during the CNS, "Magrivi would serve as the basis for political mobilization, mobilizing the Hutu from Masisi and those from Rutshuru and Bwito for unity as it was being said 'the Hutu is one and indivisible.'"[47] In reaction, "other ethnic groups, including the Hunde, Nyanga, Tembo, Tutsi, and Nande, formed an anti-Hutu coalition."[48] However, it appears that rather than the Hutu being the target of ethnic wars in 1993, ethnic groups used this as an opportunity to attack and chase any

---

42. Mathieu and Tsongo, "Guerres paysannes," 395.
43. Mathieu and Tsongo, 295.
44. Mathieu and Tsongo, 395.
45. Mathieu and Tsongo.
46. Boas, "'New' Nationalism," 28.
47. Turner, *Congo Wars*, 119.
48. Turner, 119.

other group they thought was usurping their land. Therefore, Turner reveals that "this coalition was inherently unstable, as the province was racked by a series of rivalries, Hutu vs. Tusi, Banyarwanda (Hutu and Tutsi together) against non-Banyarwanda, Nande vs. Banyabuisha and Nande vs. Hunde."[49]

From the rivalries and violence referred to above, we can easily see the reason why during this war, known as the war of MAGRIVI in Bwito, the Nande had no other choice than to leave and most of them lost their land in Bwito collectivity and went to seek refuge and livelihoods either in Lubero territory (their land of origin) or in the cities, like Goma and Butembo. They had had two enemies in the Bwito, namely the Hutu and the Hunde, whereas the latter had settled in Bwito territory many centuries before. Both the Hunde and the Hutu are farmers. This seems to have appeared as an opportunity for the Hutu and Hunde militias respectively to decide to sweep the Nande away as the Nande were trying the same forfeiture strategy. Two against one seems to have made the Nande civilians move in masses out of the zone.

The militia groups that were instrumental in this violence were mainly connected to particular ethnic groups that were aiming to either fight for their ethnic group's benefit or take revenge on any opposing group or coalition. "Groups such as the *Coalition des Patriotes Résistants Congolais* (PARECO, Alliance of Resistant Congolese Patriots), the APLCLS, and the Mai-Mai loyal to General Padiri can be traced back to this period."[50] While the ethnic war was spreading in the rural area around Goma, the cities that hosted IDPs were facing a leadership crisis. Turner states:

> About the same time as power was transferred to North Kivu leaders under géopolitique, Mobutu's troops rioted and pillaged Goma and Butembo, the two main towns of the province. Disorder spread and with it opportunities for politicians to pillage.[51]

The period from November 1993 to August 1994 was marked by the effort to reconstruct peaceful coexistence between the ethnic groups in Bashali Collectivity (Masisi) and Bwito (Rutshuru), which were the epicenter of the

---

49. Turner, 120.
50. Stearns, *North Kivu*, 28.
51. Turner, *Congo Wars*, 120.

clashes and violence. Factors that contributed toward that effort were mainly "the intervention of the Presidential Special armed Division of Zaire (DSP), a serious work was done by the civil society and Ethnic groups Chiefs' delegates in different workshops which led to an agreement for peaceful coexistence."[52] This agreement allowed populations to return to their villages but did not solve the main issue that was a land tenure issue between the autochthones and the "transplanted" Rwandophones, especially "in Masisi where Hutu chiefs had self-proclaimed chiefs at the expense of the Hunde chiefs that were legitimated by the government."[53] This would continue to be the cause of ethnic violence over land tenure issues in the region.

4.4 Eastern Congo between 1994 and 1996

The historical context of Eastern Congo in the period between 1994 and 1996 is dominated by the military operation in Masisi and Rutshuru territories, and the arrival of massive numbers of refugees from the genocide in Rwanda in 1994.

The two military operations, that is "operation Kimia (Peace) in Masisi territory in March 1996 and Operation Mbata (Slap) in the northern Rutshuru territory at around the same time"[54] were part of several operations that the Zairean armed force carried out in response to the wars that occurred in the region between 1990 and 1994. However, Stearns argues that

> these operations only compounded the violence; that in response to the mounting insecurity, the Zairean carried out several large operations in the area; the list of atrocities carried out by government forces is just as long as those carried out by local militia.[55]

Zairean soldiers seem to have been facing a challenging time in terms of care and livelihoods as well as leadership. This is what explains their "acts of riot and pillage in Goma and Butembo in the early 1990s."[56] This army, which

---

52. Mathieu and Tsongo, "Guerres paysannes," 395.
53. Mathieu and Tsongo.
54. Stearns, *North Kivu*, 29.
55. Stearns, 29.
56. Turner, *Congo Wars*, 120.

was not paid and not well taken care of, would not have accomplished the mission, instead, they showed a lack of discipline on the front lines.

From April to July 1994, Rwanda became the field for

> ... [ethnic] extremist massacres of more than 800,000 Tutsi and moderate Hutus. When the Tutsi-led Rwandan Patriotic Front seized power in Kigali and ended the genocide, about two million (mainly Hutu) Rwandan refugees flooded into the Eastern Congo to avoid persecution from their new Tutsi government.[57]

In refugee camps, there were more than 500,000 armed Rwandan Hutu alongside the civilian refugees. These armed people were mostly members of the Rwandese Armed Forces (ex-FAR) and *Interahamwe* in the dispersion. They settled in refugee camps, which they used to "reorganize themselves and prepare to re-conquer their country."[58] This alliance made up of the ex-FAR, the *Interahamwe* and other Rwandan militias would later be rebranded *Alliance pour la Liberation du Rwanda* (ALIR, Alliance for the Liberation of Rwanda) and would "become in 2001 the Democratic Forces for the Liberation of Rwanda (Forces Démocratiques pour la Liberation du Rwanda, FDLR)."[59]

In November 1994, new hostilities occurred in Masisi. They were characterized by "the looting of Tutsi pastoralist livestock and attacks on Hunde villages. The ex-FAR and *Interahamwe* ranged themselves behind the Banyarwanda of Masisi to attack the autochthones and the Tutsi."[60] In fact, "the coalition that existed between the Hutu and Tutsi groups in Eastern Congo collapsed as the local Hutu militia began collaborating with 'ex-FAR.'"[61] Apart from involving and supporting Hutu militia against other militia, these combatants (ex-FAR and *Interahamwe* in refuge in Eastern Congo) "formed enormous armed groups who based their survival on violence and looting, and used the refugee camps as rear bases from which to launch raids on Rwanda."[62] The different looting and raids within Congo in the period between 1995 and July 1996 were aiming at access to financial support to

---

57. Autesserre, *Trouble with the Congo*, 47.
58. Mathieu and Tsongo, "Guerres paysannes," 396.
59. Stearns, *North Kivu*, 32.
60. Mathieu and Tsongo, "Guerres paysannes," 396.
61. Stearns, *North Kivu*, 29.
62. Autesserre, *Trouble with the Congo*, 47.

purchase guns.⁶³ Consequently, "the large refugee camps attracted the fear of Rwandan Patriotic Army (RPA) that dismantled them in November 1996."⁶⁴

4.5 First Congo War/AFDL (1996–1997)

The growing insecurity and instability in the period between 1994 and 1995 was "a foretaste of what was to come: all-out war in the eastern Congo" in 1996.⁶⁵ This First Congo War which is also known as the "Liberation War" would have as "twin catalysts . . . the presence of Rwandan refugees and the decay of the Congolese state."⁶⁶ At the same time, "the new regime in Rwanda had to find a way to dismantle rebel groups"⁶⁷ that were established in refugee camps in North and South Kivu.

In September 1996 the "Banyamulenge rebellion" supported by Rwanda started in South Kivu.⁶⁸ In October 1996, these so-called "'Banyamulenge' (Kinyarwanda-speaking Congolese Tutsi) captured the eastern Zaire cities of Uvira, Bukavu, and Goma. They attacked the UN Refugee Camps in these cities."⁶⁹ The attacks caused "hundreds of thousands of Rwandan refugees to be 'repatriated,' while hundreds of thousands of others fled westwards"⁷⁰ and 230,000 refugees are claimed to have been killed by the Rwandan Army and AFDL in 1996–1997.⁷¹ This "'rebellion' planned and directed by Rwanda," as per the later saying of Paul Kagame in July 1997,⁷² had "Rwanda and Uganda as aggressors in the civil war which greatly worked and benefited the two countries."⁷³

According to Autessere, the First Congo War was a response of the Rwandan, Ugandan, Angolan and Burundian governments, as well as South

---

63. Mathieu and Tsongo, "Guerres paysannes,"296.
64. Mathieu and Tsongo, 296.
65. Stearns, *North Kivu*, 29.
66. Stearns, 29.
67. Autesserre, *Trouble with the Congo*, 47.
68. Reyntjens, *Great African War*, 292.
69. Turner, *Congo*, 15.
70. Reyntjens, *Great African War*, 292.
71. Turner, *Congo Wars*, 220.
72. Turner, 199.
73. Turner, *Congo*, 15.

Sudanese rebel forces, that formed an anti-Mobutu coalition, which engineered, armed and supervised various Congolese rebel groups and local militias.[74] With the support of the coalition, "the anti-Mobutu forces from the Congo formed the rebel movement Alliance of Democratic Forces for the Liberation of Congo-Zaire (Alliance des Forces Démocratiques pour la Liberation du Congo-Zaire, AFDL),"[75] created and first announced in Kigali[76] with Laurent-Désirée Kabila as its spokesman. Steams, however, reveals that the Angolan government was not part of the coalition as he states that "the AFDL was later backed by the Angolan, Ethiopian, Tanzania, and Zimbabwean governments."[77]

It is also important to note that "these forces faced an alliance of Zairean army, local militias and the ex-FAR"[78] in every step of their so-called "liberation." In 1997, AFDL liberated the rest of the country by capturing most of the major cities of the country from the east to the west, an occupation that was concluded by the fall of Kinshasa on 17 May 1997 and the swearing in of AFDL spokesman Laurent Kabila as president on the 29 May 1997.[79] It appears that this was a rapid movement of the rebellion toward the capital city due to the fact that "while the AFDL troops were welcomed by parts of the population . . . thousands of local youths joined their ranks."[80] John Clark describes the strength of AFDL:

> There were "kadogos," the young men and boys who were recruited by AFDL army in the course of its march from the east to Kinshasa. Kabila's inner circle of supporters, as well as Kabila himself, was without its own political base. Many of them had returned from exile, and this made them totally dependent on Kabila since they lacked an internal constituent base.[81]

---

74. Autessere, *Trouble with the Congo*, 47.
75. Autessere, 47.
76. Reyntjens, *Great African War*, 105, 292.
77. Stearns, *North Kivu*, 31.
78. Stearns, 31.
79. Reyntjens, *Great African War*, 292–93.
80. Stearns, *North Kivu*, 31.
81. Clark, *African Stakes*, 113.

However, the AFDL coalition did accommodate "too many components: its Rwandan backers, Congo's political opposition to Mobutu's rule, and its own military factions that ran the entire gamut from Mai-Mai fighters (local militia) to Tutsi troops and child soldiers were known as Kadogo."[82] Consequently, "their invasion threw fuel on the fire, exacerbating ethnic conflict and carrying out a series of massacres."[83] Furthermore, the ethnic divide within AFDL between Baluba of Katanga region (Balubakat) and Congolese ethnic Tutsi (Banyamulenge), as Francois Ngolet would argue, "ended up undermining the tenuous equilibrium within the movement even before AFDL troops made their triumph to Kinshasa after a grueling seven-month trek from the eastern border where the rebellion gathered steam."[84] This lack of equilibrium later became the public cause of the next war, which was trying to overthrow Laurent Kabila in August 1998.

Kabila's rise to power brought in a new episode of crisis that saw sporadic clashes in Eastern Congo. Francois Ngolet portrays that period as follows:

> The anti-Tutsi sentiment had intensified after Kabila's takeover, beginning with October 1996 insurrection. Intellectuals in Bukavu voiced frustrations against the anarchic occupation of property and administrative posts ... Civil society was also growing frustrated by new regime ... *Groupe Jérémie* publicly complained about mono-ethnic (Tutsi) composition of the AFDL and the massive Tutsi presence in the popular army. Several reports of the "Tusification" of the Kivus contained warnings of an explosion of ethnic hatred ... In North Kivu and South Kivu, violence exploded especially in the territories of Masisi and Kalehe. Tensions were so high that violence erupted over relatively trivial matters ... The Mayi-Mayi who joined the AFDL during the war of liberation then turned against Kabila and the Tutsi. From their perspective, the AFDL appeared to be composed of Rwanda forces, and thus they saw the AFDL victory in the east as simply a form of Rwandan colonization of the Kivus.... In the Masisi area in North Kivu, Hunde chiefs

---

82. Ngolet, *Crisis in the Congo*, xvi.
83. Stearns, *North Kivu*, 31.
84. Ngolet, *Crisis in the Congo*, xvi.

recruited young men to prevent the Tutsi from coming back to reclaim their grazing land.[85]

The fact is that "violence was rampant in Eastern Congo; the Congolese Armed Forces (Forces Armées Congolaise, FAC) found it nearly impossible to distinguish members of militias from the rest of the population."[86] Many civilians were consequently killed during the various expeditions and/or attacks held by the FAC against armed militias.

4.6 The Second Congo War (1998–2003)

Laurent Kabila's victory was short-lived. His government looked like a power-sharing with his allies "from Rwanda and the Kinyarwanda-speaking Congolese who held a number of key posts. James Kabarebe, a Rwandan army officer, was named the chief of staff of the Congolese Armed Force (Forces Armées Congolaises, FAC)."[87]

Soon Kabila was in a dilemma; he was trying to "frustrate the efforts of the United Nations to investigate the massacre of the Rwandan Hutu refugees in the Congolese forest" while "his regime was polarized by Rwandans and the Congolese Tutsi, on the one hand, and his Luba-Katanga community and Katangans in general, on the other hand."[88] On 26 July 1998, Kabila then announced that he was sending Kabarebe and other foreign officers home.[89] As a response to that dismissal of the Rwandan army, "the governments of Rwanda, Uganda, and to some extent Burundi, engineered a new rebel movement, the Congolese Rally for Democracy (*Rassemblement Congolais pour la Démocratie*, RCD)" which in August 1998 "launched an attack on Kabila's government thus initiating war what has become known as the second war of liberation."[90] During that first attack of the RCD, "Goma, Bukavu, and Uvira were taken."[91]

---

85. Ngolet, 18–19.
86. Ngolet, 19.
87. Turner, *Congo*, 16.
88. Turner, 16.
89. Turner, 170; Reyntjens, *Great African War*, 293.
90. Autesserre, *Trouble with the Congo*, 48.
91. Reyntjens, *Great African War*, 293.

Autessere argues that tensions arose between Kabila and his foreign backers over the dismissal of the Rwandan army, alleged support of Rwandan rebel groups and incitement of violence against Rwandans and Congolese with Rwandan ancestry.[92] The violence was committed by the local citizens as a sign of disapproval of any foreign occupation. The new rebels had taken the strategy of having Kinshasa fall under them before the rest of the country. So, "Rwandans hijacked airplanes and flew their troops to Kitona military base in Bas-Congo Province, west Kinshasa"[93] where Mobutu's army officers were being re-educated. They first flew them out of Kitona, then recruited among them soldiers for their new army force. After Kitona, they also seized the Inga electric complex, cutting off electricity at the expense of millions of people and hospitals of Kinshasa and Matadi.[94] The massacre of individual Tutsi subjects was perpetrated only in Kinshasa as a reaction of protesters in the capital city once the RCD force had just captured Kitona and was pressing on toward Kinshasa. This might have been a result of panic mixed with anger and hate through which some residents tried to demonstrate that they were not ready to receive the new rebels. This researcher recalls President Laurent Kabila calling the Congolese to defend themselves against what he called "a foreign invasion."

On 5 August 1998 "the RPA raid on Kitona was defeated by Angolan intervention."[95] This defeat would hinder the new rebellion to capture Kinshasa and thus strengthened the FAC to march against the RCD. However, from 1998 "the second war put North Kivu and a major part of Eastern Congo under the control of the RCD. Goma became the seat of the RCD's so-called 'government,' which claimed to govern the entire rebel zone."[96]

The new rebellion movement which, through support from neighboring countries, "was supposed to conquer the Congo in a few months met an unexpected opposition of forces from Zimbabwe, Angola, Namibia, and to a lesser extent Chad and Sudan; each sided with Kabila for different political, security, or economic reasons."[97] On the side of Rwanda, "once the possibility

---

92. Autesserre, *Trouble with the Congo*, 48.
93. Turner, *Congo*, 17.
94. Turner, 17.
95. Reyntjens, *Great African War*, 293.
96. Turner, *Congo Wars*, 126.
97. Autesserre, *Trouble with the Congo*, 48.

of a blitzkrieg victory had passed, a war of 'partition and pillage' set in."[98] A new movement started in the north, the Congo Liberation Movement (*Mouvement de Liberation du Congo*, MLC) led by a businessman Jean-Pierre Bemba under the sponsorship of Uganda. The Rwandan/RCD rebels were controlling an important zone of the eastern part of DRC from Oriental province in the north to Katanga in the south. Turner quotes a report entitled "Kinshasa's Missing Millions" and reveals that "the RCD, MLC, and the government zones each housed complex networks by which Congo's minerals and other resources were extracted and sold in international markets."[99] These rebel movements transformed Eastern Congo into a jungle while efforts to end the crisis were fruitless.

The SADC community and other international corps organized various unsuccessful summits, such as the summit in Victoria Falls, Summit in Mauritius from 13–14 September 1998, First Syrte Summit under Libyan auspices on 30 September 1998 and others in 1999, calling for a ceasefire between the government and the RCD troops.[100] A ceasefire was signed in Lusaka in July 1999 that "included the holding of a national dialogue and the creation of the UN peacekeeping force"; as the result, late the same year "the UN began to deploy a small observatory force in Congo called MONUC."[101] The mandate of this UN peacekeeping force to be an observatory force made MONUC unable to impact the conflict's stakeholders. Consequently, the effect of MONUC is not known in terms of ceasing the violence and fighting between groups in Eastern Congo, which continued to exist regardless the presence of the UN force.

A dispute between Uganda and Rwanda caused "the fighting between Ugandan Army UPDF and RPA in Kisangani in May-June 1999."[102] This dispute generated a split within the RCD on 16 May 1999, as "Wamba Dia Wamba retreated to Kisangani and set up the RCD-Kisangani/Liberation Movement supported by Uganda and Emile Ilunga became the Chairman of RCD-Goma, backed by Rwanda."[103] Further, splits within the RCD generated

---

98. Turner, *Congo*, 18.
99. Turner, 18.
100. Reyntjens, *Great African War*, 293–294.
101. Autesserre, *Trouble with the Congo*, 49.
102. Reyntjens, *Great African War*, 294.
103. Autesserre, *Trouble with the Congo*, 48; Reyntjens, *Great African War*, 294.

the RCD-Originale, the RCD-National, and the RCD-Populaire.[104] These splits within the RCD made the Eastern Congo into a zone with different rebel governments and challenges. Travelers, businessmen and visitors were subjected to various taxes and visit passes within the region. RCD-Goma was controlling the so-called "Petit Nord" of North Kivu, South Kivu, North Katanga, Maniema province and part of Kasai; RDC/K-ML had the control of Kisangani, the rest of North Kivu province and Ituri with Beni as its government capital and Mbusa Nyamwisi as the chair in succession to Professor Wamba-dia-Wamba, while MLC of Jean-Pierre had Gbadolite as its headquarters.

Since the ceasefire in 1999, "the government and MLC areas (respectively the southern and western parts of the country and the northern province) remained calm and relatively free from war-related violence"[105] while the areas under the RCD-Goma was "a mosaic of enclaves under the control of competing for armed bands."[106]

However, the Ugandan involvement in rebellion in the north-eastern part of Congo in 1998 "started to profoundly exacerbate an already fragile situation"[107] with an ethnic conflict between Hema and Lendu in Ituri. Turner confirms that view when he writes that "conflicts over land between the Hema and the Lendu ethnic communities had long plagued Ituri."[108] On 22 June 1999, General James Kazini, commander of the UPDF occupying force, decided to merge Ituri district and Haut-Uélé and created a province called Kibali-Ituri, appointing as its governor a Hema, Adele Lotsove, a member of RCD/K-ML. Lendu political leaders then confirmed their suspicion that the Ugandan army was siding with the Hema, a positioning which, according to Reyntjens, "it had already done during a few earlier incidents"[109] so that "Uganda began arming the Hema."[110] Consequently, "these actions helped ignite a new ethnic war."[111] It is reported that "in early July 1999, UPDF unit

---

104. Autesserre, *Trouble with the Congo*, 49.
105. Autesserre, 50.
106. Autesserre, 51.
107. Reyntjens, *Great African War*, 216.
108. Turner, *Congo*, 63.
109. Reyntjens, *Great African War*, 216.
110. Turner, *Congo*, 63.
111. Turner, 63.

killed dozens of Lendu and destroyed some of their villages. In the ethnic clashes of the following weeks, scores of Lendu and Hema were killed and thousands displaced."[112] It is also said that

> Uganda's relationships with Ituri militias continued at least until 2006. UN investigators believe that Ugandan border officers turned a blind eye on weapons shipments into Congo . . . In return for supplying arms, Uganda was plundering the area controlled by its favored rebels, becoming a major exporter of Congolese gold.[113]

Serious "tensions ran high within the Leadership of the RCD/K-ML due to the handling of the ethnic war between Hema and Lendu peoples,"[114] which made Wamba quit the RCD/K-ML as "Tibasima, a Hema, wanted Wamba to condemn the Lendu 'for committing genocide against his people,'"[115] but Wamba on 13 April 2000 attributed the killings to both parties.

The negotiations undertaken by a Ugandan senior official, James Wapakhabulo in Bunia "to mediate between the two sides within the RCD/K-ML was unsuccessful although the leaders agreed to cooperate."[116] Ntibasima and Mbusa Nyamwisi then launched a mutiny in Bunia forcing Wamba to leave as they accused him of being in collaboration with ADF rebels. This was a second event that created chaos in Bunia after the rebels "took control of a church-owned radio station and were demanding that Wamba quit as leader of RCD/K-ML."[117] Clearly, civilians were dramatically affected in many ways by this war. The triangle Kisangani-North Kivu- Bunia (Ituri) also became a battlefield, as was the area around Goma occupied by RCD-Goma during the same period. For example, people from Kisangani will always remember the massacre perpetrated by RCD-Goma soldiers under Laurent Nkunda's command; these soldiers "indiscriminately killed civilians, committed numerous rapes and carried out widespread looting in Kisangani in 2002."[118]

---

112. Reyntjens, *Great African War*, 216.
113. Turner, *Congo*, 63.
114. Ngolet, *Crisis in the Congo*, 129.
115. Ngolet, 219.
116. Ngolet, 129.
117. Ngolet, 130.
118. Turner, *Congo Wars*, 101.

The delay of the implementation of peace agreements between the DRC government and the rebel groups has always been attributed to "poor quality of the relationship between the Congolese President, Laurent Kabila, and international mediators."[119] When Joseph Kabila took over the government after the assassination of his father in 2001 "he secured the trust of most western powers."[120] The inter-Congolese dialogue then started in April 2001 in Addis Ababa. It ended the war with its Final Act in April 2003 signed in Sun City, South Africa, that outlined a framework for the transition government, an emanation of Global and All-Inclusive Agreement on the Transition in DRC.[121]

4.7 Transitional Government and Elections (2003–2006)

The peace agreement between Congolese rebel groups and the government led to the formation of a transitional government, which was a power-sharing between the government, the rebel's groups, especially RCD-Goma and MLC, and the unarmed opposition. Henceforth the DRC would be governed by a president assisted by four vice presidents as per the "infamous 1+4 settlement that emerged from internationally sponsored negotiations"[122] with Joseph Kabila as the Head of State. Stearns writes, "The head of the RCD, Azarias Ruberwa, was named as one of [the] four vice-presidents, while senior RCD officers secured not only the command of North Kivu and Western Kasai military regions but also other high-ranking positions."[123]

The peace agreement "was further cemented by bilateral deals with Rwanda and Uganda, leading to the withdrawal of their troops in 2002 and 2003, respectively."[124] This act indeed marked their official recognition by the two countries of supporting rebels' movements in Congo and even their responsibility as engineers of the two wars, the responsibility they used to deny. However, despite the formal withdrawal, their troops continued to intervene in Eastern Congo. Severine Autesserre would, for example, reveal

---

119. Autesserre, *Trouble with the Congo*, 51.
120. Autesserre, 51.
121. Autesserre, 51.
122. Turner, *Congo Wars*, 168.
123. Stearns, *North Kivu*, 35.
124. Stearns, 35.

"clashes between Rwanda, Ugandan, and different Congolese armed groups in Ituri during the war and during transition."[125]

Among the successful achievements of the transitional government, Autesserre points out the ceasing of front lines late in 2003 and the successful organization of general elections. While the ceasing of the front lines in 2003 made traveling across the country possible due to the effective reunification of the country, the elections consisted of a referendum on the new constitution of the country in 2005, the elections and the first run-off for presidential elections in July 2006 and October 2006 respectively. The successful completion of the transition was marked by the "inauguration of Joseph Kabila, the elected president, on December 6th, 2006."[126]

However, during the transition, Eastern Congo was still subjected to "massive violence to such an extent that Congolese officials still referred to the area between the cities of Kindu (Maniema), Kalemie (Katanga), and Ituri as the 'fatal triangle' of the country."[127] While the rebel movements in Eastern Congo were allowed to either top the leadership or the military command in the area, militia groups such as the Mai-Mai did not fare as well. Furthermore, "while they also received their share of the seats and positions, their lack of organizational structure meant that many groups and officers felt left out."[128] These groups would see the transitional government as a new form of the RCD continuity. As a result, "any new armed group could, therefore, draw on a large pool of former combatants."[129]

Fear and dissatisfaction permeated the RCD, especially among the Tutsi. Stearns mentions three senior military officers who defected from the Congolese army in August 2003.[130] One of them, General Nkunda, a Tutsi from Rutshuru territory, along with some members of the RCD leadership, created a new synergy called *Synergie Nationale pour la Paix et la Concorde* (SNPC, National Synergy for Peace and Concord). The uncertainty was not only the concern of the rebels but also that of their mentor. According to Stearns, "Kigali, driven by an amalgam of economic, security, and political

---

125. Autesserre, *Trouble with the Congo*, 58.
126. Autesserre, 53.
127. Autesserre, 54.
128. Stearns, *North Kivu*, 36.
129. Stearns, 36.
130. Stearns.

Historical and Ethnical Context of Eastern Congo from 1990 to 2011   137

interests, was also afraid of losing a foothold in the Kivus and threw its weight behind these dissenting officers."[131] As the result, Laurent Nkunda and Col. Jules Mutebusi, a Munyamulenge, "made a three days siege on Bukavu in May 2004 following friction between RCD officers and transitional government loyalists in Bukavu in early 2004."[132] General Nkunda was already known for the massacre perpetrated against civilians in Kisangani 2002.[133] Despite him being wanted at the Hague by the International Criminal Court, RCD-Goma had proposed him "to help lead the unified army, as were a number of officers from other former rebel groups who were implicated in war crimes and crimes against humanity over the past years."[134]

Between 2004 and April 2006, "Museveni also was backing the *Mouvement Révolutionnaire Congolais* (Congolese Revolutionary Movement, MRC) with arms, ammunition, or other military supplies."[135] This backing seems to have had a double purpose. On the one hand, Uganda became "a major exporter of the Congolese gold which was exchanged with all the supplies offered to the favored rebels in Ituri."[136] On the other hand, the Lord's Resistance Army, "a Ugandan rebel movement had raided northeastern Congo. The Ugandan army, which has driven the LRA out of Uganda, had to send several missions into DRC after the LRA."[137] The militia backed-up by Uganda would play a significant role to help in pursuing the track of Joseph Kony and his LRA rebels.

During the transitional government time, population movements continued in the war zones as well as outside the country due to various wars and clashes in Eastern Congo. Security and safety were never guaranteed for either IDPs or refugees. For example, a mass movement of Banyamulenge from South Kivu to Burundi followed the time after the withdrawal of Nkunda and Mutebusi from Bukavu in 2004. Turner notes "on 13 August 2004, [Burundian] armed fighters, the majority of them belonging to Burundi's Front National de Libération (National Liberation Front NLF) massacred at least 152 of these Congolese refugees and wounded 106 others in Gatumba

---

131. Stearns, 36.
132. Stearns, 37.
133. Turner, *Congo Wars*, 101.
134. Turner, 101.
135. Turner, *Congo*, 63.
136. Turner, 63.
137. Turner, 64.

refugee camp, near Bujumbura"[138] weakening the international relationship between Burundi and DRC. Unfortunately, according to Human Rights Watch, it appeared that "the massacre was more than another case of ethnic violence."[139] The victims were mainly Banyamulenge (Congolese Tutsi) while the killers were from NLF, a Burundian Hutu rebel group. The presence of these Congolese Tutsi refugees may have appeared to the Hutu from Burundi as a possible reinforcement of the Burundian Tutsi main enemy of Hutu militia or rebels.

The transitional government left room for the formation of an integrated national army, the FARDC. This was constituted by a mixture of soldiers from the national armed force (FAC), the rebel groups and the militia fighters. This, however, did not mean the security of the civilians would be safeguarded, especially in Eastern Congo. In mid-December 2004, for example, Turner recalls the case of "civilians at Kanyabayonga, Buramba and Nyabiondo in North Kivu [who] were killed, tortured and raped. In the course of military operations, military forces having carried out intentional attacks on civilians."[140] According to him, "these events highlighted the vulnerability of the civilian population to attack particularly in a context of heightened ethnic tensions and a lack of integrated and accountable national army."[141] Consequently, "the victims came almost exclusively from the Hunde and Nande ethnic groups. Many appeared to have been deliberately targeted on the basis of ethnicity."[142]

During the transition, the governor of North Kivu, Eugene Serufuli, also "maintained his 3,000 strong Local Defense Forces, a predominantly Congolese Hutu militia that he had created during the war and that the Rwandan soldiers had trained."[143] So, the area around Goma remained subjected to perpetual crises due to the existence of such militia in the government-controlled zone and the existence of new rebel groups in the instance of Laurent Nkunda's CNDP and the like. Therefore, Autesserre concludes that during the transition (2003–2006), "in place of war violence, there were now 'crises' such as the 'Bukavu crisis' (May-June 2004), the 'Kanyabayonga

---

138. Turner, *Congo Wars*, 103.
139. Turner, 103.
140. Turner, 131.
141. Turner, 131.
142. Turner, 131.
143. Autesserre, *Trouble with the Congo*, 159.

crisis' (December 2005), the 'Rutshuru crisis' (January 2006) and the 'Sake crisis' (November 2006)."[144]

4.8 Eastern Congo between 2006 and 28 November 2011

During the transition, "President Kabila and Vice-Presidents Bemba and Ruberwa continued behaving like warlords, to the extent that foreign military observers concluded that they all kept their best soldiers and weapons in reserve."[145] Laurent Nkunda was one of the threats that this phenomenon posed to the transition process.[146] According to UN sources, "Nkunda's troops had received weapons and support from Rwanda."[147]

Toward the end of the transitional government, general Laurent Nkunda, who during the autumn of 2005 and in early 2006 benefited from many desertions of Kinyarwanda-speaking military who were previously integrated into the FARDC, launched a new offensive in January 2006 and gained sizable territory and uprooted thousands of civilians.[148] This territory covered the districts of Masisi and Rutshuru. The latter district is one of the "substantial areas of the east [that] remained out of central government control, notably in Ituri (Province Orientale) and in North Kivu, where Laurent Nkunda continued to control territory and issue ultimatums."[149]

Having refrained from disrupting the electoral process, Laurent Nkunda, on the 25 July 2006, "announced the creation of the National Congress for People's Defense (Congrès National pour la Défense du Peuple, CNDP), and presented himself as the political protector of minorities" but did not pull out of the occupied zone.[150]

The newly elected government seems to have not been a ticket to peace. On the contrary, Eastern Congo continued to experience instability due to war. Autesserre reveals that

---

144. Autesserre, 159.
145. Reyntjens, *Great African War*, 266.
146. Reyntjens, 336.
147. Reyntjens, 213.
148. Reyntjens, 214.
149. Turner, *Congo Wars*, 181.
150. Reyntjens, *Great African War*, 114–15.

The patterns of violence and intervention during the years after transition had many similarities to those of the previous period. In 2007, 2008, and 2009, violence escalated again, and Eastern Congo (the Kivus and Oriental province) returned to all-out war.[151]

It is notable that, although "the few existing local conflict-resolution structures intensified their efforts, but continued to meet the same obstacles as before . . . the existing local tensions"[152] played a role to hinder the efforts from obtaining peace. Among the various efforts to peace was the peace conference organized in Goma in January 2008. The conference established the famous *Amani* program. *Amani* is a Kiswahili term that means peace, security, safety, confidence.[153] The principal objective of the program was to establish conditions for security, pacification and reconstruction of the provinces of North and South Kivu by ensuring the implementation of the resolutions and recommendations of the Goma Conference, as well as its rules of engagement. The *Amani* program had several difficult issues to deal with: the question of armed groups, humanitarian and social questions, reconstruction and development and pacification and reconciliation.[154] Organized by the Congolese government with the support of the UN and international diplomatic forces, the conference yielded no substantial fruits.

During this period, Laurent Nkunda and his CNDP and other militia had remained a threat to peace. In 2007, after military integration had failed, the government attempted to reduce the Nkunda threat by trying to integrate his troops further in the FARDC, using the so-called *mixage*. Rather than reaching its goal, "the process contributed to expanding Nkunda's influence beyond his base in Rutshuru territory. From January to July 2007, Nkunda controlled five brigades of troops rather than two."[155]

In September 2007, "Nkunda had a smaller DRC force siege in Masisi, and during the same month his men raided ten secondary schools and four

---

151. Autesserre, *Trouble with the Congo*, 246.
152. Autesserre, 246.
153. Johnson, *Swahili-English*.
154. Minani, *Du pacte de stabilité de Naïrobi*, 128–37.
155. Turner, *Congo*, 107.

primary schools and took children by force."¹⁵⁶ It is reported that "girls were taken as sex slaves and boys used as fighters, in violation of the international law."¹⁵⁷ The government responded to the president's order to disarm Nkunda's forces forcibly and government forces, therefore, organized various expeditions toward that process. Turner states that "fighting in the '*Petit Nord*' (the area around Goma) was estimated to have displaced over 370,000 since the beginning of the year" 2007.¹⁵⁸ That attack did not stop Nkunda. In November 2007, his troops captured Nyanzale, a town situated about 100 kilometers north of Goma. The counter-offensive by the government early December 2007 resulted in the seizure of Mushake and the call for negotiations.¹⁵⁹

The year 2008 was marked by a peace agreement signed between the government and Nkunda, which included "an immediate ceasefire, the withdrawal of all rebel forces in North Kivu province, the resettlement of thousands of villagers, and immunity for Nkunda's forces."¹⁶⁰ It is curious that "dissatisfaction on the progress and lack of resettlement of refugees caused CNDP to declare war on the FDLR (former *Interahamwe*) and hostilities to resume, including atrocities against civilians."¹⁶¹ As a reminder, the CNDP was founded as "a protector of the Congolese Tutsi minorities."¹⁶² The refugees in Rwanda who were to be resettled were from that community and in the context of Eastern Congo, the FDL who are Hutu, constituted a potential danger for their resettlement and stability. Unfortunately, "neither the FDLR nor the government of Rwanda took part in the talks"¹⁶³ that led to a peace agreement. On 28 October 2008 CNDP rebels fought against FARDC and MONUC between Kibumba refugee Camp and Rutshuru. They later captured Kibumba, and the next day they "declared a unilateral ceasefire as they approached Goma, although they still attempted to capture it."¹⁶⁴ The war made "Goma to be overcrowded by displaced people and fleeing FARDC soldiers,

---

156. Turner, 107.
157. Turner, 107.
158. Turner, 108.
159. Turner, 108.
160. Turner, 108.
161. Turner, 108.
162. Reyntjens, *Great African War*, 114–15.
163. Reyntjens, 114–15.
164. Turner, *Congo*, 109.

including their tanks and military vehicles."¹⁶⁵ However, Nkunda under the UN Security Council pressure had to create a "humanitarian corridor" to allow displaced persons to return to their homes.

At the end of 2008, the Congolese government, in search of possible solutions to end CNDP of Laurent Nkunda, used the fact that "the Rwandan government has been embarrassed by the UN report accusing them of supporting Nkunda."¹⁶⁶ It was, therefore, forced "to reach a 'secret' agreement with Kigali."¹⁶⁷ That agreement led Rwanda to "detain Nkunda and help integrate the CNDP into the Congolese army, while in return Kinshasa would allow Rwandan troops into the Congo to help attack the FDLR."¹⁶⁸ General Bosco Ntaganda, a Tutsi from Rwanda, from the Mugombwe clan northwest Rwanda (Ruhengeri), who "had been indicted for war crimes committed in Ituri when he was fighting on behalf of a Rwandan-supported, predominantly Hema, movement, UPC" took over from Nkunda to command the CNDP.¹⁶⁹

In January 2009, "the Rwandan troops entered North Kivu"¹⁷⁰ and the troops of the two countries "launched the *Operation Umoja Wetu* (our Unity) against the FDLR- while Kinshasa and CNDP signed the *23ʳᵈ March agreement*"¹⁷¹ on 23 March 2009. Stearns writes:

> This 16-point blueprint for peace, along with a subsequent deal for other militias, included an amnesty for free political prisoners, the integration of armed groups, security sector reform, and the government pledge to promote the return of refugees.¹⁷²

The joint operation started in January 2009 and was successful. It then "became *Operation Kimia 2* (Peace 2) in March 2009, before involving *Operation Amani Leo* (Peace today)."¹⁷³ The outcome of the two operations,

---

165. Turner, 109.
166. Stearns, *North Kivu*, 40.
167. Turner, *Congo*, 109.
168. Stearns, *North Kivu*, 40.
169. Turner, *Congo*, 109–10.
170. Turner, 109.
171. Stearns, *North Kivu*, 40.
172. Stearns, 40.
173. Stearns, 40.

within several months the CNDP and many other armed groups were integrated into the Congolese army.... More than 16,000 soldiers were integrated into the national army, including around 5,500 from the CNDP and 4,000 from the PARECO.[174]

Furthermore, "the operations were successful in decimating the FDLR. Between 2009 and 2012, over 4,500 FDLR combatants were repatriated through the UN to Rwanda."[175]

In 2010, "the role of Rwanda in the Congo war had attained greater visibility,"[176] and the joint forces were still within Eastern Congo. However, in 2011, "two years after the secret deal between Kagame and Kabila, it became clear to the West that the attempt to resolve the deadly conflict in Eastern Congo by military force was failing and would have to be modified."[177] Stearns explains, "This deal between the two countries collapsed in 2012, even as Kinshasa tried to dismantle ex-CNDP networks in the Kivus and integrate CNDP fighters into the national army, and Rwanda backed Ntaganda's new project, the M23 mutiny."[178] In fact, for the Kinyarwanda-speaking people, both the process of integration and "mixage" did not succeed to transfer former Tutsi rebel fighters outside the area of their interest. That would have made their movement fragile. When the Congolese government finally touched that sensitive aspect and decided to dismantle the networks, it caused a new rebellion.

The end of the year 2011 was marked by the national elections organized by the Congolese government through its National Electoral Independent Commission. Joseph Kabila was re-elected president, despite apparent massive fraud[179] on 28 November 2011. These presidential and legislative elections set off a surge in political violence[180] in the country, in addition to the existing wars in Eastern Congo. Gred Kehailia describes the elections environment and says that "the Congolese political environment quickly degraded in the

---

174. Stearns, 40–41.
175. Stearns, 110.
176. Turner, *Congo*, 110.
177. Turner, 110.
178. Stearns, *North Kivu*, 41.
179. Turner, *Congo*, 41.
180. Turner, 200.

run-up to Election Day, and the rise in election-related violence marked the beginning of another chapter of instability that continues today."[181] According to the Carter Center's final report, "forty-five acts of election-related violence were documented by the United Nations in advance of the November 28, 2011, elections."[182] It is said that "Rutshuru territory was among a handful of areas nationwide where the elections results had to be thrown out; there were numerous reports of intimidation of villagers by FARDC (ex-CNDP) soldiers, who wanted them to vote for Kabila."[183] Among the consequences of pre- and post-electoral violence, there were "hundreds of people who remained in camps for 'internally displaced persons'; some of them were attacked, raped, and even killed by armed groups who attacked the camps."[184]

4.9 Congo War Against Women and Children

While revealing that "a great many Congolese, including many women, have died during the war that began in the mid-1990s,"[185] Turner identifies "the multiple culture that underpins and justifies the war against women, summarized as the culture of impunity, the culture of violence, and the culture of rape."[186] It is unfortunate that "the violence of war and many ways in which the silent onslaught in Eastern Congo destroys society and kills the most vulnerable children and women."[187]

During the last two decades and a half, Eastern Congo became a jungle of civil war and rebellions that engaged in various fights and violence in the area. Soldiers and/or warlords who committed or were responsible for human abuses were never punished for it because the interest of the rebel groups or their backing supporters needed to be achieved while civilians' protection was not their concern. For example, the Congolese government allowed Bosco Ntaganda to play a key role in the implementation of the Amani Leo Operation, a joint operation that involved the Congolese army and Rwandan

---

181. Kehailia, "Countering Electoral Violence," 30.
182. Stremlau, *Presidential and Legislative Elections*, 46.
183. Turner, *Congo*, 200.
184. Turner, 200.
185. Turner, 144.
186. Turner, 146.
187. McCullum, *Angels Have Left Us*, 31.

army tracking the FDLR in North Kivu even though the government knew he was wanted by the International Criminal Court for Human rights abuses. The government, rather than handing him over to the Hague, made him "one of the most significant figures in the modern history of Kivus."[188] So, impunity caused cases of violence and rape to increase in Eastern Congo.

The maintenance of the so-called multiple dimensions of culture in Eastern Congo has caused "over 200,000 cases of rape reported since the war started, 8,000 cases of sexual violence have taken place yearly in 2009 and 2010 and 5,485 cases were counted in North Kivu province in 2010."[189] In his description of the war in Eastern Congo, Turner quotes Collette Braeckman's argument and says that "the war has been a 'war against women,'" that "the UN has charged that various rebel groups have used rape, cannibalism and other atrocities as 'arms of war.'"[190] He adds that "the RCD-Goma (ANC) forces 'used rape as a means to terrorize the civilian population.'"[191] In Nyabiondo, on 25 December 2004, for example, the "RCD-Goma troops reportedly raped several dozens of women and girls as young as eight. As the health centers in the region had been pillaged and destroyed, many victims were left for weeks without care and medical help."[192]

The areas around Goma have suffered much from this war against women and children to the extent that children have been forced to become child soldiers and sex slaves by rebel troops such as CNDP in the year 2007 and militiamen such as the FDLR and the like.[193] During a personal contact in July 2015 with a man who was kidnapped around Goma and detained for seven days by FDLR in Buleusa, he stated that "many kidnapped women are used as sexual slaves and the children of the FDLR use guns and are involved in raids." In fear of children being taken as child soldiers, many schools have had multiple interruptions at the expense of children's education in the zone around Goma, where many clashes and displacement movements have occurred.

---

188. Stearns, *North Kivu*, 41.
189. Burrow, *Violence against Women*, 26.
190. Turner, *Congo Wars*, 3.
191. Turner, 134.
192. Turner, 137.
193. Turner, *Congo*, 107.

4.10 Eastern Congo and a Mining War

Collier and Hoeffler assume that "resource-rich countries tend to be poorer and poorer nations and are more prone to conflict."[194] This theory was corroborated by a lawyer from Goma who confided to Peter Eichstaedt that "minerals are the source of the persistence of war."[195] The mining in Eastern Congo is highly militarized and this prolongs the armed violence. According to a Global Witness report, "In many parts of the provinces of North and South Kivu, armed groups and the Congolese national army control the trade in Cassitérite (tin ore), gold, columbite-tantalite (coltan), wolframite (a source of tungsten) and other minerals."[196] The report further argues that "the unregulated nature of the mining sector in Eastern Congo, the breakdown of law and the lack of restricted access to minerals gives them access to profits through the loot which most of the violent groups use to survive."[197] It is reported that "The RCD-Goma taxed the coltan trade, sold mining rights and demanded license fees, non-refundable deposits, various export taxes and a 'war effort tax.'"[198]

The mining industry in Eastern Congo has allowed the militia and the armed forces involved in it to encompass "slavery, killing, and genocide" for their success. Eichstaedt reports that "militias in Eastern Congo also force people into mining. When one Ugandan and Rwandan-backed militia pushed a rival out of a gold mine, the militia, having no mining expertise, coerced local miners into unpaid service as armed men stood guard."[199] There are even mines staffed by "former child soldiers, now working freely in mines owned by militias."[200]

The situation described above is proof that the mining system in Eastern Congo catalyzed the rebellions' persistence and that even the RCD and other rebel movements were benefiting from the militias' existence in mining areas. Minerals would be dug by forced and enslaved civilians for militias or Congolese army or rebels who would sell minerals to trading companies in the

---

194. Collier and Hoeffler, "Resource Rents," 625.
195. Collier and Hoeffler, 625.
196. Global Witness, "Faced With aGun," 1.
197. Global Witness, 1.
198. Reyntjens, *Great African War*, 224.
199. Eichstaedt, *Consuming the Congo*, 7.
200. Eichesaedt, 7.

city. These traders had to pay "war effort taxes"[201] in addition to many other taxes and fees to rebel movements before exporting it to the West through Rwanda and Uganda, the countries that backed the rebellion movements.

In North Kivu and South Kivu, for example, "all mining takes place in the informal sector. The minerals are dug by hand or with very basic tools by civilians known as artisanal miners."[202] However, there are a few foreign mining companies which have been in the region during war such as[203]:

1. Mining and Processing Congo (MPC), a subsidiary of South African owned Kivu Resources, registered in Mauritius and which was established in Eastern Congo in December 2002.
2. Metal Processing Association (MPA), its counterpart in Rwanda, MPA has a factory in Gisenyi (city neighboring Goma) before 2008 which used to process Congolese minerals (cassitérite and Coltan).
3. Banro, a company with headquarters in Canada, holds exploration titles in South Kivu and Maniema.
4. The Canadian registered Shamika.
5. Transafrika, a Mauritius registered company with South African interests.
6. Loncor Exporting Minings in Lubero territory.
7. Many other companies including some Congolese ones already operating as comptoirs, such as Sodexmines and group Olive.

In Oriental Province, a Human Rights Watch's report (The Curse of Gold 2005) revealed the following in 2005: first, "between 1998 and 2002, Ugandan Forces plundered the gold of Haut Uele District of a value of $9 million dollars." It is stated that during that time illicit exploitation was strengthened by the fact that Ugandan soldiers beat and arrested and frightened OKIMO's officials who tried to protest.[204] Second, the report states that "the existence of local armed groups fights for gold in Ituri between 2002–2004"[205]; while an "FNI armed group exploited and forced civilians taxes over gold exploitation in

---

201. Reyntjens, *Great African War*, 224.
202. Global Witness, "Faced With a Fun," 24.
203. Global Witness, 24.
204. Human Rights Watch, *Curse of Gold*, 17.
205. Human Rights Watch, 20–21.

Mongbwalu."[206] The same report presents results that indicate that Congolese and Ugandan traders were the main traders of that of gold from Mongbwalu and Ariwara in north-eastern Congo. The two of them, separately in connection with Ugandan army or civilians, were exporting gold to Switzerland. The National and Integrationist Front (FIN) commissioner "confirmed that they bought gold for the traders,"[207] who "smuggled it to Uganda, from where it is exported to global gold markets in Europe."[208] Unfortunately, the global markets benefit from the Congolese minerals, which have been a source of various human abuses. Eichstaedt avows that "each time we use a mobile phone, use a video game console, or open a tin can; we hold the lives and deaths of the eastern Congolese in our hands."[209]

Therefore, based on the above information, it is reasonable to conclude that war in Eastern Congo between 1990 and 2011 was sustained by the militia, the Congolese army and rebels in the interest of their political backers. Consequently, the existence of a militia in a mining zone also benefited the rebel groups who controlled the market process and whose survival depended on it.

Some organizations such as Organization for Economic Co-operation and Development (OECD) and its partners have developed policies to help mitigate abuses against children and women through their "goal of responsible sourcing of minerals from the Great Lake Region, and help them to find space for civil society to play."[210] But it is difficult to identify the effects of such efforts especially because they work for the international community which is involved in the mining trade. For example, through the "joint Aid for Trade Initiative . . . supported by OECD, donors have become more aware of African countries' lack of infrastructures as a constraint to their ability to trade and access global markets."[211] Rather than working as implementers of policies to benefit from the oppressed civilians, it is possible that they worked more as partners of the government and its partners encouraging them to establish

---

206. Human Rights Watch, 73.
207. Human Rights Watch, 101.
208. Human Rights Watch, 103.
209. Eichstaedt, *Consuming the Congo*, 5.
210. OECD, "Responsible Supply," 4.
211. OECD, 9.

"an incremental approach."[212] In such case, such organizations are likely not to help stop forced labor in mining zones controlled by militia and other rebels.

4.11 Conclusion

The historical context of Eastern Congo from 1990 to 2011, in which the eastern Congolese church has been undertaking its action (ministry and mission), has been dominated by a war that had the character of a civil war and an international war.[213] Issues of land tenure and identity have played a key role. Both the indigenous people groups and the "transplanted Banyarwanda" have been involved in wars since the mid-1990s to either protect their land against the occupation of "foreigners" or claim the right of ownership. Therefore, the major causes of war in Eastern Congo can be identified here as being the ethnic identity crisis, the political agenda of warlords and their backing countries and the multinationals' greed for the Congolese minerals. The United Nations Security Council report of the panel of experts on the illegal exploitation of natural resources and other forms of wealth of the Democratic Republic of the Congo confirmed this and said that "the wealth of the Country is appealing and hard to resist in the context of lawlessness and the weakness of the central authority."[214]

However, in such a context and in a country lacking stable and credible leadership, identity has also been used to justify the war aiming to feed political and exploitation agendas of militias, rebel groups, the government and foreign countries such as Uganda and Rwanda backing the rebel groups. The imbroglio on the battlefield makes them work for one particular purpose, trade the Congolese minerals from the forced labor to the international global markets, for their survival but at the expense of humans (civilians, women and children and child soldiers) who are victims of abuse. This research, therefore, supports Turner who says that "for the most part, foreign intervention has been disastrous for the locals, however profitable it may have been for the outsiders."[215]

---

212. OECD, 5.
213. Turner, *Congo*, 8.
214. Eichstaedt, *Consuming the Congo*, v.
215. Turner, *Congo*, 147.

Consequently, the view that some people hold that war in Eastern Congo is caused by greed around the issue of mineral resources is, therefore, not correct. Furthermore, minerals, although part of the problematic aspects of it, are far from being a major cause of war. Eastern Congo is not the richest part of the country in minerals. There are issues of land tenure and identity that should be understood as having played a role. Envy of minerals by both armed forces and militias, whether from within or from outside Congo, played a key role in war maintenance.

The wars that started in the mid-1990s around Goma were a result of identity aspects, that were mishandled at the independence of the country and which did not integrate the so-called "transplanted" Kinyarwanda speakers among the "autochthones" (indigenous) in Eastern Congo. The various vacillations in changes regarding the law of citizenship have not favored that integration to the extent that both the Kinyarwanda speakers and the "autochthones" feel insecure with one another. The war, called "the Kanyarwanda war" in Masisi between 1962 and 1965, which started with the Banyarwanda attack of the Hunde and police stations at Kibabi,[216] is connected to the war called the "war of MAGRIVI" in the mid-1990s. The latter opposed the same Kinyarwanda speakers (Hutu and Tutsi) as other ethnic groups in the Bwito collectivity (Rutshuru territory) and Masisi territory. It turned into an ethnic massacre perpetrated by ethnic youth militias aiming to exterminate one ethnic group or the other. Consequently, it caused the "beginning of civil war and killing by both parties which are said to have caused, in the six months, the loss of 7,000 people and the displacement of more than 200,000."[217] These two wars had had the same motives and same actors.

Turner reveals that Magrivi served "as the basis for political mobilization" when the Hutus began to promote the *"facteur Hutu majoritaire"* with the "slogan . . . 'the Hutu is one and indivisible,' . . . in reaction, other ethnic groups, including the Hunde, Nyanga, Tembo, Tutsi, and Nande, formed an anti-Hutu coalition"[218] which was strengthening their ethnic *mutualités*. This makes it reasonable to conclude that the eastern Congolese politics is based on an ethnic identity agenda. During the First and Second Congo

---

216. Mathieu and Tsongo, "Guerres paysannes," 393.
217. Mathieu and Tsongo, 395.
218. Turner, *Congo Wars*, 119.

Wars, the number of armed militias increased because each indigenous ethnic group would consider the rebellion as a Kinyarwanda speakers' invasion that needed to be dissuaded. The split within the RCD into many groups is an additional proof of that fact. While the Banyamulenge were leading in RCD-Goma, the RCD/K-ML was organized by Wamba (from the west of DRC), Mbusa Nyamwisi (a Nande) and Tibasimwa (a Hema) who moved out of the RCD-Goma.

The massive arrival of Rwandan refugees in 1994 marked a turning point in the history of Eastern Congo. Not only did refugees come into an area unsecured by local ethnic militias that were being tracked by an undisciplined and unpaid national force through military operations in Rutshuru and Masisi territories, but it also brought an additional armed force. That armed force, being a threat for Rwanda, was "made [up] of the ex-FAR, the Interahamwe and other Rwandan militias an alliance that formed the FDLR to liberate Rwanda,"[219] and their presence would become the motive for Rwanda to initiate the First and Second wars in Eastern Congo as it backed the Rwandan speakers and helped them address their identity issues through a military approach. It appears that the Zairian government, which was weak from the beginning of the early 1990s, had just come from the unfruitful national conference that did not accommodate the Rwanda-speakers; but it did play a significant role in this war context, having allowed armed refugees to enter Congo publicly without being disarmed.

Therefore,

> the wars of 1996–97 and 1998–2002 were civil wars, according to some. They were international wars designed to overthrow a dictatorship, according to others. They represent a continuation of Rwanda's Hutu-Tutsi conflict, pursued on Congo soil, for still others.[220]

This is why, even during transitional government time and during the government of the Third Republic under Joseph Kabila until the election on 28 November 2011, Eastern Congo was under war caused by either a new rebellion and the reaction of ethnic militias to the presence and actions of

---

219. Stearns, *North Kivu*, 32.
220. Turner, *Congo*, 8.

foreign forces and militias in the region; the joint military track of the FDLR by the Rwandan and Congolese troops through Operation Kimia in 2009 to Operation Amani Leo, which ended in 2012 and was also a war that lasted long and during which civilians and FDLR militias and their families were exposed in the area around Goma.

From the wars in the mid-1990s to the elections in 2011, the context of war in Eastern Congo has been characterized by killings and massacres by armed groups (militias, rebels or army forces) that exposed civilians to "an epidemic of rape,"[221] to the displacement of populations that created overpopulation of the city, the existence of ever permanent and mobile IDPs and refugee camps, non-schooling children and, above all, a sustainable war context and ethnic conflicts in the region. Statistics reveal that "some five million Congolese have died un-necessarily from 1998 to 2007, the worst loss of human life since World War II, yet the pillaging and looting continue at a frightening pace."[222] Sharan Burrow reports that "in illegal controlling mining activities, military elements and rebel groups commit serious abuses against the population, including murder and rape."[223] This is explained by the fact that "the mining activities incentivized different armed groups and military units to create a volatile environment, through human rights abuses, that ensures the continuation of the status quo."[224]

The eastern Congolese church experienced missions in the above context of war and has survived it. Because "events in the history of nations and peoples are historical facts and the Christian testimony is also historical,"[225] the experiences need to be recorded and referred to in this study as it would develop a contemporary, contextual missions theory that incorporates experiential, biblical and missiological perspectives on these experiences in a biblical model.

In relation to the church during this same period of war (1990–2011), the church in Eastern Congo was not dormant but organized its business in the context of war. It is important to note that "the marriage that occurred

---

221. Eichstaedt, *Consuming the Congo*, 53.
222. Eichstaedt, 1.
223. Burrow, *Violence against Women*, 26.
224. Burrow, 26.
225. Deiros, "Historical Research," 139.

between the Protestant Church and the state in Zaire"[226] during the Mobutu regime under the leadership of Bokeleale, the ECC's driving figure whose goal was "to go away with the autonomy of the denominations and create a super-Protestant Church in the nation."[227]

Therefore, by the end of that regime in the 1990s, "little were the indications of Protestant commitment to enforce decisions by ECZ at the local church level."[228] When the Laurent Kabila regime came to the place, "there has been little change either in the morality of the nation and its structures or in the significance or otherwise of the ECC. Even the Catholic church appears to have dropped its rhetoric"[229] to the extent that Congolese are wrestling with the system and with life believing less that "they will get much out of the state, nor will they get much out of official church conglomerates such as ECC."[230] The reason is that those conglomerates, especially the ECC then ECZ, "moved a great distance from its original purpose of being a collaborative body for all Protestants in the Belgian Congo to that of being one of the staunchest supporters of a harsh and corrupt regime headed by Mobutu."[231] Consequently, the church denominations, through their local churches were wrestling along with issues relating to the context of war in Eastern Congo.

In a research dealing with "Songs and hymns sung in the Anglican Church in North-Eastern Congo," Peter Wood and Emma Wild-Wood found that "both *Nyimbo za Mungu* and the modern songs and chorus present heaven as a central motif."[232] Although "the evangelical nature of churches such as the Anglican Church and the political and economic instability make this fact surprising,"[233] it means that in evangelical messages "heaven emerges as a central motif in both categories of song, presenting an eschatological theology, which offers comfort, escape and social comment" while "the ECC (Church

---

226. Garrard, "Protestant Church," 131.
227. Garrard, 131.
228. Garrard, 151.
229. Garrard, 152.
230. Garrard, 152.
231. Garrard, 152.
232. Wood and Wild-Wood, "'One Day We Will Sing,'" 145.
233. Wood and Wild-Wood, 176.

of Christ in Congo-CCC) claims to be the spokesperson for the Protestant churches of Congo."[234]

While being aware that, "Mobutu attempted to limit the categories of worship in the nation to Catholic, Protestant and Kimbanguist could not be expected to satisfy people's hopes."[235] It appears that these legal churches then were not able to respond with contextual theologies to changes and shifts brought by contexts such as that of war in Eastern Congo between 1990 and 2011. With "the church and its struggle against poverty,"[236] this might have contributed to the rise and proliferation of "prayer groups" and revival churches that welcomed the prosperity gospel.[237] Garrard attributes that phenomenon to the fact that "the Protestant theology of personal salvation and/or prosperity lacked a theology of social justice, which was certainly present in Catholic thinking."[238]

In the context of war, there were notable cases of religious mobility. For example, the period between 1990 and 1994 was marked by many "Alur Christians switching from CECA 20 to AICC, a decedent's church called Malalamiko."[239] Georges Atido identifies, among the reasons for their move "the pre-eminence of ethnic identity," "social capital," "living obligation," "nativism," "inclination to monarchial leadership" and "predilection for liturgical and sacramental worship."[240] It appears that there was a lack of "critical contextualization"[241] in some churches.

While "it was for long an assumption of the historiography of the twentieth-century African Christianity that only in the African Initiated or Independent Churches (AICs) could Africans feel 'at home,'"[242] Emma Wild-Wood's research on *Migration and Christian Identity in Congo (DRC)* with focus on the history of the Anglican Church in Northeast Congo, argues that "in contemporary Africa, as elsewhere, Christian identities are increasingly fluid

---

234. Wood and Wild-Wood, 145–52.
235. Garrard, "Protestant Church," 150.
236. Bosela, "Justice and Poverty," 30.
237. Garrard, "Protestant Church," 150.
238. Garrard, 154.
239. Atido, "Religious Identity," 67.
240. Atido, 68–74.
241. Atido, 135.
242. Wild-Wood, *Migration and Christian Identity*, 432.

and hybridized."²⁴³ It is appears that it is "the reverence instilled by Anglican liturgy and respect for order symbolized by episcopal hierarchy appeared wholly consonant with their own cultural values of dignity and authority" and that adherence "was also yoked to the pursuit of *maendeleo* (advance or development)"²⁴⁴ in their context in Eastern Congo. Unfortunately, in the same context, "some evangelicals would fear hybridity that may lead if the element added is not in conformity with the Bible."²⁴⁵

---

243. Wild-Wood, 433.
244. Wild-Wood, 232.
245. Atido, "Religious Identity," 135

CHAPTER 5

The Nature of Church Missions before and during the War

5.1 Introduction

The previous chapter explored and described the historical and ethnic context of the Eastern Congo during the period 1990 to 2011, during which the area and its surroundings experienced large-scale warfare. Hence, it provides the background for chapters 5 and 6 which explore the mission of the CBCA during this period. This chapter focuses on the nature of missions before and during the period, while the next focuses specifically on how leaders of the CBCA experienced missions during this period and how these experiences affected their understanding of missions.

5.2 Demographic Information

This chapter was constructed as the analysis of information collected from face-to-face interviews of forty-three randomly selected pastors who served before and/or during the war. They were all men, because the CBCA have only men as pastors. In addition, discussions with separate groups of men and women who were involved in church leadership before and/or during the war in various capacities other than pastoral work were conducted.

Participants in the face-to-face interviews fell into age ranges between thirty-six and eighty years. No age was below thirty-five years with large numbers of them between fifty to sixty years, the years nearing retirement in CBCA while the younger generation is missing. This is because, although there are young people doing pastoral work in CBCA churches, many of them are more interested in other careers.

All participants in the interviews were married. Only one of them had a family of three children; the rest had large families with five of them having between seven and fourteen children. Two respondents out of the forty-three interviewed had remarried after the death of their wives.

In terms of role in ministry, the majority of respondents worked as senior pastors of the selected churches, few participants were associate pastors while some served as pastors of chapels planted by selected churches. The study also included two lay persons who served as pastors of selected churches after the pastors fled the war. Of all the forty-three interviewees, seventeen served before the war and twenty-six pastored churches during the war (1990 to 2011). Three of the forty-three pastors have previously experienced a migration move of a church from a war zone to another location.

All respondents affirmed their membership of the CBCA, most of whom became members through baptism. However, although few of them knew they became true members the year of their baptism, they were members by birth through their parents' membership. These are the participants who, with a laughter followed by a response, expressed church membership with a sense of ownership. The threshold for membership seems then to value membership by birth although baptism is the official entry certified by a baptism card.

5.2.1 Codes and Usage

Interviews and focus group discussions were coded. Face-to-face interviews are coded as I1–43 with initials of the respondent's name C for CBCA then the initial of the local church (e.g. I26NyaCKab). Focus group discussions are coded as FGDMen or Women together with the initial of the local church (e.g. FGDWomenBut). The number in parenthesis is a code supplied by the software to distinguish entries, for example [11203–11750]. The reader will find in this work references like I16KerCKak [17767–17885] or FGDMenBir [1105–1367] which refer to the entry from thematic analysis of data from face-to-face interviews or focus group discussions respectively. The reader will also find a few references like I16KerCKak, 5; this refers directly to the interview and indicates the page on which the information is found.

5.3 Nature of Missions before the War

To identify the nature of missions in Eastern Congo, thirty-nine respondents from the CBCA were considered. Information related to the nature of missions before the war was provided from fourteen of the seventeen pastors who served selected churches during that period while the twenty-five pastors who served the same churches during the war provided information related to missions during war. The imbalance in terms of the number of respondents which initially was meant to be equal for the two periods is due to the fact that the majority of pastors who served the particular churches before the war had passed away. On the nature of missions, this study limited itself to the description of oral witness, discipleship and the church's involvement in social concerns.

5.3.1 Oral Witness before the War
Sharing the gospel through sermons

Before the war in Eastern Congo, the main role of a pastor was preaching the gospel through sermons. The majority of pastors would do so either on Sundays and/or during weekly occasions in their church settings (i.e. chapel and group meetings). Since chapels within CBCA are used for morning gatherings of church members from the same neighborhood, all did not meet daily, while some organized a morning and an evening session at that time. It was not an issue finding a senior church who "did not yet preach, since preaching was for the pastor" (I23LukCBa [2869–3031]).

The other occasion that offered opportunities to one-third church leaders to share the gospel is when "pastors would get involved in outreach ministry on the sister church's invitation along with their church's choir" (I14MuhCKak [3926–4077]). However, although 21 percent of pastors from the CBCA delivered sermons in their churches, theses were not opportunities for sharing the gospel. Such "maintenance Christianity mentality" in the eastern Congolese church, therefore took its roots in the church during peaceful times.[1]

Sharing the gospel one-on-one

This practice of sharing the gospel one-on-one aims to persuade individuals about Jesus and this includes sharing your testimony with them (Acts

---

1. Musolo, "From Maintenance Christianity," iv.

28:22–23). Before the war in the 1990s, that practice was either daily, weekly, monthly or several times to individuals as was the lifestyle of an 86 percent majority of church leaders. Pastors "could meet often with people at their homes and others on the road and share the gospel" (I21KavCBa [2486–2634]) and wherever they went they used every single occasion "to preach the word of God depending on the subject which the host brought or depending on the subject that they identified" (I2LukCBi [5297–5543]) and could challenge people for salvation (cf. I39MuhCBi [3976–4305]). There was a team for evangelism which, sometimes together with a pastor, would go out on an evangelistic trip to preach the gospel and there they would have an opportunity for one-on-one evangelism (cf. I8MusCVi [4492–4704]).

Therefore, as the result of the pastors' commitment to the one-on-one sharing of the gospel, the church grew in terms of attendance and discipleship was impacted to the extent that pastors even "sent some disciples to Bible school" (I21KavCBa [2486–2634]) and pastors reached out to "tribes that were not at CBCA through one-on-one evangelism" (I16KerCKak [4549–4664]), an indicator for genuine conversion that might have led the move from ethnic churches to multiethnic churches.

Church members' involvement in sharing the gospel one-on-one

It was found that before the war church members, in the majority of cases, were not involved in sharing the gospel one-on-one with individuals. This practice aims to persuade individuals about Jesus and this includes sharing your testimony with them (Acts 28:22–23). The reasons of not involving the practice are attributed to the fact that either members were not used to the practice or they needed to be assigned before they act accordingly or share the gospel one-on-one as was the work of an evangelism team. Being involved in one-on-one meant that only "following a specific program that the church leadership set" (I14MuhCKak [5233–5280]; I8MusCVi [5080–5447]) demonstrates a lack of commitment from church members.

Planting new chapels were part of the outcomes of evangelists' outreach. Although church members were not committed to sharing the gospel one-on-one as their lifestyle, at "that time the church was flourishing" (I37KilCBa [3123–3339]) as a result of the commitment to one-on-one evangelism by occasional teams doing outreach. During the occasional crusades most church members were involved in the running of other crusades activities, such as "serving food and receiving guests in their homes" (I19MbaCKak [3317–3513]) while the "group of evangelists could go all over the city evangelizing and afterward bring the reports to the pastor" (I2LukCBi [6227–6591]).

Organization of open crusades

Before the war church leaders were assertive and committed to organizing evangelistic crusades. Because of the culture of baptizing new believers every six months, most of the churches, therefore, "organized open-air crusades twice every year during baptism festivals" (I37KilCBa [2831–2995]). In addition to the routine of running crusades during baptism festivals, other churches used many kinds of occasions such as Easter, Christmas and the like to organize crusades. During festivals, pastors involved sister churches within their denomination by calling for "ambassadors (evangelists) and choirs to come and lead" (I39MuhCBi [4565–4873]).

Church involvement in short-term missions

Before the war, churches were involved in short-term missions. That involvement of the 57.8 percent of churches was catalyzed by a local church partnership in the running of open-air crusades and the church's involvement in establishing new chapels. In most cases, involvement meant sending a team out between two to three times every year for short-term missions, which is likely to be closer to the number of times the churches were having baptism festival every year. This was a support team "called 'ambassadors,' to a neighboring church where it went to assist in ministry work" (I19MbaCKak, 3) and whenever there was an invitation for "a church choir group to go and do evangelism there" (I8MusCVi [6510–6783]).

Church involvement in sending long-term missionaries

When it comes to long-term missionaries sent out before the war, only few isolated cases of long-term missionaries appear to have been sent from CBCA Bambo and Goma. Long-term missionaries were sent in areas that were unreached at that time. For example, "three were sent from Bambo to Mwenga" (I22NyaCBa [4544–4558]). Sent from the prestigious fertile Kivu mountains and climate they went to minister to people from other ethnic groups and cultures in a humid zone deep in the mining forest at the far extreme southwest of South Kivu Province. These long-term missionaries "sent to Mwenga mission were sent by the regional office" (I23LukCBa [4418–4568]) because any cross-cultural missionary sending process was to be under the responsibility of the regional office of the sending church.

Although "it was the responsibility of the *Poste* (region) to deal with the case, if a local church wanted to send someone somewhere" (I2LukCBi [7157–7355]), the policy was not always observed. Respondents from CBCA Virunga mentioned one pastor sent from Goma to Idjwi as a church planter in the year 1984 without the support and involvement of the Goma regional office. The church, which at first started sending short-term teams for evangelism to start a chapel, later sent a resident pastor who led the church to grow and has since multiplied (cf. I8MusCVi [7256–7868]). This imbalance demonstrates a lack of the denominational leadership with respect to the tasks of missions.

Missionary support before war

When it comes to how the few missionaries were funded on the field once they were sent, the case of the missionary to Idjwi illustrates the approach. The local church was responsible for funding the survival of the sent person who also had to contribute to his livelihood through farming. That sending church's support consisted "for the first four years to send him, whenever possible, some money labelled 'Sabuni' (meaning 'soap') as a token of encouragement while he was forced to rely on farming for his survival" (cf. I8MusCVi, 6). A four-year support might have enabled the cross-cultural missionary to focus much more on ministry instead of struggling to raise funds. However, the word "Sabuni" in Congolese Kiswahili meaning "soap" is sometimes used as a pejorative word for salary. Sending a long-term servant without any guaranteed support was a sign of lack of commitment to support him. The pastor would not have succeeded if it was not for his farming activities.

5.3.2 Discipleship before the War
Helping new believers interact with God's word and apply it in their context

Before the war church leaders used catechism and post-catechism classes and seminars to train believers to help new believers to interact with the word of God and apply it in their context. First, pastors took new believers through catechism teachings that would lead to baptism followed by post-catechism sessions. Candidates were called "'students of the Bible' or 'Walomba'" and the baptism class was meant to prepare new believers to mature in the knowledge of the word of God and a path to their integration into ministry such as "initiation to preaching by assigning them to preach." Therefore, upon baptism the person could join church life and be part of the task force, for example, "work as a member of the choir; join the prayer group, Bible study and the like" (I37KilCBa [4151–4540]).

Second, pastors organized seminars for spiritual growth. These seminars would benefit not only new believers to grow spiritually but also the whole church to interact with the word of God and practice it. Therefore, teaching the word of God was key for the church leaders before the war for the development of believers' spiritual maturity. In addition to that, in some cases leaders would jointly visit new believers in their homes.

Discipleship classes

Before the war discipleship was managed at two levels. The first is discipleship, a six-month class called Catechism that prepared new believers for baptism upon successful completion. Enrolled students based on their faith in Jesus would be under observation for six months (see I11BakCBut [7474–7611]). The second class comprised various seminars, which the pastors would organize for the spiritual growth of his congregants. In addition to that, seminars would be brought to the local church from the denominational level (I8MusCVi [15985–16058]) in order to assess the growth at the church level. In some cases, seminars forced members to attend literacy classes so that they could read and write during the seminars (cf. I16KerCKak [11639–12064]).

The third class was a discipleship class through the youth ministry, and was preparing young people for life by involving boys in "constructing a house and teaching girls to assist women who just delivered in gathering firewood, peeling cassava roots, and the like" (I14MuhCKak [11649–12381]). This strategy might have attracted many young people to church membership due to its free entry (I14MuhCKak [12626–12709]).

However, no curriculum was used for these discipleship classes within the CBCA in the period before the war although a respondent revealed the existence of a Sunday school for adults prior to the normal Sunday service.

A prayerful life

Before the war, with regard to prayerful life, chapels' meetings conducted in the morning were known as "morning prayer," hence, in their mind prayer goes hand in hand with church meetings. But because "prayer was seen as another church in the making..." (I30BihCKab [6426–6550]), "those days the CBCA church was not allowing prayer groups outside the church setting" (I16KerCKak [8194–8616]). Some pastors taught their church members how to pray while and/or organized a prayer group in church (intercessory team) and involved all church members in regular weekly prayer meetings.

Members fasting and seeking God

Few were churches that would organize a prayer chain involving all members. With a low emphasis on prayer from the church leadership, the majority of church had their members who either did not fast or did fast whenever there was a call to fast from the head office or themselves had a problem urging them to pray.

Pastors fasting and seeking God

It is curious, apart from a quarter of pastors who did not fast at all, that the same majority of pastors who would pray and fast did not have a fasting program in order to seek God in their ministry. Some of them occasionally fasted depending on the nature of their pastoral work "fasting on those items which were seemingly tough" and some others rarely fasted (cf. I14MuhCKak [8298–8410]).

Discovering and using spiritual gifts

Before the war, for church members to discover their gifts, the majority of pastors did not act except for few of them who taught others on how to discover their spiritual gifts. A minority of pastors helped their church members to discover what their gifts were. While some of them would assign work to people according to their interest because "they had a lot of service in the church through which everyone could serve" others, and other pastors allocated work to members as a test of their gifts before they assigned them according to the identified gifts (cf. I37KilCBa [5546–5668]).

Fellowship and the community of believers

It was found that, before the war, in order to encourage members to have fellowship with one another the majority of pastors taught them, encouraging them towards unity and the minority either started small groups or just used morning chapels meetings as an opportunity for fellowship. The teaching on unity implies that the ethnic conflicts existed even before the war. It is curious that within such a context, only a quarter of pastors acted to encourage their church members to fellowship as a community of believers through organizing prayer cell groups as a follow-up of teaching on unity (I16KerCKak [10890–11326]), collective work, especially in the rural areas (I23LukCBa [8859–9078]), and members' visits and assistance to needy members (I23LukCBa [8859–9078]).

5.3.3 Involvement in Social Concerns before War
Teaching members how to love the poor

In order to teach their church members on how to love the poor, 60 percent of pastors organized seminars and taught their church congregants. Among them, one participant specifically focused on teaching his congregants how to be self-sufficient in order to help the poor (I14MuhCKak [13766–13959]). However, while these pastors focused on teaching love to the poor, the rest focused on teaching through actions. They specifically acted towards widows and orphans through helping groups initiated within the church. In the rural areas, the support consisted of church leadership "to assign each group of five people to help in farm work for one of them" (I19MbaCKak [8118–8265]). In the city, by contrast, the list of widows was first established, then, "whenever a widow had a problem, the church tried to see how to intervene, as there were few help groups" (I39MuhCBi [11699–12156]) in the city to help them. Therefore, 20 percent of the church taught its members to love the poor by teaching and leading them to action toward widows, orphans and the aged who were known as the poor at that time.

Church action to demonstrate love to the poor

Because church leaders and members had not experienced war and suffering because the country was still stable, there was no action oriented to people other than widows, orphans and the aged. Thus "they gave themselves out"

(I16KerCKak [14984–15493]) for the limited number of poor people while they had the ability to help due to their limited knowledge of "the poor as the physically challenged" (I14MuhCKak [14159–14987]). Church's actions were limited to "organizing them in the church and donate food to the widows, and some helped in farm work" (I16KerCKak [14984–15493]), although "the church was economically strong and the economy had not gone down" (I16KerCKak [14984–15493]).

Stories of love to the poor

There are numerous stories from those times about people who either helped to meet the pastors or the church members with their needs or took care of the widows by giving clothes and other things such as salt (I16KerCKak [16098–16424]). There were also stories of individuals who used to fill the gaps to help the needy people on behalf of the local church (I39MuhCBi [12909–13520]). For example, a respondent told the story of a church member who mentored and paid the dowry for a poor young man (I30BihCKab [12524–13571]), taking charge like an immediate father would do in that cultural context, thus holding himself accountable to the family of the boys' bride. This would tie him for life as he took the fatherly responsibility for that marriage.

Love, peace and unity

It is true that love, peace, unity and justice were needed in this community. However, before the war, 36 percent of pastors did nothing to promote these and 36 percent only preached on unity while a few of them either promoted community help to the poorest (I14MuhCKak [17232–17584]), organized the so-called "Likelemba," a rotative loan within members' group associations, or simply used the "Upendo," a church service running door-to-door in members' homes during which participants may share food, bring gifts and the like.

5.4 The Nature of Missions During the War
5.4.1 Oral Witness during the War
Sharing the gospel through sermons

Among those practices of oral witness used by the church before war, sermons remained the excellent mean to share the gospel by 100 percent of pastors within CBCA during wartime. Sharing the gospel one-on-one and organizing outreach preaching and crusades became less relevant practices during wartime. From Monday to Sunday, preaching was used in the routine of the pastor's work and therefore, the church's pulpit was its avenue (cf. I4KavCBi [2445–2578]).

The war added an overwhelming need for church participants and thus a need to bring the gospel from the church pulpit as part of the church's response to the context of war. The major change has therefore not been in the activities of the church, but rather in the emphasis on sharing the gospel in their regular preaching. The pastor gave sermons, sharing the gospel with groups of people and presented seminars to them in small groups, mostly about war, that is, teaching them planning as well as self-reliance' so that they will access means "to fund their livelihoods, abandon war practices and work for peace among people" (I24MunCBa [2720–3099]).

It was noted that during the ethnic war the Sunday service sermon remained the best way to share the gospel. Because of the problems around ethnicity the pastors feared to interact with people outside the church building by fear of being stigmatized along their ethnic affiliation. They then "presented the gospel in relation to the current context" (I33BalCBu [4947–5268]) of ethnicity every Sunday, as people could no longer share it one-on-one avoiding to be seen as supporting the political side or the tribe of the person they were seen sharing with (I33BalCBu [4947–5268]). It is good to note that, in Eastern Congo, in some pastors' cases, ethnic conflicts reached the extent that even "pastors could not be seen together and seeing you with the tribesman meant you coalesced with that tribe" (I33BalCBu [4947–5268]). Therefore, pastors generally used the pulpit as the best way to share the gospel message.

Because church attendance during the war was surprisingly high, the church used every routine church meeting including "prayer sessions, Bible studies and biblical devotions" (I13KiwCBut [2120–2258]) as an opportunity "for sermons and all were focused on the gospel" (I18KasCBut [2453–2548]).

Therefore, preaching was central to every gathering and the word "Bible study" might have implied a Bible exposition.

In one church, refugees and IDPs would come to pastors who "preached the gospel to them how they could come to the Lord, and on the occasion distribute food to them" (I43MisBut [3152–3892]). Some churches in Goma and Kiwanja were able to "accommodate refugees from different places, and to provide them with foodstuffs and also share the word of comfort to them" (FGDMenBir [1105–1367]). The church at this stage became aware of its need to make faithful disciples of Christ in their particular challenging context among those who attended church; pastors focused on initiating and preaching to groups of believers called "Wa fidèles" meaning "the faithful" (I29KaiCKab [3260–3546]) who were different to other church goers.

However, war added another avenue for preaching sermons, these were the occasions of "burials and funerals in the homes of church members and others who were killed" (I1WabCVi [4793–5175]). In that particular context "even though the war was gathering pace, the people gave themselves to come and worship God and thereafter return to their homes" (FGDMenKak [3364–3576]) and the "ministers kept on preaching to the people that God is the savior of their lives" (FGDWomenKak [1366–1510]).

The church, therefore, became a mission field where the pastor who could not reach out to people one-on-one because of ethnic barriers but used the pulpit to reach out to many people coming to seek for help, hope, peace and community life in response to the suffering because of the war. Thus, the church pulpit/setting became the center of the church action (ministry and mission) in responding to the context war.

Sharing the gospel one-on-one

As stated above, sharing the gospel one-on-one was no longer among relevant missional practices during wartime. During that period, due to the ethnic character of the war, sharing the gospel one-on-one did not capture the interest of church leaders who substituted it with church visits to church members for pastoral care. While senior pastors felt more responsible for pastoral care, the task of sharing the gospel one-on-one then remained perceived as part to duties of associate pastors and/or church elders who would occasionally reach out to non-believers as they also provided pastoral care to their church members. Thus, the majority of them, in fear of insecurity, only visited their church members for pastoral care during the war (cf. I12VinCKak [3054–3435]). Thus, to the role of the evangelistic team, who rarely run one-on-one evangelism during outreach activities, added to its role to pay visits to their church members in time of suffering (who the team felt needed it) and pray for them. Visiting Christian and non-Christian families then became "part of their portfolio" (cf. I4KavCBi [2707–2985]) and pastors, therefore, needed to "contact new people as they preached to them" (I18KasCBut [2637–2778]) as well as providing pastoral care through home visits.

Therefore, these pastoral visits are an ingredient or one reason for the survival of the churches during war to the extent that in one church in Kiwanja reported the increase of the number of students of the Bible increased because of going to them simply because in that context of war pastors, "almost every day visited believers, praying for them and teaching them the word of God" (cf. I9MahCBut, 4; I9MahCBut [3442–3703]).

However, even associate pastors only used migration for that task. It seems that, like senior pastors, ethnicity closed the possibility for outreach and they could only connect with IDPs who were coming to church to seek help and then shared the gospel one-on-one with them (cf. I7MuyCVi [3346–3838]).

Church members' involvement in sharing the gospel one-on-one

While church members used to commit occasionally to one-on-one evangelism as the church's outreach team went out before the war, during the war members of the church took it as the duty of the church leaders' and "members in the CBCA really did not know one-on-one evangelism" (cf. I7MuyCVi [4208–5050]). The then added task of pastoral care and visiting Christian and non-Christian families to the pastors' duties might have launched, and be attributed to, a culture that has established itself within the CBCA claiming that sharing the gospel one-on-one is not members' responsibility but that of church leaders. Therefore, the research showed the limited involvement of church members in sharing the gospel one-on-one during war.

Consequently, sharing the gospel one-on-one being the duty of church elders, one-fifth of the respondents' churches had a team in charge of that, and therefore, church members could only get involved in such activities during a special door-to-door evangelism occasionally while only one pastor "initiated members to carry the gospel individually" (cf. I33BalCBu [6255–6775]).

Organization of open crusades

Wars in eastern Congo between 1990 and 2011 did not hinder the running of open-air crusades during wartime, rather the crusade revival in the 1990s affected that practice regardless of the context of war in the region. It was revealed a high commitment to open-air crusades during the war compared to the period before the war, with even a more inclusive strategy from the local church at the denominational level. The exception is only four pastors out of twenty-five who did a crusade once for their term. In addition to the two annual crusades that the larger majority of pastors routinely organized, additional crusades were organized as follows: pastors either had a crusade three times per year, had an open-air crusade every two months or had a crusade monthly. Local churches organized only two annual crusades over the baptism seasons (I40JohCBu [4554–4769]) during which "pastors were invited from afar to help them for crusade" (I13KiwCBut [2802–2972]).

A new kind of open-air crusade was introduced in the 1990s by the CBCA and was practiced by some church leaders involved in this study during wartime. Called "mukutano mkuu wa injili," this crusade brought the responsibility of evangelism crusades to the church district or the church head office, while it also channeled "seminars to different groups" (I29KaiCKab [3894–4153]). Therefore, while local churches organized baptism festival crusades, the region and/or the CBCA head office organized one crusade in partnership with churches in the region.

Church involvement in short-term missions

During the war, the practice of the local church being involved in short-term missions continued and was being catalyzed by an invitation for preachers and choir teams to attend or to animate crusades outside their zone (in 48 percent of cases). The church used this opportunity to collect and send short-time missionaries with funds and food to go to targeted locations for which some of the church members were involved in planning evangelistic trips (cf. I1WabCVi [6953–7586]). In three local churches, the mobilization of food and funds rather consisted to send some church members either to a Bible school or to a training conference, assuming that was missions.

In the same vein, there was a particular custom among the churches in the region that consisted of sharing resources for the sake of planned events "as the custom of sending singers whenever it was necessary. They could go even up to Rwanda to evangelize where they had some churches' twinning partnership" (I5MulCBi [4127–4316]). The second group made up churches that recalled the involvement of churches in short-term missions to initiate new churches. For example, a pastor stated that:

> In regards to missions, we used to go to preach the good news in a place called Nyamwisi near Uganda-Butogota. Immediately we got a group of new believers we began looking for a church plot . . . They still fellowship there except that I hear the ministry has weakened owing to war. (I15KiyCKak [7004–9687])

Church involvement in sending long-term missionaries

War affected the long-term mission endeavor within CBCA in that it shifted from focusing on reaching out to the unreached (before the war) to becoming a voluntary adventure carried out by individual believers in search for subsistence. Thus, the majority of Christian leaders (64 percent) who pastored churches during the war period said that their churches had not sent a long-term missionary. One church only sent people to Bible school in preparation for pastoral ministry.

However, the search for survival and livelihood exposed individual believers to mission. That's why individuals who went for their personal business then did missionary; then a majority (60 percent) of their churches used that as opportunities to send a planter to join business believers in the mission field and half of them participated in funding this missionary work within their region. The church denomination realized that "individual believers took isolated initiatives to plant churches in new mission fields without following any norm and even without any financial ability."[2] Therefore, it involved churches that "were able to send missionaries to start new chapels and they remained and worked there" (I42KunCBu [4326–4377]). In this case, CBCA Bunia appears to have sent the highest number of church planters during that

---

2. Kighoma, "Rethinking Mission," 7.

period with six people sent for the long term from Bunia (cf. I36ChaCbu [4322–4409] and I33BalCBu [7529–8224]).

Missionary support during war

The funding of missionary endeavors did not change, in the contrary short-term and long-term missionaries did rely on occasional support from their sending churches. In addition to that support, the number of self-supported church planters increased during war, as individual believers would support their isolated initiative of church planting through their business activities.[3] Those who were sent from the head office or through a local church initiative faced support issues. It was reported that for ten years a certain church failed to participate in supporting missionary work in Maniema through the head office (cf. I10KamCBut [5618–6643]), meaning that the missionary structure lacked a missionary support system. This confirmed the need for a mission strategy as stipulated by the CBCA 2010 General Assembly's report.[4]

That's why, with regard to the survival of the few sent missionaries, "the support for their living was discussed in district's meetings, with a promise to help him with a little money as church support to him and sometimes the church did sent something to help them" (cf. I29KaiCKab [5539–5797]). This illustrates weaknesses in the sending church council and a lack of an effective mission support strategy resulting in financial struggles for the missionaries.

5.4.2 Discipleship during the War

Helping new believers interact with God's word and apply it in their context

In order to help believers to interact with the word of God and apply it to their context during wartime, church leaders continued and maintained the catechism and post-catechism classes (which they called follow-up classes). However, although the format of discipleship was still the same, the content was affected by war. New believers were encouraged to read the word of God and practice it in their context of baptism classes, commonly known as "Katekisimo," and follow-up. During the six-month class, pastors had them join the Bible study every week (cf. I5MulCBi [4694–4864]). After baptizing

---

3. Cf. Kighoma, 7.
4. Cf. Ngayihembako and Midiburo, "Communauté Baptiste," 10.

them, the pastor "organized around two follow-up sessions strengthening them so that they too become able to share the word of God with other people" (I6SyaCVi [7739–8423]). These two classes substituted the post-catechism classes that used to be offered after new believers' baptism before the war.

It is good to note that seminars for spiritual growth continued to be run during wartime, except that church leaders focused more on hope through the reading of the word of God. During wartime, in addition to the weekly meetings on Sundays and morning devotions, church leaders drew members into the routine of church life which, in most cases, also comprised the organization of teaching and seminars focusing on fostering hope in the Lord. One Christian leader argued that it is "because they were in a war zone, they used to bring Christians together and encourage them to depend on the Lord in their life" (I40JohCBu [5741–5941]). Therefore, "the church used prayer to galvanize groups to pray for the churches and the enemies, and to plead with God to deliver them from the situation in which they found themselves and to change it" (FGDWomenBut [1124–1311]).

During that period of war, the CBCA designed a pre-established discipleship curriculum that is titled *Kitabu cha Mafundisho Kuhusu Imani Yetu* (CBCA 1996) which was meant for discipleship but, instead, was used by a few pastors for catechism (see I9MahCBut). Consequently, Bible studies were delivered by pastors at the center of the discipleship process with the pastors' teaching aiming at hope and firmness of believers facing challenging issues.

Therefore, although only a few pastors followed the existing discipleship curriculum, Bible study groups were the platform together with church meetings to help new believers join the community of believers (see, for example, I4KavCBi, 4; I5MulCBi [4694–4864]) and helping them to mature in the knowledge of God in a context of war. This kind of discipleship was watered by various contextual seminars at the church level. Even during displacement and refuge, the emphasis remained on the word of God given through circumstantial meetings and baptism classes in the jungle (cf. FGDWomenKab [1550–2334]; FGDMenKab [1693–2498]).

Discipleship classes

There was, therefore, a dynamic revival of discipleship within the CBCA church during the war. New believers had to go through the catechism classes, which led them to baptism. In the year 1996, in response to a felt need, the department of Christian education of the CBCA designed a curriculum called "Kitabu cha Mafundisho Kuhusu Imani Yetu"[5] and made it publicly available to CBCA members. Drafted primarily "to be used for the spiritual growth of all believers,"[6] it was found that no pastor used it to teach his church members, while some used it only to teach Catechism and post-catechism (cf. I27KalCKab [4329–4532]). This book, known by some as the "book for followers of the Bible (another meaning of baptism candidates)," helps pastors teach them "doctrine, the works of a Christian and about judgment" (I9MahCBut [4856–5359]). After baptism, the newly baptized people were taken through a teaching series as a continuation of the baptism class aimed at encouragement, to be well grounded in the word of God and fellowship with the church community for their spiritual growth (cf. I15KiyCKak [11171–11760; I33BalCBu [13016–14042]). Thus, while catechism focuses more on doctrinal teaching, the post-catechism is oriented towards spiritual maturity and equipping new disciples to be able to witness to other people.

At the local church level, seminars were organized to foster an eschatological hope for believers in the context of war through added teaching on love and unity as a response to the context of ethnic conflicts. But in terms of discipleship classes, local churches either used their own initiative or imitated what another sister church was already doing. Bible studies provided discipleship training, since most respondents organized weekly Bible study meetings (I5MulCBi [4694–4864]). The eschatological hope also brought the commitment to church life, for leaders could say, "if they die in the war for the sake of the good news – so be it!" (FGDMenKak [6681–7236]).

Therefore, as the war continued, the good news continued through crusades and the pulpit as the result of that commitment to church missions, which, according to some pastors, "were able to baptize more people in the course of the war than in peaceful times" (FGDMenBut [3415–3504]). This success was also due to strategies used by pastors for new church membership. The church recruited new candidates for catechism through newly baptized members who were asked to "exercise to evangelize other people who then registered for the class" (FGDMenBir [2216–2617]). When the threshold for

---

5. CBCA, *Kitabu Cha Mafundisho Kuhusu Imani Yetu*, 6.
6. CBCA, 3.

membership is built on evangelism then the church is likely to grow even in a context of ethnic conflicts because individuals reach out to others from inside their own cultural circles.

Another dynamism that came about during this period is that a kind of Bible school was organized at the local church level. This kind of theological education, called "Niveau 1" (Level 1), benefited more believers who were involved in ministry and to be trained, any person who has done at least the sixth year of primary school was also allowed to take the training, which lasted six months (cf. I18KasCBut [6854–7069]). Some churches opened the class "to all believers and to people from other church denominations to respond to a felt great need for ministers" (I33BalCBu [8416–9548]).

Another book in the hands of pastors of the CBCA, entitled *Mwongozo Kuhusu Mwakawa Mabadiliko na Upatanisho* 2015,[7] was used for purposes of educating members. During one meeting, the deputy president of the CBCA and director of the Department of Evangelism, Mission, and Life of the Church (DMVE), told the researcher that "this humble contribution to the building of the church aims to respond to local pastors' limits in designing a church teaching program." The theme for 2015, for example, was "Change and Reconciliation."[8] In the view of the researcher, the guide covers the gaps of the catechism curriculum of discipleship, but it did not take care of the context of displacements and mobile churches. For example, during data collection visits, the researcher interacted with church leaders in Bwalanda a day after the IDP camp was burnt down and left the Christian migrants from the CBCA Kabati homeless; many of them were still hiding in the bush where they had run to escape (interview I26NyalKab, 1). The interview with the few women leaders revealed their permanent fear "to be locked up in their sanctuary which was spared by the fire and stabbed with knives" (FGDWomenKab, 3) in case they attempted to attend or hold a church meeting. Curiously, the orientation that the Muongozo had suggested for that particular week was far from the context in Bwalanda. The week was supposed to be a week for youth camps and the guide planned for a fasting week with topics for sermons such as "assurance of salvation" among others.[9] It is clear that in Bwalanda,

---

7. CBCA, *Mwongozo Kuhusu Mwaka wa Uamsho*.
8. CBCA, 130–44.
9. CBCA, 133.

the youth were hiding in the bush out of fear of being a target of the militia, and homeless families might have seemed irrelevant. Thus, due to such risk the youth would encounter, the discipleship class through the youth ministry that aimed at preparing young people for life was affected and no longer existed within CBCA. Fortunately, the establishment of the "scout movement" and the mentorship of the so-called "juniors" and "cadettes" (teens at their tender age of youth), as a means for youth discipleship took over from the previous youth discipleship class. Its aim was "to mobilize their youngsters not to take weapons as their response to the foreign aggression of the country"; having a church program training the young people ethical ways of life and self-sufficiency was a right response to stop young people being recruited into various rebellions and militia groups as they were involved in "many tasks they were being taught" (I10KamCBut [10534–10945]).

However, in the church leaders' view the church did nothing for discipleship during the war and participants believed God sustained the church. It is true that "the grace of God enabled their church throughout the war" (FGDWomenKak [1593–1706]) and it did survive, but some church leaders would reveal that at that time "discipling people was very hard and the church deteriorated, and at that time the church went down" (FGDMenBam [2436–2642]). The church leaders' emphasis was not on evangelism and discipleship.

A prayerful life

The war context forced the church to focus more on prayer and also allow prayer groups outside the church setting as church leaders taught church members in view of fostering their hope in the Lord. During war, Christian leaders used four methods to inspire believers to a prayerful life during the time of war.

1. Some pastors taught on prayer and organized prayer sessions weekly.
2. Other church leaders set an example of commitment to prayer by being committed to prayer.
3. A considerable number of pastors (48 percent) organized an intercessory program at the church with weekly prayer sessions or a prayer chain involving a group of members.
4. Few pastors organized prayer meetings in their church every day.

Members fasting and seeking God

In addition to the above information, a larger number of pastors involved in this study (55.5 percent) had church members who frequently fasted (twice per week, once per month, four times a year, or once per year). There were even churches whose members would occasionally pray whenever the "church top leadership asked that they fast because the wars have worsened the times" (I4KavCBi [6457–6697]). Therefore, one is likely to conclude that wars informed the prayer life of church members.

Pastors fasting and seeking God

Before the war, pastors were used to not having a fasting program and rarely fasted for matters pertaining to their ministry. But war exposed pastors to encounter challenges and problems and made them learn to fast and seek God in prayer. Pastors personally fasted to the extent that would be a frequent fasting program, the majority of them fasting every week and others fasting once, four or five times every month, and the like. Some pastors had to fast for ministry-related challenges, which "pushed them to organize personal prayer and fasting sessions" (I34SyaCBu [6016–6284]). Other church leaders, however, fasted for their family or personal challenges brought by war contexts. There was a case of a pastor whose wife was beaten by rebels (see Interview I15KiyCKak) and had to "pray for her in her condition of sickness" (I15KiyCKak [13372–13838]). Therefore, the war affected both the church leaders' prayer life and that of individuals due to the permanent challenges and suffering to which their ministry and lives were exposed.

Discovering and using spiritual gifts

To help their church members to discover and use their spiritual gifts, respondents used the following six ways:

1. The formation of clusters or small groups provides each member with an opportunity to serve. Church leaders "found that by shrinking the church through sending members to start chapels the gifts were available where they started the chapel" (I7MuyCVi [7408–7740]), but other church leaders chose to assign people to groups within the church to allow "everyone be posted at their

suitable place according to their gift such as prayer group among others" (I10KamCBut [8707–9085]).
2. The leaders spent time with their church members to discover their gifts. The purpose of this approach enabled the pastor to help members discover their spiritual gifts.
3. Some pastors assigned certain tasks to members in order to identify their gifts.
4. Pastors taught their members how to discover and evaluate their spiritual gifts. This strategy, allowed participants "to ask questions as they identify their gifts" (I26NyaCKab [9017–9235]).
5. Church leaders initiated Bible studies in their church and attendees were then assigned work in chapels. This was likely to identify people based on the level of growth the pastors thought they have reached in terms of interpreting the Bible message as "they assign them as preacher for morning chapel meetings" (I17WayCKak [6399–6634]).
6. Some pastors held discussions with church members to help them discover their gifts.

Love, peace and unity

Ethnic conflicts existed before the war but, as minor issue, a minority of church leaders would encourage believers to fellowship as a community. The context of war brought new practices of being a community church in a zone torn by clashes, violence and suffering. To help their church members to fellowship with one another, the majority of pastors taught them unity in Christ, while others organized and supported church members through the church whenever anyone was facing challenges. This support would reach the person through the Upendo, a church visit to their home. Furthermore, in some cases, whenever conflict arose between two members, the church leadership sat down to reconcile them, sometimes a few churches would organize a party called "Agapao" for all church members, friendship was initiated within the church, or the pastor served as a role-model for relationship.

When it came to helping church members' fellowship as a community of believers, two major strategies were used: teaching church members their unity in Christ and organizing and supporting any church members whenever facing challenges. These two strategies were followed by the strategy for church members to come together and do community work and the pastor encouraging members to be part of a help group (called "Likelemba") that would help members to obtain small loans, then with the organization of the Upendo, the solving of conflicts by the church leadership, and the church organizing a feast occasionally for the whole church called Agapeo (I40JohCBu [7249-7481]).

5.4.3 Involvement in Social Concerns during War
Teaching members how to love the poor

During the war, the church did not change its practice of teaching its members love to the poor through organizing seminars on love, instead the number of pastors running such seminars increased 16 percent. It is curious that none of this larger majority of pastors taught church members through action and services of love. While some of them organized seminars on love to the poor, few other organized seminars for and with poor members from their churches to encourage them, and one pastor organized seminars to teach his church members how to fight poverty in groups (cf. I15KiyCKak [20964-22607]).

However, war brought the minority of the churches' leaders to work toward the "formation of communities accepting the values of the kingdom" and "church responses to human needs by loving services"[10] to the discipleship teaching seminars held at their churches. These churches called members to action, to offer what they had, including services to the poor. One pastor welcomed IDPs "in the church compounds and asked believers to give something for them" (I34SyaCBu [8317-9242]); another one had his church members make voluntary donations to the poor in the church; and three pastors organized members into small groups to help the poor through farming during the agricultural season. "The deacons' ministry could make the list of vulnerable and assigned them to groups to help them to farm" (I17WayCKak [8057-8404]).

Church action to demonstrate love to the poor

In addition to the few calls to action, seminars on love had a big impact on church members' attitude and practice in their communities. During the wartime, as the result of the church mobilization toward the poor, 80 percent of

---

10. Zink, "Five Marks of Mission," 152.

CBCA pastors led their churches to act to demonstrate their love to the poor, in addition to the traditional poor with "donations and distributions of items to IDPs, injured people, victims of lootings" (FGDMenKak [8933-9295]) where needed. But because "everyone in the church was affected by the war and was vulnerable" (I15KiyCKak [23260-24405]), special offerings aimed to establish a treasury to help the poorest were now of a complex nature. This helped the CBCA to develop its program of "diakonia" that works to provide support to the most vulnerable people. The program then led local churches to "plan for a day to help the poor during which members brought stuff and various utilities; the church distributed them to the poor who were in the church" (I13KiwCBut [8907-8993]) and "half of the collection was sent to the church department in charge to distribute to the poorest" (I15KiyCKak [23260-24405]).

Different to the period before war, actions targeted the neediest people including widows, orphans and the aged. Having experienced war and suffering, church leaders and members thus "gave themselves out" (I16KerCKak [14984-15493]) for the limited number of poor people while they had the ability to help due to their limited knowledge of "the poor as the physically challenged" (I14MuhCKak [14159-14987]). Churches' actions were limited to "organizing them in the church and donate food to the widows, and some helped in farm work" (I16KerCKak [14984-15493]).

Stories of love to the poor

"Yes, during that catastrophic time, there are people who took care of children of deceased persons; today those children have grown up. We, therefore, had to teach love towards orphans, towards foreigners . . ." (I3LiCBi [11061-11274]). The experience of war taught individuals to give in a sacrificial way (cf. I4KabCBi; FGDMenBir [3824-4054]). The quote above indicates further that individual believers exercised love to the poor in a context where most of the church members were also vulnerable. Speaking of herself, a woman had this to say: "Some had their houses burnt down; when they came to us some of them rented houses owned by Christians. They could share the little we possessed in the house, they became as our own people" (FGDMenKak [9303-9491]). In her context, welcoming people was among the riskiest actions, but individual believers took the risk to protect families or individuals that were homeless, hungry and desperate.

It was established that actions of some individual believers changed into either a help group action or a local church action as a sustainable way of helping the poorest. This is the case of a church leader, two women in his church joined efforts to help people living with HIV/Aids in their neighborhoods (cf. I4KavCBi [11589–12015]).

Love, peace and unity

When it comes to the church's involvement in social concerns during war, the CBCA built on its practices during the time of peace, that is, the organization of a rotative work or loan within members' group associations and cells meetings called Upendo. The experience of war, and suffering pertaining to it, led the church to develop five practices that allowed members to develop love, peace and unity among themselves, and the context of war, therefore, exposed the church to exercise the third and fourth mark of mission during the war, where as it used to focus more on evangelism and discipleship (teaching) believers before the war.[11] The five categories or practices that help the church to promote love, peace and unity in the church during wartime are presented as follows:

1. Upendo: The church members used Upendo as a major means for them to promote love and unity and interpersonal relationships. These meetings were opportunities for members to "stand in unity as they work together in unity as a small group" (I4KavCBi [12172–13321]).
2. Different meetings – in cells: Different to Upendo for its broader audience depending on the purpose for a home visit, the cell group's meeting is an ordinary church meeting or Bible study run by and for a small group of church members who lived in the same neighborhood.
3. The pastor preached the message of reconciliation and reconciling people in conflict: The church was not made of one tribe and the two majority tribes of the CBCA were accusing one another of the responsibility for the war, the Nande being accused of supporting

---

11. Cf. Ross, "Introduction," xiv; Niringiye, "Proclaim the Good News," 15; Zink, "Five Marks of Mission," 152.

the Mayi-Mayi militia and the Hutu being either accused of complicity and involvement with the foreign rebels or backing the Mayi-Mayi/Nyatura (cf. I16KerCKak, 7). Pastors, therefore "spent time to reconcile people who had conflict" (I29KaiCKab [14943–15229]).

4. Helping members in need: For example, three out of the fifteen respondents (20 percent) had to show the example of love by visiting and supporting the sick, the bereaved and the like. This action was extended to the enemy, "whenever an enemy of the peace died the church would go there and console" (FGDMenKak [10650–11097]) his family as an exercise for ethnic reconciliation.

5. Initiated members visiting members: In the culture of the CBCA, church members expect their pastor to visit them regularly. So, this initiative to have church members visiting other members might have been a way to show trust and consideration among church members because the pastoral visit is done to a family which is identified with the local church. Thus, this approach was a way to build mutual acceptance and confirmation of the church being a stakeholder of a new identity in Christ.

Advocating for peace and justice

During the war, the church was able to advocate peace at the church members' level as the result of work of three stakeholders for peace and justice in the region: CBCA Commission of Justice, Peace and Safeguard of Creation (JPIC) from the CBCA denominational level, the partnership between CBCA and a peace organization called APRED and an international Christian organization called World Relief. The church developed a teaching on reconciliation building from the training done by World Relief in the zone formerly occupied by the M23 (cf. FDGDMen [7413–7723]). In Goma, the effects of the JPIC and APRED have been perceived as having laid the church foundations for peace and justice within the local churches.

The combined impact of these efforts led to the initiative of the "cellule de paix" (peace cell) in some parishes to help solve conflicts among believers and even among outsiders, and work for peace (cf. FGD-MenBam [7220–7598]). However, partnership was still lacking between the church and other stakeholders in peace building. It was noted that JPIC, the head office arm for peace and justice promotion, was less active in the zone that suffered most during the war while it had not partnered with World Relief, which was active in educating the church and creating clubs of peace. Therefore, the church lacked more efforts in advocating for peace and justice in that region and left it to the only local pastors.

In many cases, some local pastors of CBCA experienced the pain of seeing their members threatened by ruling rebellion imperialism and thrown into prisons. They had to advocate for justice in favor of the believers through building relationships with the rebel's administration or the government local administration "in order to shield the people from the adverse effects of the war that was likely to lure them into rebel groups or prejudice" (FGDMenBut [6257–6530]).

5.5 Summary

In order to describe the church's response to the recent wars, chapter 5 mainly focused on identifying the nature of missions before and during the war in Eastern Congo from 1990 to 2011. War informed the nature of missions by affecting its witnessing, discipleship and the church involvement in social concerns. During wartime, the practice of sharing the gospel through sermons in the church's setting continued and was most used by Christian leaders as one-on-one evangelism, outreach and crusades became less relevant in an insecure context brought by war. Thus, the context of war changed the church from being a mission force to being both a mission force and a mission field where believers and non-believers came in search of comfort, livelihood and the gospel. Most of the church leaders that used to go out for door-to-door evangelism, together with pastoral care to their members, before the war also became less involved in sharing the gospel one-on-one and focused more on providing pastoral care to their church members, either at home or even during displacement.

The open-air crusades had always been organized during the baptism festival, around which the church purposed to make new believers through evangelism and organized discipleship seminars. This activity has played a key role as an avenue for short-term missions and was a channel for the local church to launch new chapels. That practice of running crusades survived the war due to the open-air crusade revival called "Mukutano mkuu wa Injili" introduced to CBCA in the 1990s. However, although during the war the regional church and the head office became involved, it turned out to be a mission activity of the church that did not really consider the context of war and thus exposed short-term missionaries and participants to risk of insurrections, looting and kidnappings.

The war continues and the gospel continues to be spread in Eastern Congo. In addition to the pastor's pulpit that plays the role of reaching out to people in need of comfort, the church developed a dynamic discipleship approach, through teaching and seminars to create hope and Bible studies as the central task for pastors to disciple all believers. Although church leaders did maintain the format of discipleship classes, its content during wartime was different and innovative compared to the one used before the war. To new believers, catechism and post-catechism classes continued to be taught by using a designed curriculum. That curriculum helps students to be grounded in biblical doctrines, the post-catechism class aiming to equip them for outreach. The culture within CBCA, which recognizes one-on-one evangelism as the role of a group of evangelists and not as a task of every ordinary member or believer, has hindered members to share the gospel one-on-one to their ethnic friends and brothers in a context of ethnic wars.

In the displacement context, however, the emphasis was put on the word of God present in context. Baptism classes and church meetings were organized in the bush. Rather than the church disappearing because of wars and repeated displacements, the study found that the church survived and even baptized more people than before the war, the reason being that the gospel spread as the preachers were ready to expose their lives for the demands of the gospel (see FGDMen Kak [6681–7236]). It is also the Scripture presented in seminars and Bible studies that had the eschatological character that might have awakened people to change and get baptized.

Catechism has been the entry point to disciple new believers and to prepare them for baptism. During the war, a discipleship curriculum was drafted and published in 1996 to benefit all believers but was only used by a few Christian leaders to teach catechism. Although that curriculum and the teaching guide called *Muongozo* are needed, they are yet to respond to the context of war and migration in Eastern Congo. Christian leaders have responded to the context with a contextual discipleship, which included teaching on various topics to respond to current issues. Theological education was then brought to the local church in the form of a discipleship class called "Niveau 1" to help equip local church leaders. With the need to recruit new believers, post-catechism and the "Niveau 1" were contributions that would help CBCA work toward members' appropriation of one-on-one evangelism.

While before the war some Christian leaders acted to help their church members to discover and use their spiritual gifts, during the war, except for few Christian leaders who did not act, the majority acted to help their church members discover and use their spiritual gifts. Results show that emerging themes before the war were more of involving the believers by either assigning them to work to do according to their interest or allocating work to test their gifts. But during the war, Christian leaders added teaching to members on how to identify their gifts, discussion during Bible study, and dividing people into groups. The strategy focused on church service activities and mainly pointed to preaching or being part of a group within the church.

When it came to the church's involvement in social concerns, before the war a majority of churches focused on teaching members on how to demonstrate love to the poor and the minority of churches mobilized their churches to act towards them. These were mainly orphans, widows and the aged. However, during the war most church members were poor and church members had learned to sacrifice to the poorest of the poor who were the IDPs and refugees, people injured during clashes, those whose belongings were looted or stolen, returnees, orphans and widows of war. Curiously, a majority of church leaders concentrated their effort on teaching their members how to help the poor and some got involved practically. Consequently, there are stories of individuals who sacrificially exercised their love to the poor during the war, people whose actions brought about change in communities. It can be interpreted as a demonstration of love to their enemies.

Before the war, the promotion of love, unity, peace and justice was mostly done through sermons which, to some extent, were preached on love and unity. During the war, the local church initiated justice and peace cell groups as a result of the support and advice of JPIC and APRED in Goma and the work of World Relief in the war zone in Rutshuru. These peace cell groups educated church members on Christian ways of conflict resolution. In the war zone, on the other hand, pastors advocated for justice in favor of their members when falsely accused or arrested by rebels or the government armed force. They also organized prayer rallies to advocate against the war, and lastly, some of them had to develop a friendship with the governmental administration for the safety of the church. Therefore, this local advocacy against war contributed to the survival of the church during the war, the pastor being key in the advocacy process. It might have increased the ownership of church missions among members as well as building trust from the local ruling governments.

Thus, the church experience of war and suffering pertaining led to the development of five practices, that is, the "Upendo" or "Likelemba"; meetings in cell groups; preaching the message of reconciliation and reconciling people in conflict; helping members in need; and the initiative of "members visit members" to enhance love, peace and unity within the community of believers in the context of war. That has therefore allowed the church to upgrade its missional practices from evangelism and discipleship to also practicing the third and fourth mark of mission.[12]

---

12. Cf. Ross, "Introduction," xiv; Niringiye, "Proclaim the Good News," 15; Zink, "Five Marks of Mission," 152.

CHAPTER 6

Christian Leaders' Experiences of Missions before and during the War

6.1 Introduction

In the previous chapter of this study, in order to describe the CBCA response to the wars between 1990 and 2011, the nature of missions from field data were described and analyzed. This chapter is the continuation of that descriptive presentation of the church's missions before and during the war in Eastern Congo from 1990 to 2011. The chapter presents a synthesis of the experiences of the Christian leaders who were involved in church missions during and in the context of war. Focusing on the experience of Christian leaders, the church position on the war and the church's survival during the war, in this chapter, it argues for God being in mission in the midst of the war.

It will be shown that the experience of war affected positively the knowledge of missions, from a narrow understanding to a broader, holistic and contextual understanding, and it also affected the church position on war and thus guided the praxis that determined its survival during the war. Primary source information was accessed from twenty-five Christian leaders who served in the selected churches during the period between 1990 and 2011 with additional information accessed during gender-based focus group discussions that included church lay leaders who served in various capacities during the same period.

6.2 Experiences of Christian Leaders Involved in Missions in the Context of War

In this part of the study, the experiences of Christian leaders involved in missions in the context of war are synthesized. Their stories reflect their experience as well as their suffering, that of their families and of their church members. It will lead to the argument for the presence of God in mission in the context of war. It entails that God is at work during war to rescue the missionary and the task of missions.

6.2.1 Stories of Christian Leaders Involved in Missions during War

The task and the missionary

> The story I have brings me worry. Upon graduating from Bible school, I was sent to Buramba. The war broke out and the enemies killed the senior pastor and injured his wife with a bullet in the knees. The CBCA administration asked that I take over his responsibilities . . . after two years in Bunagana, a new war broke and we had to run to Uganda empty-handed. We went up to Mbarara. I, my wife and children then spent a whole week sleeping in an open parking lot and struggled so much to access food and unsuccessfully asked the police. It was hard for us to communicate to people in Kiswahili or Kifumbira while they spoke other languages. From there we traveled to Congo through the town of Lubiriha-Kasindi, it is then that the church leadership asked me to serve as a pastor in that area around Beni. Posted in Mwenda and later in Oicha I experienced suffering, all my children suffered severe malnutrition (*kwashiorkor*), three of them and my brother's wife died. After a lot of suffering, I asked to be transferred back here where I was born. Although I live here in Buturande, the war has left trauma. (I13KiwCBut [10569–13413]).

Like the pastor who undertook church missions in the context described above, many Christian leaders witnessed their colleagues being murdered on the mission field and still had to carry on the task of missions, a task that exposed them to experience displacement, suffering and even death of their loved ones. It is evident from the above story that war has the effect of discouragement, trauma and readiness to abandon almost everything for the sake of their own survival on pastors. This Christian leader in need for pastoral care said that "it is when he is telling what he went through that he feels a relief from the wound the events did on him" (I13KiwCBut [23705–24101]).

From his story, one would think that God is a selfish God who only cares about his mission but does not protect the missionary in context. He allows the missionaries to suffer the effect of the war as they are trying to rescue the task of missions in war zones or places of refuge. In the same vein, a respondent shared the story of his experience of a war that broke out during an open-air crusade week, specifically during the time they had started baptizing new believers. He narrated the following:

> Once I was called to preach the gospel during baptism in Buramba . . . The time we were baptizing people, suddenly the fight/war came in and we had to interrupt the baptism church service and therefore we also had to transfer baptism candidates to another sister church outside our area for baptism. On another occasion the day we were in church running a baptism service; I was teaching at the 2 p.m. service. Then soldiers came in the village, intimidated people and looted the food reserves. Because we were in rebellion context, immediately the Mayi-Mayi militia came to the rescue of the population against the army and chased the soldiers who ran away. Now from the military camp soldiers went to organize revenge and they came back shooting many bullets and the senior Pastor was killed. I ordered the church members to run and we went to hide in the hills, . . . around 150 people were killed that day . . . (I15KiyCKak [34901–36033]).

Once again, it is erroneous to construe success as only having baptized people when the pastor and church members were killed among the 150 people during raids of the government's army and the militiamen. But it is good to notice that these stories reveal both the commitment, the courage and determination of church leaders who continued to manage church life in a very demanding context. Therefore, as the war context continued to be sustained and causing the death of many people, including pastors, the church continued with its mission of making disciples. This is explained by the fact that the first pastor took over the reign when his senior pastor was killed, and pastored that church for one more year before he moved on to another post (see I13KiwCBut [23705-24101]) and the second pastor finding solutions to accomplish the tasks in such a context.

Surviving risk and ill-treatment during war

A pastor was assigned to a local church in a certain region (Poste) that was highly affected by the war. He said that due to war, most of his colleagues migrated outside the region, but he never fled. When the situation became unbearable, he had no way out except that he "asked God for protection in that context . . . but God kept him alive and helped him persevere" (I32NzuCKab [11210-11938]) as "they had to start building the church again" (I32NzuCKab [11210-11938]) in a situation when ministry was already seen as very problematic to fulfill.

"Look at my hand [showing the way his hands had changed] they broke it using a rod and today I am crippled. There are so many suffering, I was beaten when I was in the church of . . ." (see I32NzuCKab), he said in order to indicate how tough that time was. During his time as pastor in that particular church, the FDLR crippled his hand and the FARDC broke his leg because he tried to advocate justice for the people. Government soldiers were also mistreating and raping people pushing citizens to flee into the forest. As the pastor, he invited them to come back, not only to live a "normal life" but also because they were spending nights in the bush out fear of the armed force (cf. I32NzuCKab [12069-14108]). Beaten almost to death, with even the dowry of his daughter taken by the militiamen, this pastor said, "when we arrived there, we suffered but many ministers had suffered ahead of us, the so and so who were there before had already suffered, so . . . we simply persevered" (I32NzuCKab [12069-14108]).

Such perseverance was not a fruit of preparation; it was the result of comfort that he took from his predecessors who, ahead of him, went through such a challenging ministry but did not quit. Just as the Ephesians were "built on the foundation of the apostles and prophets, with Christ Jesus himself as the chief cornerstone" (Eph 2:20), the example of the experiences of predecessors has helped Christian leaders to persevere with church missions in the context of war. Therefore, war has informed the construction of the eastern

Congolese church missions in context. Such experience serves as impetus for other Christian leaders to risk their lives for the sake of the gospel in the war zone. One pastor whose church covered a battlefield area shared his experience and had this to say:

> I kept going from the dangerous areas to Rumangabo to teach. Amidst gunshots God protected me. Being a pastor of both Nande and Hutus, I had to bring reconciliation whenever they conflicted. . . . I took some out of rebel's prisons. I could go to them whenever a believer had been arrested and they could be released without payment. . . . Whenever there was a torturing fighter I could do all I could to have him arrested by his colleagues. That is what put my life in danger. They began looking for opportunities to kill me (cf. I15KiyCKak [27732-30484]).

It appears that courage and the passion for the lost enabled pastor "Kahindo Uwizeye" to reach out to the people on the front line. His neutrality as far as the ethnic conflict was concerned might have been part of the factors that worked for his security in this dangerous zone where he was doing ministry. In most cases in Eastern Congo, rebel groups and militia were associated with ethnic groups. A respondent shared his experience describing that period of war as "a very sad time because at that time, to be a member of a particular tribe you immediately become enemy from another tribe while you do not even share their history" (I33BalCBu [18822-20554]). Any Christian leaders involved in politics supporting his ethnic group or any other would not have been able to preach the gospel in war zones such as Rumangabo; he could have been seen as a spy for the opposite armed group. Therefore, political neutrality enabled some pastors to continue church missions in conflict zones.

Christian leaders were, however, also exposing their lives as they tried to use their advocacy position in society to rescue people wrongly arrested. As it is the case for "Kakule Uwizeye" whose life, at some point, was in danger, they overused their position and warlords would attract them closer to their regime at the expense of the credibility of the church with its involvement in politics. But Christian leaders who were apolitical were able to contribute truly to building a community of believers that was a multiethnic church. This is the case of a Christian leader who did pastor a church in Bunia, during the ethnic war between 2002 and 2005, and built his ministry on love and unity to the extent that believers from both ethnic groups sought refuge in his house (cf. I33BalCBu [18822–20554]). From the above two experiences, it appears that a church leader who had in mind the church as a new community of believers not only succeeded to reach out to people in their context but also contributed to the church becoming multiethnic where it was needed.

This is not arguing that exposure to risk meant that a pastor was connected to warlords, but the context of ethnicity itself exposed many to danger as they undertook missions. A pastor, for example, trying to access medical support to rescue the lives of people who "were being shot by bandits regardless of their church and ethnic group" (I4KavCBi [13541–15162]) was wanted by the Mayi-Mayi militia who were from his tribe. They accused him of "serving the MAGRIVI, their enemies, after they shot them so that they go and die but now the pastor was working to bring them to life" (I4KavCBi [13541–15162]). The pastor was the leader from whom church members and the rest of the community could expect solutions to rescue them from a miserable situation and that exposed Christian leaders to danger although it allowed them to continue church missions. Therefore, the story of the spared lives of the above three Christian leaders is a testimony that missions and the missionaries survived in the process of God leading the church to reconstruct the story of his mission in Eastern Congo. It built on the experiences of leaders who persevered to serve God in the context of war.

Forced bi-vocational lifestyle for Christian leaders during war

The context of war in Eastern Congo brought a fear and a threat to the pastors' security because the enemies were sometimes church members and subjects of church missions; the context also exposed the ministers and their families to a high risk of poor livelihood and other challenges. When 97 percent of the DRC population was estimated to be Christians in the year 2000,[1] this meant there were Christians who were involved in the war at the expense of thousands of believers and non-believers exposed to suffering and death. Upon graduating from Bible school in 2010, the then twenty-seven-year-old pastor assigned in Bwito, shared his experience saying: "I came here with so much fear, I had never seen even the FDLR. But as I continued to serve here and see them face-to-face, it gave me also the strength to serve here although

---

1. Barrett, *World Christianity Encyclopedia*, 758.

I still feared" (I27KalCKab [11203–11750]). For this pastor, "seeing the FDLR face-to-face" simply meant that he experienced their incursion, looting and other ill-treatment, and the fear of them made him spend nights in the bush (see I27KalCKab). In fact, he was interviewed an hour before he started a baptism seminar on a tensed day after an IDP camp was burnt down in an ethnic clash in the same locality. This was a sign that from his experience he was convinced of his calling to serve there and, therefore, that war does not have to hinder discipleship, only that it motivates it.

During wartime, most pastors experienced a ministry at risk of danger. Some of them were mistreated by members of their flock. Trying to be neutral could lead to being a target of the suspicious camp of people involved in the dirty business of war. This was the case of a pastor whose church members plotted against him after he had warned them for their misbehavior against others. He was rescued by a policeman from the people who conspired that "he knew much history of all that happened there, by eliminating [him] nobody would tell their ill-actions" (I24MunCBa, 11). This shows how involved believers were in the militia and ethnic clashes that killed people and that the army was not always part of the destructive corps in Eastern Congo. Some in armed groups did protect citizens against danger.

Pastors working in a warzone struggled to meet the basic needs of their families. During war, pastor Isa (a false name) shared that in living in places with the scarcity of food like Rwindi, believers were few to cater for his family upkeep that increased the challenges facing missionary work. He did food crop business as a secondary means for his and his family's subsistence. "I left the flock to look for my survival" meant bringing fishes from Vitsumbi and bringing them to Rwindi and then to Butembo (cf. I17WayCKak [11985–13088]). In CBCA, all pastors are in full-time service. This, however, re-confirms that CBCA lacks a missionary support strategy and that in a context of such a strategy, pastors who hustle to meet the needs of their family are likely to resist on the field because of their access to resources to sustain themselves.

Experience in translating the message during war

The stories of Christian leaders are full of insights about how their experience of war informed their transmission of the gospel message as well as their own understanding of the scriptures. A respondent told of the shift in the phrase "Watu wa uku," meaning "people of this area" in Congolese Kiswahili, had on ministers after the ethnic war in the Ituri province: "initially it was never an issue but during the war, if you said: 'people of this area,' it was like an insult to them" (I42KunCBu [15408-15908]). Therefore, the war helped with the need to analyze the context at the same time a pastor analyzes the biblical text in the process of transmitting the Christian faith. Some respondents said that their experience of war made the word of God more real to them. They are no longer preaching the word of the God in an ambiguous way, but whenever they read the Bible and asking to love their enemy they really began to understand the message in their context (e.g. I40JohCBu [19088-19966]; I7MuyCVi [18935-19310]).

War and acting pastors

The CBCA church ordains its ministers before assigning them for any pastoral work. That ordination requires three years internship under supervision to which holders of a theological education certificate from a Bible school or theological seminary are subjected. It was in the year 2010 that the Department of Evangelism and Mission started to organize "seminars to train the lay church planters"[2] and also ordain them not as ministers but as evangelists in charge of church plants (Evangelistes Responsables – EVARES).

Whenever there was a fight in a region some pastors were displaced together with part of the church members. Pastors' displacements became an avenue for lay pastors to act as senior pastors and some led churches for years. The researcher identified two lay pastors in Bunia who pastored the church of Bunia for three years in 2002 before another ordained minister was re-deployed there (see I40JohCbu; I41DavCBu). One of them shared his experience and said:

> Before the war I was a church elder, then we ran, . . . [by] the time I came back the church had already been dispersed. I was obliged to bring the few people that were available together, and we started the ministry in ministering to people here in church . . . I served as a senior leader for three years because there was no minister (I40JohCBu [2278-3254]).

---

2. From the interview with the secretary of the Department of Mission and Life of the Church, July 2012, in Goma at the head office of the CBCA.

The church members' ownership also contributed to the survival of the church. This would work well when the layperson is from an indigenous ethnic group. For example, church leaders from a local church believed that "it is God that used a young man to spare the church, as the militia group would come in they did not destroy the church or loot anything because they found he was from their ethnic group" (FGDMenBu [7261–8115]). Although the church building was rescued, highlighting ethnicity in this context has no biblical support, especially in such a multicultural context.

6.2.2 Personal Suffering Related to Missions during War

During interviews, Christian leaders said they did experience suffering for church missions. Their description of these sufferings is summarized together with the themes from the data analysis:

1. Pastors "exposed [their] life advocating for members in danger of and imprisoned by rebels": some pastors took the risk to approach the administration of either rebel groups or the governments whenever their members were accused or jailed. "People were put in prison anyhow, and we went there so that the people may find some assistance and be safe" (I10KamCBut [16218–16661]).
2. Pastors were "accused and / or arrested for [their] church members' association and/or involvement with militia": in this vein one of the respondents was arrested and detained by the local authority, accused of "hiding enemies in the church his security was no longer guaranteed and many times he then used to sleep hidden in the bush" (I13KiwCBut [13631–13992]). Not only did he suffer the stress brought by the service of intelligence but also the impression ministry efforts looked like a failure to the extent that members were suspected to be part of the rebel movement. One pastor expressed his discouragement and said, "I see, it is like we did not teach people well, there's nothing we did before the war . . . the people we preached involved war" (see I16KerCKak, p5).
3. Pastors "risked [their] life during a mission/church event trip or while on transfer to a dangerous location": among people who experienced this kind of suffering are those who, for example,

met or were evaded by bandits/rebels, others escaped bullets fired against them by enemies while on missions trips, among others. In this category is a pastor who "fought the battle with armed people the whole night, when he went to minister somewhere" (I15KiyCKak [30768-31258]) and those who experienced "incursion of the Mayi-Mayi militia during baptism session" (I15KiyCKak, p23).

4. Pastors suffered witnessing people being murdered or losing church members who were killed to the extent that one of them "was tempted to quit pastoral work when he witnessed for the first time in his life someone being slaughtered" (I34SyaCBu [11968-12361]).

5. Pastors suffered hunger: due to war church members could not be able to pay their pastor who had to struggle for his family needs. This was the case (in interview I24MunCBa) of a pastor who ran a mobile business to meet his family needs while doing ministry. Pastors from this group who did not fill the gap with an income generative activity had to abandon their ministry. One of them "had to quit his ministry in the Virunga National Park to rescue his family from suffering to a safer place" (I18KasCBut [10756-11175]).

6. Pastors found "the ramping made me suffer": From the French word "ramper" meaning "to crawl" participants to the study used the word "ramping" to express a practice they did as they tried to hide in the bush running away from the raids of rebels or militia or sometimes FARDC soldiers against villagers. Citizens would spend their daytime in the village and in the evening the entire family would go and hide in the bush for the night, mainly raids happened in the nights. A pastor described his experience and said: "sleeping in the jungle (Bush) made us suffer during the war. At a time like this (evening) it could rain, we leave the house and go to sleep in the bush with the children" (I29KaiCKab [18408-18771]).

7. Pastors "suffered rejection and [were] in danger because of my ethnic origin": One pastor expressed his frustration as "people [members] were not ready to receive him in their

homes" (I42KunCBu [11680–12003]) and another pastor had "to be evacuated outside the city for his security" (I36ChaCbu [9823–10213]).
8. Pastors faced a lack of support of the church administration during hardship: some others suffered lack of comfort from their leadership; there were also challenges of communication of the gospel caused by "pastors' inability to translate the message into the local Kiswahili" (I36ChaCbu [10227–10507]). This calls for the idea of strategy; the lack of preparation made pastors to be sent without a plan to learn the language.
9. Pastors were beaten to death or humiliated by rebels or militia or the government soldiers: reasons included advocating for justice (e.g. mentioned from I32NzuCKab [12069–14108]) and a few were exposed to public humiliation such as taking the clothes of people during the looting raid in front of their children (cf. I32NzuCKab [12069–14108]).
10. Pastors lived in constant fear: Christian leaders lived "in constant fear of war" (I5MulCBi [11645–12104]).
11. Lastly, some pastors suffered looting in repetition: pastors were vulnerable whenever "everything in their homes was taken by the rebels, militiamen or soldiers" (I26NyaCKab [25001–25439]).

6.2.3 Family's Suffering during the War

Christian leaders described their family's sufferings as follows. (1) Some leaders pointed to internal displacements, which in many cases caused separation with the husband or parents. In many cases, families were moved either outside the zone and the pastor would be left taking care of the flock or the whole family would move. (2) In the case of displacement, families suffered from unmet basic needs and support for their subsistence. The pastor "could get crops to send to them but had no possibility to visit and bring it to them because the road was blocked" (I4KavCBi [16258–16616]). As for separation, pastors' families were also exposed to "ramping" and did suffer from the lack of shelter, sleeping in the forest caused some people to get sick (see I15KiyCKak [32425–32730]). (3) The education of the children of some pastors was endangered by war. Regular displacements hindered the children from pursuing their education and if they did, it did affect "most of them to never reach the level of education they expected" (I12VinCKak [13193–13635]). (4) Some pastor's family members went through trauma and frustration, "suffering during displacement brought internal wounds" (I13KiwCBut [14074–14489]). And lastly, (5) pastoral families were overwhelmed by the needy; one used to "share his children's food and rooms with the many and regular poor needy people, and some overstayed in the family for refuge" (I43MisBut [13993–14541]).

6.2.4 Suffering of Church Members during the War

Pastors described their church members' suffering during the war and listed displacement and refuge, the so-called "ramping," the murder of loved ones, food scarcity and famine, poverty and others as contributing to the suffering. Since "it was very difficult for members to access their farms, which brought hunger, and because the pastor gets his pay from believers," (I12VinCKak [13745–14296]), poverty at the church members' household level also affected the subsistence of pastors' families.

However, the list describing their suffering from the interviewed pastors misses the effects of war on women and children, the reason being that pastors did not have reported cases of violence to their church members as women were not ready to speak out or the gender gap in the communities of believers made them not to speak out whenever one was a victim of abuse. Thus, from group discussions, the study identified the effects of war on the lives of individuals and families, which are interconnected, within the following categories: (1) Death, migration and refuge, hunger and poverty; (2) effects of war on children; (3) church members' involvement in militia and kidnappings; (4) arising new conflicts and a culture of mistrust with IDPs as a result of war; and (5) enmity and tribal hatred.

To begin with, first, during the period of the war, "many people lost their lives and housing, many houses were shut up and families perished" (FGDWomenBir [9808–10027]). "The war first forced people to leave their village or town and relocate to a different place" (FGDWomenBam [7634–7708]). In these conditions, some respondents recalled their experience of having been forced to live in a small IDP camp, which caused diarrhea and people suffered the lack of intimacy (see FGDMenVir [10726–11218]; FGDMenKako [19364–19392]).

The immediate consequences of war and displacement are then poverty, food scarcity and hunger with a score of sixteen – meaning sixteen of the respondents reported these experiences during group discussions. For respondents in the city, "war destroyed property and income generative activities to the extent that after the war most of the church members subsisted by selling remaining items and suffered more" (FGDWomenBir [13026–13407]). The enemies (militia and FDLR) made their habitat in some forests, thus preventing families in rural areas to have access to their farms and exposing them to hunger; others had to move to the city at the expense of church life (cf. I10KamCBut [176443–18231]).

Second, war had effects on children and women. This includes sexual violence and rape (with a score of nine); children's education was affected by war (with a score of three); the increase of the number of widows and orphans (with a score of four); children separated from their parents as they fled from war zones (score one); children and mothers killed (score one); women carrying the responsibility of family alone because of war (score one); women traumatized by the war effects (score one); and women saying that the war affected their marriages (with score two).

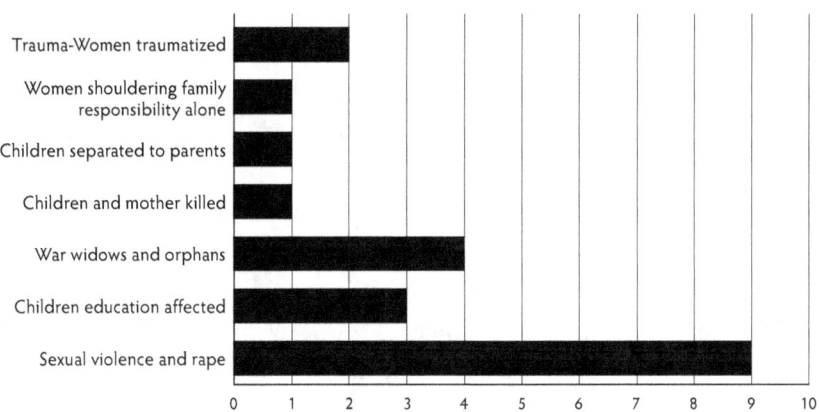

Figure 2: Effect of war on women and children in Eastern Congo
Source: Field data analysis

The scoring in the graph indicates the number of times a theme was pointed to by focus group participants. Sexual violence was placed first as the major suffering women experienced during the war. To express how rape and abuse was a war by itself, a respondent described the context in Rutshuru territory as follows: "The women were raped quite a lot. You go to the Lutare (a place to search for firewood) and they rape you there. And the sexually transmitted disease increased as a result of the rape cases" (FGDWomenKak [7118–7333]). In Goma, water scarcity "exposed women to rape on their way searching for water" (FGDWomenBir [13501–13770]) from tap stands early in the morning.

It is unfortunate that rape is much attributed to armed people among which even the soldiers of the government armed forces (FARDC) are guilty. This was confirmed by a woman who said that even today, "if you see a man in the uniform of a soldier you will be seized by the fear that they might rape you" (FGDWomenKak [7118–7333]). Rape and sexual abuse also relate to "youth who had [been] wayward to the extent that pregnancies, for example, arising from rapes or the underage catching pregnancies, were high" (FGDWomenKak [12794–12994]). The youth recruits into the rebel movements and militia also had an effect on their sexual behavior.

In addition to rape and gender sexual violence, participants mentioned widowhood and orphanage; according to them, "during the war, many people were rendered widows and much more orphaned, some of them were left psychologically disturbed as a result of encountering the horrors of the war" (FGDWomenKak [7715–7930]). In the same vein, it has become hard for church members to educate their children and some of them had quit school (FGDWomenKab [8527–8597]) because "people stayed for many years wandering and the children were not going to school nor faring well, some children's intellectual ability went down because of the effect of the war" (FGDWomenBam [7782–7950]). It is possible that children experienced being lost during displacement (see FGDWomenBam [7782–7950]) or witnessed many cases of abuse to the mentally affected. Women also revealed that many marriages "died" as an effect of war as "some people were forced to abandon their inter-ethnic marriage from ethnic groups in conflict" (FGDWomenBu [10637–11038]) and other "men remarried after their spouse went on displacement thus creating a chaotic situation whenever spouses came back" (FGDWomenBu [10225–10629]).

Third, other effects of war that caused family members to suffer fall into the category of church members' involvement in militia (with score two) and kidnappings (score one). During war, some family members who became desperate and felt that the government had failed them decided to joined in the rebellion (cf. FGDMenKak [19676–19872]). Others, however, joined for the purpose of having access to guns for robbery; having joined the "band of armed thieves, they had no other option but joining a rebellion to make ends meet" (FGDMenKak [19404–19666]). With citizen involvement in militia for such ill-reasons, believers and non-believers suffered the kidnapping of members of their families who were then freed with much pain and a huge amount of money as ransom. This practice also hindered farming and movement within the region (FGDWomenKak [8255–8441]).

Fourth, the next stage, new conflict arose and IDPs suffered mistrust as a result of war. During displacements, accusation and suspicions of camp dwellers made new conflicts to arise as "war bore the hallmark of an ethnic war" (FGDWomenBut [12162–12420]). It is useful to note that international policies conflicted with national ones that sustain conflicts between camps dwellers and the host communities as far as security was concerned; this conflict is often what caused the clash between IDPs and host communities in Bwalanda, and the host communities accusing camp dwellers of hiding militia.[3]

Finally church members suffered enmity and tribal hatred (with score five) during war. That tribal hatred endangered those who were betrayed by people from other ethnic groups, for example, some "suffered their crops harvested by force as an expression of hatred" (FGDWomenBam [8046–8475]), and this explains the frequent lootings from the participants (with score two).

6.2.5 Effects of the War on Witnessing, Discipleship and Social Involvement

When it comes to witnessing, the war has, to an extent, made Christian leaders share the word of God with much confidence, having experienced the presence of God in their lives and ministry during war. A respondent had this to say:

---

3. The researcher witnessed debates in Bwalanda, the host accusing that rebels were hiding in the IDP camps, whenever the population and the police wanted to catch bandits, they would run back to the camp which was protected by the international policy which, according to them, does not allow armed persons, even from the government, to enter the camp.

> But the way to testify, I saw that it was also a way through which the Lord could also re-write, in a proper manner, the life of each of us. I read in the Bible people who went through very difficult situations, so we had also seen the hand of God. We do not tell the story of God that is in the Bible, we also have personal experiences where we saw the hand of God working in our lives (I33BalCBu [24242-24736]).

It is true that the experience of war led to boldness to share the word of God, but it also appears from the quote that the story of missions during the war in Eastern Congo is a book written in the hearts of Christian leaders and the experience of the church, just as in the Bible where experiences were recorded as a testimony of God's presence with biblical characters during their missions.

It was found, however, that the war negatively affected the Christian leader's plans for church life and evangelism as the implementation was sometimes interrupted and postponed due to sudden incursion (see I15KiyCKak [36095-37366]). In addition to "many plans which came to a standstill, the church had a deficit" (I9MahCBut [14440-14908]). It became a normal phenomenon for local churches, such as CBCA churches, which "only rely on the offering of the church [whose] developments were very slow" (I9MahCBut [14440-14908]) due to high expenses and poverty levels among the members' family caused by war.

The war had an impact on the way of doing discipleship in the period between 1990 and 2011. The church needed to provide a biblical response to suffering that was the immediate effect of repeated wars in the region. Because "during hard times as challenges increased people came closer to God to seek and plead their cause to him" (I6SyaCVi [27565-28820]), church attendance went high as the church was overwhelmed with people in search for hope. The war then "taught pastors to teach that the existing trials and sufferings do not cancel the reality of the existence of God" (I6SyaCVi [27565-28820]) and that also "helped them to profoundly study the experience of the Bible characters who went through suffering before they preached" (I6SyaCVi [27565-28820]); "from their experience of suffering, they got a message to teach their members" (I20MweCBa [26557-26638]).

The experience of war also negatively affected the Christian leaders' commitment to discipleship due to the debilitating effect of war that some leaders encountered. After all efforts to disciple church members, a pastor was frustrated to "discover that people whom he took through catechism class, later joined rebels in the jungle"; it hurt him and affected his ministry to witness Christ as he saw they had left because of suffering (I13KiwCBut [15892–16437]. In the same vein, a woman said in Katwe after the interview:

> Pastor, the war is bad, women have been raped and when those "Wajambazi" (enemies) are doing their forfeit you cry to God, "Jesus help me," and they finish their business on you while you are praying when you wake up you discover you did not die.[4]

In the context of war, it is possible to question whether God is with those suffering on the church's mission field. In hearing the women, however, it was concluded that it is when discipleship goes beyond blessings and suffering that people began knowing who God is. Continuing to confess Christ after a failure in discipleship or after rape means you have understood that suffering is not the indicator of the absence of God. Jesus predicted a similar context of war as he warned disciples about what would happen at the destruction of Jerusalem and the temple. He told them to flee because of the terrible tribulation that was coming. Jacoby states that because "the urgency of leaving the city was to be great . . . Jesus warned the believers not to descend to retrieve their belongings even if they happened to be walking immediately above their own homes."[5]

When it comes to effects of the experience of war on the church's involvement in social concerns, the study identified that before the war, the church was not locally involved in supporting the poor other than care for orphans, widows and the aged. From the war experience, both church members and pastors learned to give to the poor (I4KavCBi [17731–18546]). The many opportunities to learn to give and showing love to the refugees, to the IDP, the sick and the like led church leaders "to organize seminars on love and to call believers to help, for example, Rwandan refugees" (I43MisBut [15628–15945]).

---

4. See additional note on FGDWomenKab.
5. Jacoby, "Destruction of Jerusalem," 4.

6.3 The Effect of the War on the Understanding of Church Missions

6.3.1 Christian Leaders' Understanding of Church Missions before the War

Before the war, church leaders described what they understood as church missions as spreading the gospel. The analysis of their knowledge of church missions is described in different themes/characteristics presented in the following set of tables.

Table 1: Face to face participants' understanding of missions before the war

Understanding of missions before the war	Score	%
Mission was preaching the gospel for people to be saved and be heaven minded	23	59.0
Mission was the pastor being on the frontline of every initiative	1	2.6
I understood church mission as a good job to serve the Lord and I could encourage people to join us	6	15.4
Our focus was on the local church, we had few missions to the outside of the church	2	5.1
The church mission focus was mainly on the life of the church	2	5.1
I thought the church was a missionary church locally and outside	1	2.6
Church mission was someone being sent out	4	10.3
Total score	39	100.0

It appears from table 1 that for the majority of interviewed pastors as preaching the good news was "the only mandate of the church and that God was to do all the other" (I10KamCBut [20130-20275]) things as the church pointed to "heaven as their home where they shall live away from earthly troubles" (I16KerCKak [17767-17885]). Not only pastors but also all the other church leaders, who are in the majority, knew missions was spreading the good news, as is also evident in table 2.

Table 2: FGD Participants' understanding of missions before the war

Understanding of missions before the war by FGD participants	Score	%
Mission was spreading the good news	13	72.2
The objective of the church was development	1	5.6
Missions aimed at behavioral change	4	22.2
Total score	**18**	**100.0**

However, for focus group participants, missions was known as "spreading the good news" and connected to behavioral change, with a score of four. A new church seemed to have focused on cultural practices such as marriage among others. That is why participants said that "they discovered many men lived with women and did to have a wedding, then we found that we had to plant a church here and that was going to be a model for others" (FGDWomenBu [12885–13104]). When there was not yet a curriculum, this church seems to have concentrated more on people gaining moral standards than discipleship.

6.3.2 Church Leaders' Understanding of Church Missions during the War

The understanding of missions shifted from spreading the good news before the war to a larger range of knowledge about missions after the war, as indicated in table 3, with the high scores pointing at themes such as missions being known as a very hard task due to the dangerous environment created by the war (score seven). That understanding was followed with church mission being reconciliation (with score seven), the church denying its missions when pastors got involved in the war while serving the church (score four), and church missions being a holistic mission in the context where politics formed part of missions (score four).

Table 3: Face to face respondents' understanding of missions during war

Understanding of missions during war	Score	%
Mission is to minister even as a migrant church	2	5.6
During war, the pastor should have the word to minister to people in a hard time	2	5.6
The church denied its mission-pastors involved in war while preaching the gospel	4	11.1
Church mission is to encourage people unity	1	2.8
Church missions is a war for peace and unity	2	5.6
The mission of the church is to pray	1	2.8
Mission is when someone is sent to preach and the sender sometimes sending support and catering for his transport	2	5.6
I discovered missionary work is very hard – war creates a dangerous environment and it requires sacrifices	7	19.4
Mission is holistic – church missions is informed by the political state of the country-church	4	11.1
I discovered our church was not a missionary church and thus needed to be mobilized	1	2.8
Church missions focus much on discipleship – during war believers are committed to the word and prayer	2	5.6
The church missions consist of reconciliation – it requires the preaching of reconciliation, peace, etc.	5	13.9
During war, I understood the need for missions – multiplying the sharing of the gospel, training and praying	1	2.8
The church missions need to be purpose-oriented in the context of war	1	2.8
The church is a problem solver (diakonia)	1	2.8
Total score	**36**	**100.0**

It is curious to note that mission was understood as reconciliation at 37.9 percent in group discussions as indicated in table 4.

Table 4: FGD participants' understanding of missions during war

FGD participants' understanding of missions during war	Score	%
Church missions is to spread the good news	6	20.7
Church mission is reconciliation	11	37.9
Mission was holistic – education, pray for people, etc.	6	20.7
The church mission is to pray for the world	1	3.4
Church mission is to give comfort and hope to people	4	13.8
It is the work of God in the context of difficulties	1	3.4
Total score	29	100.0

This information is not contradicting the church leaders' understanding of missions as a difficult task. The fact that "church mission being reconciliation" comes second after "mission is a very hard task" with Christian leaders weighing the sacrifices required to serve God in the context where "even the minister permanently runs the risk of being kidnapped and therefore responds to any ministry calling with the fear" (I13KiwCBut [17664–18036]), a context in which "whenever there is a crisis the church is called by both believers and the world to act at the forefront" (I4KavCBi [19878–20318]).

The specific context of ethnic crisis and wars required a specific action of reconciliation through preaching reconciliation and peace, which introduces the idea of missions being a "war for peace."[6] As for the experience of some respondents, "missions was informed by the political state of the country thus required the church to influence the politics" (I37KilCBa [9675–11012]).

The long list of themes describing what participants and members understood as church missions expresses, therefore, a calling of the church in Eastern Congo to a contextual ministry in war, to which, unfortunately, the church to some extent (with score four) responded by denying its missions and becoming involved in the war as it carried out its evangelical mandate of sharing the gospel message. That is why one would say that "during the war, people join evil people and pastors are in possession of weapons. They belong to rebel groups while at the same time are pastors in church"

---

6. Polat, "Peace as War," 318.

(I15KiyCKak [40262–41370]); "God fights for whoever is fighting for himself" (see I15KiyCKak [40262–41370]).

The experience of war brought changes to both Christian leaders and church members in terms of their understanding of church missions. Apart from 13.5 percent of church pastors who said that "nothing" changed in their understanding (score five), the majority of respondents (86.5 percent) did experience a change in their understanding of church missions and data analysis led to the identification of a long list of themes or characters presented in table 5.

Table 5: Change in pastors' understanding of missions as a result of the experience of war

What changed in your understanding of missions as a result of your experience of war?	Score	%
Nothing changed	5	13.5
Interacting with other tribes and nations brought experience that our difference does not make God different	2	5.4
We knew how to adapt to other culture and identify with it	3	8.1
Regret – we did not prepare the church well to deal with it	2	5.4
Believers persevered in faith and did not take revenge	1	2.7
We discovered the need for trauma healing in the church after displacement and refuge	1	2.7
Our prayer life changed	2	5.4
I understood that politics can be missions	1	2.7
The church has become self-dependent more than before	1	2.7
Mission is a difficult task – it requires us to mobilize believers for the task	4	10.8
The context of war informs church missions – the Bible's message is better understood because it is really just like those of biblical people and their experience in their context (it informs the transmission of the gospel)	8	21.6
My understanding of tolerance changed to mutual acceptance of our ethnic differences within the church	2	5.4

I discovered that missions focus on the small group to be effective during war	2	5.4
I discovered that God owns missions; it is his own work	1	2.7
I had to cooperate with rebels for the sake of the church to survive	2	5.4
Total score	**37**	**100.0**

From the data in table 5, it appears that the highest score (score eight) is from the pastors who noticed that the Bible's message became real and they better understood it in light of their experiences of war which informed their ministry of preaching. This is confirmed by the idea that "it [the war] brought the experience of knowing that the holy scriptures are true because they talk about what happened . . . one has to concentrate on God so as to remain faithful" (I36ChaCbu [13931–14294]). One respondent used his experience and the interpretation of Psalm 23 and had this to say:

> Before the war, we were not preaching about God as the protector. We never used to talk about his protection like today. Before we preached the gospel without precision. When we ran from the war, those that we ran with some die some went through. When you tell somebody "the Lord is my shepherd, he passes me through the valley of the shadow of death" you have a new understanding more than before when we had no experience of the war (I40JohCBu [19088–19966]).

Therefore, the experience of war not only informed the transmission of the biblical message which became real in their context; it also helped Christian leaders to acknowledge the presence of God in their missions in that context.

"Mission is a difficult task – it requires us to mobilize believers for the task" (see table 5). This was leading the church toward a shift from church missions being a task of the minister to becoming a task in which everyone is called to participate. In September 2011 it was said that 40 percent of the pastoral force would retire in the next ten years. However, the situation led the youth to enroll for theological education and local churches to invest in

Bible study.[7] Instead, the church should have involved every single believer in one-on-one evangelism and this direction was to be watered by "Bible school called 'Niveau1' (Level 1) as part of the discipleship which trained enrolled members for six months" (I18KasCBut [6854–7069]; [13016–14042]) as a result of the experience of war.

The third theme on the list of changes is the "Christian leaders know how to adapt to and identify with other cultures" (with score three). Migration made many "who left their zones to get used to people they didn't know and they also went to preach the word of God and they were as people born there" (I25MatCKab [15076–15319]). This was made possible by the system of the CBCA which continues to transfer its pastors within regions and outside regional boundaries during the war.

From the focus group discussions, however, participants' responses brought out new insights of what changed in their understanding of church missions with emerging themes being "prayer life changed" (score three), "leaders spiritually matured even in their exercise of love" (score three), and "church attendance increased" (score three) as seen in table 6.

Table 6: Change in FGD participants' understanding of war as a result of the experience of war.

What changed in your understanding of missions as a result of their experience of war?	Score	%
Our prayer life has changed	3	17.6
We gained boldness in sharing the gospel	1	5.9
Invested in reconciliation	1	5.9
We spiritually matured, even in our exercise of love	3	17.6
Our church attendance increased	3	17.6
There was an increase in love; we protect and we value lives	2	11.8
We understood that church mission should be holistic	1	5.9
We started reaching out to people from other ethnic groups and we have other tribes now in the church	2	11.8
People adopted Christian values	1	5.9
Total score	17	100.0

---

7. Cf. CBCA, "Brief Survey," 10.

6.3.3 Effects of War on Christian Leaders' Practice of Church Missions

The research results led to an identifying of the effects of the experience of war on the practices of both Christian leaders and church members. Themes in table 7 present the different practices by church leaders from their experience of war.

Table 7: Face to face interview respondents' current missional practices resulting from their experience of war.

What are you doing differently now as church missions as a result of your experience of war?	Score	%
Doing nothing.	4	10.5
We don't segregate people.	1	2.6
We don't insist on implementing church activities according to our plans but according to current realities (what we have).	1	2.6
We just pray for conversion out of fear of being kidnapped.	1	2.6
We teach unity and forgiveness.	3	7.9
Addressing trauma for healing through seminars.	1	2.6
CBCA has developed more autonomy in initiative than before. We have started to gain a little support for outreach.	3	7.9
I encourage believers to join politics.	1	2.6
We encourage people who are discouraged in their faith.	2	5.3
The experience of war gives us new strategies for missions; discipling believers through small groups (cells).	5	13.2
We now accept and respect the culture of people around us.	2	5.3
We have started giving to missions because of our experience of war.	2	5.3
We promote child protection.	1	2.6
The church is no longer sending out someone without theological education.	1	2.6
I am no longer taking initiative. I just focus on routine activities which have been established as planned.	3	7.9
Focus on pastoral care to heal the traumatized.	2	5.3

The message we preach is alive and contextual.	2	5.3
We serve but we have too much fear now.	1	2.6
I am investing in empowering natives for church sustainability.	1	2.6
Prayer.	1	2.6
Total score	**38**	**100.0**

Table 7 indicates both positive and negatives effects of the experience of war on the church's missional practices. On the one hand, the negative effects of the church's experience of war lie in the fact that some church leaders no longer took initiative but "focused only on what their predecessors have started" because they feared to risk waste resources in the context of instability (cf. I17WayCKak [1905719682]). Next followed pastors (with score one) who do not insist on implement their plans but are driven by current realities and therefore "due to financial challenges they only ran church activities depending on the available funds" (I14MuhCKak [20504-20781]). It is also clear that the fear of some pastors in their churches (score one) is part of the reason other respondents "just pray for the salvation of people out of fear of kidnappings" happening in the region. Prayer works, but the ministry of presence is not implemented during the war and consequently, there are people who may not hear the gospel because the messenger is not available.

On the other hand, the experience of war informed the strategies of discipleship (score five), building hope (I21KavCBa [11802-11988]), the teaching of unity and forgiveness (I19MbaCKak [11968-12212]; I30BihCKab [17161-17572]), pastoral care ministry to the traumatized (I18KasCBut [15351-15645]), among others. Consequently, having started a contextual discipleship strategy, respondents revealed that CBCA has developed more than before, with local churches having the autonomy to take initiative, in a mobilization fund locally available for outreach, and "pastors focusing on the Bible in the preaching" (I15KiyCKak [42915-43840]). This "has made the church grow more than it was before" (I32NzuCKab [19949-20006]).

6.3.4 Participants' Suggestions for the Improvement of Missions

During face-to-face interviews and discussions in the focus groups, participants suggested what needed to be improved in terms of missions for their church in the context of war. The analysis of their suggestions led to the identifications of themes presented with their scores as indicated in table 8 and table 9.

Table 8: Face to face participants' suggestions for improvements for effective church missions in the context of war

Face-to-face interview participants' suggestions for effective church missions	Score	%
Improve evangelism	7	17.9
To promote love	2	5.1
Pastors should invest in teaching the church members to avoid members' involvement in war	2	4.7
Prayer	2	4.7
Mutual support from different churches in the region	2	4.7
To increase teachings on love, unity, peace and reconciliation	2	4.7
The church should work with and be the adviser for people in politics	2	4.7
The church should come back and promote theological education for illiterate people who feel called to ministry at the same level as theological education to French-speaking people	1	2.3
There is a need for a mission committee at every local church level	1	2.3
Pastors need more training	3	7.0
Access to financial resources to fund church missions	1	2.3
Work to abolish ethnic barriers within the church to be able to plant churches in many provinces	2	4.7
Improve the giving toward missions	3	7.0
Train children and youth	1	2.3
The church to invest in teaching of the word of God during war	3	7.0

The church to involve its members in income generative activities	1	2.3
CBCA is to integrate other ethnic groups into the church leadership	3	7.0
Church building	1	2.3
Pastors' well-being to be improved	1	2.3
The church missions should invest in equipping natives for missions	1	2.3
Discipleship	1	2.3
More pastors to spread the mission of God are needed	1	2.3
Total score	**43**	**100.0**

From table 8, it appears that evangelism was suggested to be improved with the highest score (score seven). This suggestion is followed by three needs, all with score three: pastors' need for more training, improving the giving toward missions, and the need for the church to invest in teaching the word of God during war.

Table 9: FGD participants' suggestions for improvements for effective church missions in the context of war

FGD participants' suggestion for effective church missions	Score	%
Promote teaching on love	3	15.8
Promote Christian involvement into politics	1	5.3
Improving missionary service	2	10.5
Promote the theological education	3	15.8
We need missionary support projects	1	5.3
Improve discipleship teachings	4	21.1
Increase evangelism occasions	1	5.3
New ways of evangelism	2	10.5
The church to assist churches in war zones	1	5.3
Patriotic teachings need to be taught in church	1	5.3
Total score	**19**	**100.0**

From table 9 it is evident that participants in group discussions suggested that the church improves discipleship teaching with the highest score (score four) followed by the need to promote theological education (score three) and promote teaching on love (score three).

Taken together, it appears from the tables that a few suggestions were shared, which means they might be the priority regardless of score given to each. There is also an inter-connection between a certain number of suggestions. Therefore, the following insight can be drawn from the above information.

First, to improve evangelism. Because of the war context, "pastors abandoned going out for the gospel, thus the church outreach has gone down" (I11BakCBut [12809–13071]), there is need to increase evangelism occasions in addition to crusades done during baptism festivals (FGDMenBu [14189–14524]) and to initiate new ways of evangelism, for example, "through developing community projects for income-generating activities" (FGDWomenBu [16339–16420]) and the like.

Second, the need to invest in discipleship. Participants complained that "discipleship program is not given enough time" (FGDMenBu [14742–15174]) and therefore called for an increase of discipleship-oriented teachings (FGDMenBu [14742–15174]). This is supported by the pastors' call for the church to invest in teaching the word of God in a contextual way during the war (I17WayCKak [20015–21016]) as they address current issues related to their context.

Third, the place of theological education. Participants called for "an increase of pastors to meet the needs of new church plants especially for the interior" (40JohCBu [20973–21386]). While one participant expressed the "need to streamline the theological education program" ([17313–17495]) women presented the need for "women as well who are in need to have a proper foundation in the Bible" (FDGWomenBut [17506–17569]). A retired pastor pictured CBCA with a majority of its members being illiterate or with a poor level of education among whom are people with a genuine call to missions. According to him, CBCA is no longer accommodating people who only know to write and teach Kiswahili in the existing Bible school. He then suggested that the church should come back and promote theological education of this category of people alongside the existing program (cf. I38MuvCVi [12994–13758]). This is a call to develop either Oral Bible Schools and informal theological education in addition to improving the existing theological training that has to be able to teach theology in context.

Finally, the church to contribute financially towards missions. According to respondents, "church members should be led to exercise giving because evangelism requires money" (I12VinCKak [20945–21029]). However, this can only work if the church has a missionary support system, which also calls for a mission strategy.

6.4 Church Position on War

The results indicate that war has negatively affected the position of the church concerning the nature of missions as a result of war. Although the church did maintain the nonviolence position as the majority position, the war's effect on the local church's position determined its involvement in war with implications for its survival.

6.4.1 Church Position on War before the War

Before the war, the church's position was mostly that of the nonviolence theory of war. Table 10 presents the respondents' views on their church's position during that period.

Table 10: Church's position on war before the war

Theological position on war before the war	Yes	No	Total
Christians should be involved in war for a just cause and attack the enemy for the right reason.	1	13	14
Christian should respond to war with a peaceful attitude and not enroll in the military.	6	8	14
Christians should be involved in holy wars.	0	14	14
Christians should respond to war with non-violence.	14	0	14

It is evident from table 10 that one out for the fourteen pastors who served the church before the war supported the view that Christians should be involved in war for a just cause and attack the enemy with the right intention. Six out of fourteen pastors said their church's position was that Christians should respond to war with a peaceful attitude and not enroll in the military. None of the respondents supported the view that Christians should be involved in holy wars, and all the fourteen pastors said their church supported the view that Christians should adopt a nonviolence approach to war.

The following reasons were given for the views in favor of why they answered "yes" to the positions described above:

1. The respondent who supported the first position argued that "the Bible says whoever kills with a sword will die by a sword" (I30BihCKab [21325-21411]).
2. For the second position, supporters of this position argued that "the Christian must defend his homeland in a peaceful way denouncing evil" (I37KilCBa [13584-13980]). However, holding that position, a majority of them still maintained a possibility for a Christian to enroll in the army arguing that "even many biblical characters such as David were in the army but served following God's will, and that even in their time whoever joined the army for himself did not come back alive" (I30BihCKab [21495-21773,19MbaCKak [16493-16606]). With this position, therefore, the church did not support the pacifism theory, which denies believers the freedom to join the army.
3. To the position of holy wars, the majority of pastors either laughed before they said "no" or said, "no" with a categorical emphasis arguing "there's no holy war, all wars are evil" (I38MuvCVi [15522-15660]).
4. For the last position, a majority of respondents argued for nonviolence attitude and prayer as the only Christian response to war. Using Ephesians 6:12 some of them could say, "You know scripture tells us that our fight is not against blood and flesh, we cannot involve such business because Jesus Christ fights and wins for us" (I25MatCKab [17718-18089]). "The church knew their work was to pray and that of the government was to protect and defend its citizens" (I37KilCBa [15394-15777]).

6.4.2 The Church's Position on War during the War

Contrary to the period before the war when the large majority in the church support nonviolence theory, the church's position on war during the war changed as follows. Out of twenty-five respondents, one did not support nonviolence (4 percent), six (24 percent) supported the just war position, thirteen (52 percent) supported the pacifist position, and two (8 percent) supported the holy wars position, as shown in table 11.

Table 11: Church's position on war during the war

Theological position during war	Yes	No	Total
Christians should be involved in war for a just cause and attack the enemy for a rightful intention	6	19	25
Christian should respond to war with a peaceful attitude and not enroll in military	13	12	25
Christians should be involved in holy wars	2	23	25
Christians should respond to war with nonviolence	24	1	25

The following reasons were given by respondents for their respective positions on war.

The just war position

Those who supported the position that Christians should be involved in war for a just cause and attack the enemy for a rightful intention were motivated by the desire to see the war come to an end: "having suffered a lot, they wanted that war to come to an end. There were some Christians who left to go and fight against the machinery" (I10KamCBut [24885-25096]). It appears that the church as a denomination did not shift to this position, which was held at local church level as an effect of war. That is why one respondent said, "CBCA in the whole nation, during the entire war we never taught people on how to take weapons into their hands or it's time to use weapons" (I20MweCBa [28808-29122]), while another laughed and said, "that issue, me when I talk about it, saying the Christian shouldn't attack his fellow Christians but he must attack considering the state of war if he wants to save their life, but it is not good" (I24MunCBa [22490-22685]). The local churches' support of this position led those churches to agree with ethnic militiamen who, for them, "really seemed to be the men who people needed at that time" (I4KavCBi [22905-23458]) against the rebels who were backed by foreign forces.

Pacifist position

According to some pastors whose churches supported the pacifist position, "the church had but one position, to continue with prayer, and church members were spending their daily time in prayer asking God to do something for the enemies" (I10KamCBut [27929-28044]). Some of them "were teaching that if you enroll in the army you are like having two tendencies: if you are in the church and you also go and be incised for military militia recruitment you ran the risk of being killed with a bullet" (I20MweCBa [29334-29630]), portraying, therefore, the joining of the army or militia or rebel group as evil. However, a group of pastors among them, though not supportive of Christian enrollment into the military, indirectly cautioned their youth to join the militia for a while and fight to defend their country against occupation arguing that "they fought the war as civilians . . . they had no gun . . . they used machetes or arrows, that happened in here in Congo" (I10KamCBut [26763-27765]). Although the church did not allow them to do so officially, the attitude of the pastor implies that he approves of taking up arms in some conditions.

Christians should be involved in holy wars

The reason one of the three respondents gave why Christians should become involved in a holy war is that "whenever the Christian finds that his freedom is in danger, he must commit himself directly to fight for it" (I4KavCBi [25138-25313]). This explains the attitude of the second respondent who, proudly could say "that they did, indeed they fought [laughs]" (I10KamCBut [26130-26193]). Curiously it is the same person who partly supported pacifism. It, therefore, appears that some church leaders agreed that one could join the militia for patriotic reasons although they did not have theological support for their position. This illustrates the inner conflicts and contradictions that war fosters within church leaders and in their theologies. Therefore, it is the role of the church to guide its leaders towards consistency and a commitment to the virtues in a state of war.

Nonviolence position

Of the respondents, 96 percent supported the nonviolence view. Among them, we can categorize five groups based on the reasons given for their position. The first group is that of pastors who believed in the transformation of the gospel message which shows the Christian distinctiveness, "in war and during peace, because of the life that has changed" (I6SyaCVi [36317–36984]). Therefore, "because of the love of God for them in John 3:16, Christians are to love the enemy . . . showing people the Spirit of forgiveness and grace" (I18KasCBut [16889–17419]).

The second group is pastors who believed in prayer as the Christian response to the war in search for peace (cf. IKunCBu [22345–22823]). Supporting their position with Romans 12:19 – "Do not take revenge, leave room for God's wrath, for it is written: 'It is mine to avenge; I will repay,' says the Lord" – they said, "mission is not putting people in the military but to preach the word of God for people to get saved" (I15KiyCKak [46562–47395]). "This stand for searching for peace through prayer required the Christian not to have had a side they were supporting" (I42KunCBu [17745–18192]).

For the third category, the war created one local church (4.1 percent of the respondents) that was heaven oriented. There is no need to fight back because "people who were killed and buried with the hope to see them in heaven" (I3LiCBi [24717–25191]). It seems that for this view members had to endure ill-treatment for heaven's sake.

The fourth category is that of the church that supported nonviolence as part of the wars, stating that their church activities mattered. Consequently, "any reaction to the war that favors the gospel was commendable" (I4KavCBir [25791–26208]). The fact that this comes from the same primary source supporting the militia as a means to revenge against the enemy makes the researcher think that the true position of that church under the leadership of the interviewed pastor supported the just war.

The last category (25 percent) is that of pastors who supported the nonviolence position while allowing freedom to believers to join the national army. A church in this category could show kindness "to soldiers returning from the battlefield by providing water and food for them" (I13KiwCBut [22341–22600]). The churches that held this position also argued "against church members joining rebel forces because they were tribal oriented" (I33BalCBu [32008–32613]) and "pastors feared to be seen as advocating for Satan" (I29KaiCKab [30848–31196]).

6.5 Summary

6.5.1 Experience of Church Leaders Involved in Church Missions during the War

The experience of war is an account of God going into mission with the church and taking care of both the task of missions and the missionaries as they respond to the missionary mandate of the church in context. Synthesized stories of Christian leaders presented the context of war as the world in which they lived an ordinary life, exposed to the same challenges and risks like everyone else but committed to their task that was informed by their experience and the context of war. The secret of their surviving the ill-treatment and suffering in their ministry was perseverance shaped by the experiences of their predecessors (i.e. others who suffered before them) in the context of war. The survival of the church is, therefore, a story of the reconstruction of church's missions on the basis of the experience of perseverance of Christian leaders in serving God in the context of war as the church exercised its love for God and the poor.

The experience of war caused Christian leaders to adjust church activities and led some pastors to adopt a different lifestyle such as becoming bi-vocational. This meant that, while continuing to take full responsibility for their ministry, they also became involved in another job that provided some income to enable them to continue their ministry and afford the subsistence of their families in the context of CBCA lacking a mission strategy and consequently missionary support strategies. The experience of war also informed the leaders' translatability of the Christian message in context. Therefore, during suffering, they would preach a God present in the midst of the turmoil of his people.

From the stories of Christian leaders, this research identified that the experience of war affects church members' commitment to church life and, therefore, their church ownership. It is then during the war period that the CBCA church made room for committed lay members, committed to EVARES (Evangelist in Charge), who were allowed to pastor chapels and setting some church ordinances.

Christian leaders did experience suffering in relation to missions in the context of war. Some of them witnessed the murder of their colleagues, others exposed their lives trying to free their falsely accused church members and still others suffered the pain of a ministry that impacted discipleship, which was hard to measure in a context where the same people could enroll in the militia or rebel groups or the like. The pastors' family and his church members encountered serious suffering as well as displacement and the seeking of refuge when looted (the so-called "ramping"), the experience of death, poverty, food scarcity and famine at the family level.

Women and children were the most affected. Women suffered sexual violence and rape, and children's education was adversely affected by war. The latter caused widows and orphans to increase, separation from parents, increased killing of other women and children and many marriages were adversely affected by either the absence of the husband or ethnic separation, and women with family responsibilities were abandoned and left at the mercy of their assailants.

The shock caused by what a minister calls a failure in discipleship in a context of war (I13KiwCBut [15892–16437]) and believers who continue to believe that God exists beyond their experience of rape and pain (see FGDWomenKab) captured the interest of the researcher. He was led to conclude that discipleship in the context of war stretched beyond pains and suffering, and beyond joy and peace.

6.5.2 The Effect of the Experience of War on the Understanding of the Church's Missions

Before the war, the majority of respondents knew missions as "spreading the good news," but the war changed that perception into a very contextual understanding that included missions being a very difficult task. It required church members to be mobilized for it; mission became reconciliation, and mission being a war for peace, unity, comfort and hope to people. In addition, church mission was understood as difficult because not only did some pastors deny mission by being involved in the war, but also because they denied the need for it to be purpose-oriented in the context of war. The church being the problem solver become diakonia, but the task of missions is on discipleship and being holistic. That holistic and contextual aspect of missions highlights the idea of a contextual theology of missions.

Changes in the understanding of missions mostly comprise of effects on the church's missional practices – the experience of war informed the strategies of discipleship with the teaching focus becoming on hope and addressing current contextual issues such as peace and unity, among others. It had a negative effect because it hindered initiatives and creativity of church leaders who exercised a routine implementation of church life. Hence, participants suggested four major areas of improvement for the church to be effective in its missions in the context of war, which are: evangelism, discipleship, theological education and the church's financial contribution towards missions.

6.5.3 The Church's Position on War before and during the War

It was found that across the two periods, CBCA has maintained the nonviolence position concerning war. However, the war affected the position of the church negatively to some extent. The local church's position on the war changed 4 percent from 100 percent during the war and support for a just war position moved from 7.1 percent before the war to 24 percent during the war; the pacifist position changed from 42.8 percent before the war to 52 percent during the war; and the position favoring holy wars from 0 percent before the war to 8 percent during the war.

Churches supporting the just war position supported the position with the last part of a message from Mathew 26:52 that says: "for all who draw the sword will die by the sword." The text was also used to support revenge against the enemy. Based on the misunderstanding of this text, this group supported militia groups such as the Mayi-Mayi who has been heavily involved in witchcraft. Results reveal that of the 52 percent of respondents who supported the pacifist position, a few of them used Ephesians 6:12 to say "our fight is not against blood and flesh" (I25MatCKab [17718–18089]) and that during war Christians have to play a role in praying for the war to end (see I2LukCBi [24463–24744]). This group supported the view that it was the government's task to protect its citizens (I37KilCBa [15394–15777]) but did not support believers' enrollment into the militia.

Although the Christian leaders who supported the holy wars did not have any theological foundation for it, they did have a political one. The major reason being that whenever freedom is threatened one should fight for it (I4KavCBi [25138–25313]). This is the self-defense argument, either armed or non-armed. Self-defense has to be legal and any possession of a gun should be legal; but in the context of Eastern Congo the possession of guns by civilians is dangerous because of the ethnic character of the wars in the region. And, unfortunately, the crisis in leadership and governance favored the existence of armed self-defense groups.

The researcher identified groups among the 96 percent of respondents supporting a nonviolence position. The first group took the side of non-involvement in politics and argued that Christian transformation leads to a spirit of forgiveness. The second group pointed to prayer as the Christian response to the search for peace and used Romans 12:19 to reject vengeance. The third group, being heaven oriented, did not allow people to fight back. The fourth group cared about missions no matter what position is taken about war. The last group left room and freedom for individual believers to join the military. However, the same group did not allow their members to join the rebellion and militia forces because of protecting the testimony of the church in the context of war. Therefore, the study concludes that the experience of war affected the church's position on war and that CBCA as a denomination was unaware of the decline of the local church's stand on war. Consequently, there are churches supporting positions that led them to get involved in war or to encourage others' involvement in the war.

6.5.4 Church's Survival during War from the View of Respondents

From the perspective of the respondents, God himself is responsible for the survival of their churches and community life. The research, however, links the survival of the church to the following points: (1) during war, eschatological hope contributed to keeping church attendance and the commitment of both Christian leaders and believers; (2) some churches survived by moving from very insecure to less insecure zones; (3) focus on discipleship in context contributed to survival to the extent that their growth was a measure not of suffering or prosperity, per se, but because of God's presence in the midst of their suffering; (4) pastors' and individual involvement in war contributed to the survival of some churches; and (5) churches survived the war because their Christian leaders were politically neutral and preached peace, unity and justice, therefore, being the reason that members of different ethnic groups identified with their own church.

Some of these churches mobilized their members for Upendo (love), Likelemba (collective effort) and promoted fellowship at both individual and community levels. In short, the survival of the church in Eastern Congo during the war depended on both positive and negative factors. On the one hand, there were churches that decided to remain focused and disciple its members in context. On the other hand, there were churches that survived because of their involvement in the war.

6.5.5 Survival of the Church during War

Looking at participants' views on how the church survived the war, the experience of its survival in the context of displacement and lessons learned by Christian leaders from their experience opens room for a contextual approach to church survival during war.

Some church leaders' view of their church survival

During focus group discussions the researcher asked participants how their church did survive the war. In this section, he describes the various views of participants of the survival of the eastern Congolese church.

From the respondents' views, "God himself took care of the church during the war, the Word of God practiced by church members as preached upheld believers of the church and therefore made it strong" (FGDMenBir [8837-9281]). The idea of the survival of the church does not seem to lie in the effort of the minister, but is rooted in God's desire to survive and sustain the church. That is why a respondent said, "many things that we learned during the war show that God is together with us and that he is just so powerful" (FGDMenBir [8517-8814]). Thus, while the war continued, church missions also continued because as God was teaching the workers in the church that they were not responsible for its survival but responsible for teaching the church to abide in the word of God. Therefore, "applying God's word just like the early church practiced it, allowed them to be part of the story of God in their context" (FGDMenBir [8517-8814]) having discovered "they could hardly survive as a church without God" (FGDMenBir [8288-8507]). The seminars to provide hope to people were actually to demonstrate to church members that God was with them in the midst of suffering, and so they did not have to fear (FGDMen Kak[2370-3578]) and the word was used in the church's effort to unite people from different ethnic groups involved in conflicts (see FGDMenBir [9292-9509]).

The researcher has also identified that, in the case of CBCA, eschatological hope contributed to the church's perseverance. It is in such context of trial and violence that Jesus repeatedly calls believers to persevere in their hope as he addresses the seven churches in Revelation: "to him who overcomes . . ." (Rev 2–3). To the question, "Don't you think that the gospel has space because people fear death and eternity?" one pastor answered:

> Of course I do, because it's a good thing to think about that. If we live without thinking about what will come after death, then we are like we are not alive. So what'll come tomorrow it's what makes us prepared to confront life today. So eschatology has its place, because if I know that Jesus is coming back tomorrow so I have to live in consequence. But if I know he will not come back then I will live as I want [laughs]. (I4KavCBi [26312-27155])

In the same vein, the second pastor said that "whenever there is war, pastors should wake up and preach the gospel otherwise many people will be lost forever" (I6SyaCVi [37119-37417]). Consequently, during war people think about death and heaven and therefore are ready to listen and give their lives to Christ. This explains the increase in church attendance (FGDWomenVir [7793-8882]).

Church ownership by its members helped the church to survive as an institution especially in the context of displacement in which members identified themselves with their denomination. That is why churches like Kahunga and Kabati also moved and transplanted in Kiwanja and Bwalanda respectively with their members and pastors (I11BakCBut [11333-11790]; FGDWomenKab [4398-4694]). Members could "sacrifice anything they had to access a place to build a sanctuary there" (FGDMenKab [6178-6730]) in the context of IDPs due to that ownership.

For the church to survive as a local community, members had to remain neutral and some of them had to "decline to join political meetings and prayed to God to keep them from falling into this trap" (FGDMenKak [13976-14547]) of tribalism. Tribalism is the value behind leading ethnic politics and led the church members to unite as a community of believers worthy of the gospel and not as belonging to an ethnic group. However, in some cases, ethnic membership did spare some churches from destruction by an ethnic militia. This was due to the fact that whenever people fled, some who were of the ethnic group leading the rebellion would remain behind and continue their church life (see FGDMenBam [8152-8765]). A research participant said, "if the church would have been of one tribe it would be finished . . . people were sharing information from their ethnic groups and would tell brothers from the other ethnic group to hide or leave" (FGDWomenVir [6115–6715]).

To the question, "People say that the church sometimes survived due to ethnic grouping. Do you think the same applied to your church?" respondents from Bunia said, "it is not all the churches in their area under the Hema militia which had Hema people that secured them, but some did survive" (FGDMenBu [17286–17978]). However, "the survival of the church lies in God's hand who cares about the church" (FGDMenBu [17286–17978]). The only strength of ethnicity that came from the group discussion was "diversity which helps people to understand the gospel as members of the same community of faith helps interpret scriptures and bridging the message into their cultures through their tongues" (FGDWomenBu [18157–18403]).

Displacements and church's survival

Apart from the few churches such as CBCA Kabati and CBCA Kahunga whose members moved with the pastors and established themselves in the new areas (FGDMenKab [6178–6730]; I11BakCBut, p5), there were many CBCA church members from local churches who experienced the displacement and migration whether within or outside the region. The "deposit of the word of God in their hearts sustained their faith wherever they went" (FGDWomenBir [8475–8806]). Some could gather other IDPs and establish a fellowship or church for IDPs in case they fled with a pastor (see FGDMenKak [17213–17452]). This was the case for an ordained pastor who found himself with many believers in an IDP camp and he planted an IDP church that he "pastored for seven months because CBCA regional administration encouraged a church not to mix with another church" (FGDMenKak [17855–18680]). Such cases of transplanting a church might not have helped the churches in the city to interact with the migrant believers and "both call the local church to new ways of being church."[8] However, other respondents "fellowshipped with existing CBCA churches as they were welcomed and hosted by believers from those localities" (FGDMenButur [8598–8803]).

---

8. Bevans, "Themes and Questions," 13.

CHAPTER 7

Toward an Understanding of Church and Mission in the Context of War

7.1 Introduction

This chapter attempts to discuss and critique the church's understanding of the church and mission. It incorporates experiential, biblical and theological perspectives that are based on the experience of the eastern Congolese church and on what can be learned from the Bible regarding a Christian response to church, violence and war. By addressing the implications of the church's encounter with war for this study, this chapter also discusses the tensions between local theologies of missions, biblical perspectives on being the church in the context of violence and war and selected contemporary missiological models. In the process of integrating the local experience with the biblical and theoretical models of missions, it will be argued that the local experience of church missions in the war context corresponds to a large degree with the biblical theology of missions and war.

7.2 The Experience of Missions in Eastern Congo and the Biblical Perspectives on the Response to Violence and War

7.2.1 Tensions between the Local Missiologies and Matthew 5:38-45

In light of Matthew 5:38-45, which presents the biblical non-retaliation command and the law of love for the enemy, some tensions appear between local theologies of missions and war based on the church's experiences and biblical models themselves. First, it was found that, rather than responding to violence with non-retaliation and love from the perspective of the OT and NT, believers (pastors and members) responded to war with silence and acceptance of the violence. The powerless believers and pastors were not in a position to fight back against the armed enemies; they, in other words, passively accepted the violence and with resignation. For example, one woman (FGDWomenKab) who was raped found it hard to forgive the enemy who committed the act but nevertheless prayed for him; the pastor who had his leg and hand broken by rebels and the national armed force soldiers continued serving God with a strength hidden in the eschatological hope that his predecessors, who went through the same violence in that same zone, also had (I32NzuCKab [12069-14108]). They also "succeeded to persevere through the experiences they underwent because they were heavenly bound" (FGDWomenBut [16105-16338]). Thus, the local theology might have been the reason that 7.1 percent of the interviewed CBCA churches did not encourage their youth to join the militia or rebel group to fight the foreign oppression (see FGDMenBir [1855-2136]).

It is no wonder that local theologies reflect diverse opinions about responses to violence and mistreatment of enemies in the warzone, and why Christian leaders shifted their understanding of church missions as a good and enjoyable work to one of being a very difficult task. Although the enemy was a foreigner, sometimes the enemy was the church members who planned to kill their pastor because he was from an unwanted ethnic group (see interview I24MunCBa, p11). Sometimes it was the government militaries who were supposed to protect the community that actually mistreated them (see I32NzuCKab [12069-14108]). Other Christian leaders refused to fight back and, instead, choose to use their pulpits for teaching unity, love, peace and reconciliation (cf. tables 5, 6 and 7).

In agreement with the biblical teaching on non-retaliation (Matt 5:38–42) and the law of love in both the OT and the NT (Lev 19:18; Matt 5:43–45), Christian leaders in Eastern Congo understood that, in the context of ethnicity, teaching on love, unity and reconciliation as the way to respond to violence constitutes a theology of peace. While they themselves were subjected to violence, they used the only option left open for their church members, namely, to advocate for peace. In situations where the pastor's enemies were church members, such teachings were the demonstration of love for the enemy and evidence of their eschatological hope.

A second tension between local theologies and the teachings of Jesus in Matthew 5:38–45 was found in the reaction of those Christian leaders and church members who, after identifying the oppressors as foreigners and witnessing the suffering they had caused, encouraged their members who joined militia to fight back, either out of patriotic consideration to the country (cf. I24MunCBa [22490-22685]) or to avenge the killing of their family members (see I10KamCBut [24885-25096]). Pastors from this group were then supportive of militia groups such as the Mayi-Mayi, who would use witchcraft against the enemy (the rebels and their backing armed forces) simply because "they were considered and seen as the people needed for responding to the enemy" (I4KavCBi [22905-23458]). These pastors then, believed in the power of witchcraft even while they preached the gospel message of Christ.

It should be obvious that these views and practices clearly conflict with the love command in the Bible (Matt 5:45) – "an expression of love and forgiveness which goes to the extent of embracing our enemies."[1] The biblical model of non-retaliation and love for the enemy "is possible to those who are Spirit led," thus wholly opposed to local theologies building trust in witchcraft as a means to resist the enemy.[2] Curiously, while doing so, church leaders still support the nonviolent approach (96 percent) and pacifism approach (24 percent) to war. The reason is that their belief in the power of traditional forces is an individual matter to them, and it conflicts with their biblical stance on violence. Although held by a few pastors, this kind of local theology is not only dangerous, it also contradicts the non-retaliation command of scripture. In different words, it indirectly supports retaliation; individuals

---

1. Upham, "Forgiveness," 278.
2. Upham, 278.

are not fighting their enemies, but the church encouraged members to join forces seeking revenge while they, at the same time, promote syncretic beliefs. Furthermore, the church is exposed to the danger of pastors who appear as the main communicators of the gospel message while communicating these beliefs "as an integral aspect of the message and cause a syncretistic inclusion of it as cultural heritage."[3] This is nothing but a hindrance to the proper transmission of the gospel and the church's mission during war.

The last conflictual theology is held by pastors who had guns in their houses and partnered with the militia to fight back in case of an attack by the enemy (e.g. the five pastors in interview I15KiyCkak). In the context of Eastern Congo, hiding guns to a certain extent denoted secret membership of either a militia group or a rebels' movement. Their local theology is rooted in the belief that God only helps those who help themselves (see I15KiyCKak [40262–41370]). This belief allows the individual the right to retaliate in case of an assault by the person they assume to be an enemy. But it is also possible that these church leaders may have opted to retaliate because they have ceased to believe in God's power – "his ability to do what he will."[4] Waiting a long time for the war to end, they may have concluded that God was absent from the war context and, therefore, decided to act contrary to Jesus's command about not fighting your enemy.

7.2.2 Tensions between the Local Missiologies and Acts 18:1–4

Both the eastern Congolese church and the Corinthian church in Acts 18:2 are examples of the "temporary establishment"[5] among migrant refugees and IDPs. However, while the Corinthian church comprised of migrant believers, victims of identity conflicts (e.g. the Jewish Christian couple banished from Rome) and believers not affected by the conflict (e.g. Paul, a Roman citizen reaching out to multicultural communities), the eastern Congolese church developed understandings of missions that is conflicted in some respects with the biblical example. Rather than planting churches in a migrant context, the church in Eastern Congo used a transplanted church or migrant church

---

3. Hesselgrave and Rommen, *Contextualization*, 1.
4. Grudem, *Systematic Theology*, 222.
5. Culy and Parson, *Acts*, 344.

as a church planting model. In some cases, due to insecurity and war, local churches relocated from insecure to less insecure zones with their pastor and members. In other cases, members of the same church denomination gathered in IDPs' camps and formed a fellowship as CBCA churches, especially with some "CBCA administrative leaders' ideal of a migrant church not to merge into another church" (FGDMenKak [17855–18680]). This model of the relocation of a church is, therefore, a more denominational oriented model. Its weakness is that, in the context of ethnic wars, the transplanting church may not allow the church to become multiethnic, as the migrants and the host community may prefer.

Paul and Priscilla and Aquila used their craft as tentmakers to survive as missionaries (Acts 18:3) because they benefited from their "Jewish custom which encouraged children to be taught some trade"[6] and also the "Jewish law which required classes on trade to theological students."[7] In contrast to the Corinthian church, the church in Eastern Congo seemed not have a theology of ministerial survival. That is why a respondent recommended that "pastors' well-being should be improved" (see table 8) and four pastors called for the "improvement of the giving toward missions" and an "access to financial resources to fund church missions" (see table 8). However, from their experience of war, some local churches incorporated the youth mentorship process (e.g. the so-called "juniors," "cadettes," and the "scout movement") to teach young people professional skills in addition to basic education (see I10KamCBut [10534–10945]). In addition to preparing the youth for bi-vocational living in the context of war with its vicious circle of poverty, food scarcity and hunger, professional training prevented youth recruitment into militia and rebel movements.

Acts 18:1–9 presents a scenario whereby the host family (Priscila and Aquila) also benefited from Paul as they engaged in missionary work in their own country. This scenario fits the context of the Eastern Congo which has experienced repeated migration movements inside the country. This may suggest welcoming fellow workers as an avenue for missions or a missional

---

6. Schaff, *Lange's Commentary*, 835.
7. Gaebelein, *John-Acts*, 480.

practice[8] rather than waiting for the government or the church head office to provide support to incoming IDPs.

Finally, the example of the Corinthian church in Acts 18 highlights that (scenario); while the Christian leaders regularly discussed (διελέγομαι) the message with both Jews and Gentiles in public, it was also a meeting place for social groups, a place where "people with the various trades sat together."[9] In Eastern Congo, while church leaders were restricted to one-on-one evangelism due to ethnic barriers, especially because of the fear of being stigmatized as in support of a particular group, they limited themselves to share the gospel through sermons in their church building. They made use of the vulnerable state of the people – being poor, hungry, heartbroken, often facing death and lacking hope – and their hunger to hear God's word. It brought believers and non-believers to the church and so served as an opportunity for missions.

However, it is unlikely that in a situation of ethnic conflict as, for example, at Bunia, people from other ethnic groups would attend church, even though they had the desire to hear the message of hope. But for CBCA local churches around Goma, there were at least two leading ethnic groups in the area – Hutu and Nande – involved in the wars in various ways since the 1990s[10] and also represented in every church. In such case the pulpit, then, can be seen as a safe opportunity for Christian leaders to argue for unity, peace, justice and reconciliation while making the local church a peace and justice cell (JPIC) affecting the entire community.

7.2.3 Tensions between the Local Missiologies and Hebrews 10:32–34

Theological responses to ill-treatment

The biblical perspective on a Christian response to ill-treatment in light of Hebrews 10:32–34 assimilates the many conflicts and sufferings that believers endure to "the singular self-sacrifice of Jesus, whom God made perfect through 'sufferings,'"[11] which he quietly endured. Like, Jesus, the Jewish believers, permanently exposed to suffering and public persecution "had stood

---

8. See Minatrea, *Shaped by God's Heart*, 184–95.
9. Williams, *New International Biblical Commentary*, 314.
10. Cf. Stearns, *North Kivu*, 27.
11. Heil, *Hebrews*, 2993.

by those who were publicly humiliated and have sympathized with those in prison."[12] Different to non-retaliation that suggests that vengeance should be left to God who will make enemies "to reap what they have sown"[13] but leaves room for the government to punish people for their wrongdoing (see Rom 13:4), this model suggests enduring the pain in silence as Jesus did on the cross.

Similarly, silence is the local theological response to ill-treatment from the leaders and believers' experience of violence during the war. This theology of silence, although not in contradiction with the biblical response in Hebrews 10:32–34, is rooted in the fact that the powerless believers concluded that God is silent during the war and the injustice supported by a non-responsible government whose soldiers are sometimes the oppressors. Taking the example of rape, which was a common practice in war zones, women revealed that rape was an epidemic threat in war and that reporting the people who raped a relative could bring insecurity because those accused of rape were often released, even without being sentenced by the government (cf. FGDWomenBut [11719–12162]).

In their context, the enemies had a gun and could not be fought by a powerless woman believer, and whenever they cried to God, he was silent and did not miraculously rescue them, although some were, miraculously, not raped and only beaten (see I15KiyCKak [32425–32730]). As Barbara Taylor suggests, the silence of God has not been interpreted on the ground as the inactivity of God or his retirement.[14] She interprets the death of Christ as "three days of complete quiet, after which the word rose to break the silence and once again his voice was heard and commissioned disciples to make disciples, teach and proclaim."[15] By contrast, the eastern Congolese Christians did not believe that God was dead, but rather that he is alive but silent. This explains why a woman chose to pray during the act of her rape, asking Jesus to help her (see FGDWomenKab, 4); she even believed that although God did not do a miracle for her, he kept her alive. While Schaeffer argued that, before

---

12. Kassa, "Hebrews," 1530.
13. Chianeque and Ngewa, "Deuteronomy," 252.
14. Taylor, *When God Is Silent*, 43–82.
15. Taylor, 47.

the wars, "the infinite-personal God is there but also he is not silent,"[16] this woman believed that God was there but was acting in his silence. Therefore, in addition to the Bible that encourages responding to mistreatment with a no-retaliation attitude and leaving it to God to punish at the last judgment and to the government to recompense each citizen according to their wrongdoing, this local theology is one of the responses to today's gospel of prosperity in the DRC. In sum, the experiences of war highlight the insight that God is present during tough times and that a silent response of God to the cries of Christians does not diminish the reality of his presence or our personal relationship with God.

Strength of belief in the incarnate God during suffering

Throughout the OT (e.g. Exod 15, Deut 20, Josh) and the NT, "God is presented with the character of a warrior who has never sanctified war but whose presence and activity in an evil world has given hope."[17] If so, then Hebrews presents God in his incarnation in the context of suffering and trials (Heb 10:31–32). Believers should not revenge and Hebrews 10:32 uses the contractive conjunction δὲ to encourage them to act with the strength of being in the presence of God.[18] That theology of gaining strength in God incarnated, who suffers persecution with recipient believers, is not in conflict with the local churches model. In reflecting on the group discussions, face-to-face interviews and a synthesis of the church leaders' experience of war, it appears that the pastor is the symbol of God's presence and that his members' comfort not only lies in the encouragement from him but also that "God is present and requires sanctification in such context" (e.g. I6SyaCVi [27565–28820]). The fact that he is present in their sufferings created hope in, and the understanding of who God is.

A few examples may help to understand the implications for a contextualized theology of mission during war. First, during interviews and group discussions the researcher identified that in CBCA the experience of war established a custom: whenever war broke out, the pastor should not be the first to flee, and in most cases, they did not (e.g. I32NzuCKab [11210–11938];

---

16. Schaeffer, *He Is There*, 10.
17. Perdue, "Problem of War," 446.
18. Wallace, *Greek Grmmar*, 671.

I1WabCVi [19106-19653]). Second, most of the churches that migrated were churches that survived because their members fled together with their pastor. For example, the CBCA Kahunga moved from Kahunga to Kiwanja and CBCA Kabati moved from Kabati to Bwalanda in the IDP camp (cf. interviews I12VinCKak and I26NyaCKab). Third, even when a group of displaced people moved without a pastor, they would form a fellowship. The fellowship would call for a pastor to be their leader and it would immediately be accepted as a church. For example, the church in the IDP camp that existed next to the UN camp in Kiwanja had a pastor who was suggested by the region (see FGDMenKak [17855-18680]). Last, lay people who acted as senior pastors whenever a pastor was displaced (see I40JohCbu; I41DavCBu; I40JohCBu [2278-3254]; FGDMenBu [7261-8115]) is additional proof that church members believed God is present through the presence of their pastor sharing their suffering.

Some pastors were victims of murders (e.g. of the pastor murdered during a baptism festival in Buramba [I13KiwCBut]) and others were beaten and abused to the point of being left with physical handicaps (I32NzuCKab [12069-14108]). Yet local church pastors continued church missions in the same context through tasks such as organizing discipleship classes in the so-called "ramping" areas (sleeping in the bush). It is curious to note, for example, that immediately after the murder of the pastor in Buramba, the visiting guest pastor had to take the lead and was the one who ordered church members to flee (see I15KiyCKak [34901-36033]). In another, similar case, an assistant had to immediately take over the responsibility of the pastor (I13KiwCBut [10569-13413]). This confirms, therefore, that the incarnate God is presently sharing the suffering of believers and is also manifested in the image of the Christian leader, specifically the pastor, who silently suffered the same trials and pains, thus building the strength of the believers to endure and persevere as individual members of the community.

Hope in the eschatological blessing

As a response to suffering, Hebrews 10:32-34 calls believers to endure suffering, trial and exposure to risks because of their eschatological hope in an eternal reward, a hope that they will one day dwell in a city built by God (Heb 11:10, 16; 13:14). Perseverance should be nurtured by the believers

(Heb 10:32) using as examples the heroes of faith and through their active participation in the life of the community of faith.

The experience of the church in Eastern Congo conflicts with the nature of the church as a community of believers. On the one hand, believers and unbelievers, refugees and their hosts, rebels and other militias, all meet at church to seek comfort, salvation and the wish to have their physical needs met. As a result, pastors used the opportunity to share the gospel through sermons and to disciple the congregation. On the other hand, for the pastor, whose enemies are part of the church he is pastoring, it may be very hard to rely on the fellowship of church members for comfort in order to endure suffering. The danger of and exposure to suffering in the church (I32NzuCKab [12069–14108]), a lack of experience of war or of a predecessors' experience of mission and suffering from which a new church leader could learn, are also contributing factors hindering the church to act as a genuine community of believers.

The local eschatology, however, converges with the biblical model because church leaders use difficult times as an opportunity for people to come closer to God and seek him (see I6SyaCVi [27565–28820]); pastors "teach and encourage them that the existing trials and sufferings do not nullify Gods' existence" (I6SyaCVi [27565–28820]). Church attendance was not motivated by the desire for eternal reward, but by fear of death which was real and frequent for everyone, including Christian leaders (see I5MulCBi [11645–12104]). This became an avenue for church leaders to use the biblical model calling believers to exercise a life of "sanctification and of understanding Scripture in light of their context" (I6SyaCVi [27565–28820]). This kind of discipleship was confirmed by 16.7 percent of the respondents and messages might have activated boldness to engage missions. One focus group discussion revealed that during war, church attendance increased and that members continue sharing the gospel with an attitude of readiness to sacrifice for the sake of the gospel (see FGDMenKak [6681–7236]). Therefore, rather than pointing to the eternal reward which every believer is promised and called to desire, this local theology uses the fear of death, meaning the fear of eternal damnation, to point people to Christ and his promise of eternal reward to those who persevere in their faith as they endure suffering.

7.3 Missions in Eastern Congo and Contemporary Missiological Models

This section revisits the contextualized understanding and practice of mission in Eastern Congo during a period of war in view of the models inspired or developed by Bosch, Bevans and Escobar.

7.3.1 David Bosch's Emerging Model and *Kenosis* Theology

Addressing mission in a time of testing, Bosch identifies the presence of a crisis of a major proportion consisting of the failure of science, technology and industrialization to address events that have shaken the west to their fundamentals.[19] These include two devastating world wars; Russian and Chinese revolutions; horrors perpetrated by countries committed to communism, nationalism, fascism and capitalism; the increase of the imbalance between the rich and the poor; and ecological disasters among others. He says that, while it was absurd that the Christian theology and mission would remain unhurt by the crisis, the results of many disciplines had a lasting influence on theological thinking and developments within the church theology and mission have had equally far-reaching experiences. Therefore, the church lost its position of privilege, thus an ever-increasing tension between the church and secular authorities has been observed, the missionary became not central but an embarrassment, etc.

In trying to respond to the crisis, the church made a lot of mistakes for which it has to repent and that "repentance has to begin with a bold recognition of the fact the church in mission today faces a world fundamentally different from anything it faced before."[20] Consequently, a new understanding of church mission is needed. Bosch states that as the church is facing "a time of transition, a time for a paradigm shift, a time of crisis during which is the point where danger and opportunity meet."[21]

Addressing missions in that context, Bosch, therefore, advocates an emerging model of mission[22] which has to take into account both the centripetal and centrifugal forces of the paradigm shift which, according to him, "always

---

19. Bosch, *Transforming Mission*, 363–67.
20. Bosch, 366.
21. Bosch, 366.
22. Bosch, 363–67.

include continuity and change, faithfulness to the past and boldness to engage the future, tradition and transformation."[23] The mission of the church has not remained unscathed by the drastic changes the world is experiencing. To this should be added the vulnerability of missions that contributes to "a creative tension, which is a way to help the church begin theologizing meaningfully for our own time."[24]

With this argument, Bosch is advocating for what this chapter calls local theologies or models, which consist of the local understandings of missions in their particular context. These contextualized theologies or models emanate from the local church leaders' experience of and reflection on mission in the context of war as they struggled to connect their church tradition with the future of their ministry. The church leaders in Eastern Congo have maintained that mission was spreading the good news (see tables 1, 2, 3 and 4) but shifted that understanding from being at most "preaching the good news" before the war to a very contextual understanding that includes addressing current issues of Eastern Congo such as the promotion of peace, unity, reconciliation and discipleship in context.

The war generally had a positive effect on the understanding of the identity and functions of pastors. During the war, for example, churches allowed lay people to become pastors when no ordained minister was available. When a pastor was displaced, churches appointed one of their members as their pastor. Such openness for change and transformation was created by the local theology of God incarnated, expressing his participation in our suffering through the presence of the pastor, who represented God as he experienced suffering with them.

However, the eastern Congolese church has also gone in a different direction from Bosch's ideas in some ways. First, while Bosch emphasizes the fact that the church begins theologizing through creative engagement with the tension between the past and the future, continuity and change, constancy and contingency and the like, it was found that in Eastern Congo the experience of war instructed the church leaders and led them to practice new models of missions. But, since the beginning of the war in 1990 to recent years, the CBCA, for example, as a structured church denomination, has not been able to reflect

---

23. Bosch, 366.
24. Bosch, 367.

on or creatively think and theologize about missions in its context. It is one reason why the church lacks a mission strategy[25] and why church leaders identified a lack of a missions' support strategy (FGDWomenVir [16571–16824]).

Second, looking at the nature of missions before and during the war, it also appears that maintenance of traditions has successfully helped church leaders to organize church missions and that, although committed to engaging with missions, the church has not been consistent in addressing the need for missions nor does it have a contingency plan for churches related to the war context. For example, before and during the war, churches have been committed to sharing the gospel through sermons – with 78 percent and 100 percent of pastors using sermons before and during the war, respectively. The culture of using baptism festivals to organize crusades also covers the two periods, the only difference being that during war, the church introduced the approach of the mega crusade. Sending short-term mission teams has not been dynamic but followed the custom of sending teams of choirs and evangelists to help in crusades during baptism or in the process of planting new chapels. The one-on-one sharing of the gospel was not seen as the responsibility of church members in general or that of the pastors (cf. I15KiyCKak [6046–6269]), but rather of church elders and evangelistic teams (see I14MuhCKak [5233–5280]). Had it been seen as part of the normal lifestyle of believers to share the gospel one-on-one, it might have been less risky for them to do so during the war, especially if based on friendship. Unfortunately, the church generally persisted with a tradition that had a negative effect on its missions.

In summary, comparison between Bosch's idea and the practices of the church in Eastern Congo during war reveals that the local theologies emerging model of mission is in mostly aligning with the local theologies that emanated from the local experience of mission in the context of war. That experience revealed the positive effect of war on the pastors' identity and tasks. However, the church's consistency in addressing missionary needs in context did not take care of Bosch's ideas continuity and change of its traditions and practices as well as boldness to engage the future of mission.

In 1991, Bosch gave a public lecture at Selly Oak, Birmingham, during which he dealt with missions in the context of suffering and social concerns.

---

25. Cf. Ngayihembako and Midiburo, "Communauté Baptiste," 10.

With a reference to the statement Vatican II Pastoral Constitution on the Church in the Modern World saying that "the joy and hope, the grief and anguish of the poor or afflicted of our time, are also the joy and hope, the grief and anguish of the followers of Christ as well," he argued that "we (Christians) are profoundly involved in all pains occurring anywhere in the world."[26] For Bosch, the Christian mission's reply to the crisis is the fact that, "in the suffering Jesus, God embraces the suffering of the world for the sake of humanity."[27] Therefore, he calls the church to *kenosis*, or "self-emptying," demonstrating that Jesus came to the world to give away his life and identify with his followers. He, therefore, argued that Jesus saved us in and through suffering and was left with scars that proved his identity after his resurrection.[28]

On the one hand, *kenosis* theology gives room for the church to address the suffering and afflictions that individual believers are subjected to, and on the other hand, it gives room to the holistic mandate of the church's involvement in social concerns. As Bosch's *kenosis* model states, "the affliction which the missionary is subjected to is closely related to his missions."[29] The pastor in Eastern Congo lived to organize church missionary work in the context of suffering. Some pastors were ill-treated by rebels and government forces while taking care of their flock in the war zone, while others walked through dangerous war zones to reach out to people in villages and cities under the control of militia or rebels (see I15KiyCKak [27732–30484]). The collected stories of the experiences of pastors and leaders during war show that suffering was an integral part of their missionary task.

On the other hand, the *kenosis* model of missions is a call to the church's involvement in social concerns. This idea is supported by Bosch who argues that for "Matthew's Gospel making disciples is inclusive of telling them to exercise the call to doing justice toward the poor."[30] Results from this research have revealed that the experience of war informed the active involvement of the church in Eastern Congo in social concerns. For example, before the war, the church was involved in helping the poor by giving occasional offerings to

---

26. Bosch, *Vulnerability of Mission*, 3.
27. Bosch, 7.
28. Bosch, "Vulnerability of Mission," 356.
29. Bosch, 356; *Vulnerability of Mission*, 8.
30. Bosch, *Transforming Mission*, 81.

orphans, widows and the aged. During the war, when the majority of church members were vulnerable, the church developed a mechanism to help the poorest, such as IDPs and those who were victims of lootings, in a sacrificial way (see FGDMenKak [8933–9295]). The experience of war was then instrumental in the initiative of the service called "diakonia" that provides support to vulnerable church members.

In its engagement in missions in the "hurt world"[31] of Eastern Congo, the CBCA encountered displacement, suffering, abuse of women and children, lootings and much more (see chapters 6 and 7). This is in agreement with the *kenosis* model and contradicts Mwikamba's view of church missions during a crisis. He argues that "revolutions forced the churches to become defensive and withdrawn from the world."[32] Mwikamba, who focused in his research on the industrial crisis, hypothesizes that during war, churches may have become "sanctuaries, places of refuge in hostile environment(s) that it could not address mission outside its comfort zones."[33] However, the present study, which also focuses on circumstances during the war, found no evidence that the church was subjected by warlords or other militias to any forced tasks. It found that the church used meetings and the pulpit as a secured, strategic base from which it initiated change, as people had come to find refuge and hope in the church. The church's comfort zone in that context of war had become, therefore, the mission field, as even unbelievers attended churches during the time of the war.

Thus, to the sufferings underlies from wars in Eastern Congo, the church has mostly responded in the same line as the *kenosis* model suggested by David Bosch. The pastor and other Christian leader silently suffer among community members; such a self-denial has grown to the extent of not only some pastors emigrated with their members but also the local church pulpit and buildings did become a center where the church shares the gospel to all people and provides hope to the poorest of the poor.

---

31. Steffen and Douglas, *Encountering Missionary Life*, 296.
32. Mwikamba, "Shift in Mission," 12.
33. Mwikamba, 12.

7.3.2 Samuel Escobar's Migration Model

Samuel Escobar, exploring how the church spreads the Christian faith, in response to contemporary issues with specific attention to poverty and globalization, suggests the use of the migration model with a special focus on the fact that "the poor of the world are now the great missionary force of the present stage in the mission history."[34] He argues that, although in many nations people of all classes are attracted to Christ and respond to his call, people who are open to the gospel and enthusiastic about the faith are found among the poor to the extent that "churches are growing with outstanding vitality in this world of poverty."[35] He further observes that, in the Majority World evangelicals have found receptive hearts among millions who moves from rural areas to the city while in some regions of the world churches in other segments of society tend to decline.[36] The reason behind this success is that the churches of the poor have learned to respond to the challenges with their acquaintance with the language of the masses in the city to which they neutrally offer fellowship while they mobilize church members to reach out to the city and sacrificially give toward mission.[37]

The second argument he uses to support his view is that "missionary initiative expressed in numbers of missionary volunteers' work appears to be passing from North to South at a time when the South is increasingly poor."[38] Within this context, of the two models of mission that have developed so far, the migration model is admired as a response to the need for a mission model, not only because it "had functioned admirably through the century and is also an avenue for mission in our days,"[39] but also because the cooperative model, being experiment by some organization, poses questions among which the raising of support for non-western participants as its focuses on encouraging people from rich nations to bring material resources to be added to human resources of the churches in poor nations in order to serve in a third area.[40]

---

34. Escobar, *New Global Mission*, 64.
35. Escobar, 64.
36. Escobar, 65.
37. Cf. Escobar, 65
38. Escobar, 65.
39. Escobar, 66.
40. Cf. Escobar, 66.

He, hence, suggests the migration model that utilizes Christians migrating from poor countries to carry the gospel and Christian initiative to where they move in search of subsistence.[41] Escobar further support his argument with historical facts of the experience of Christians migrants from their homeland to other countries where they contributed to the establishment of the church, although their missionary activities have not been recorded. Their list includes the Moravians who moved from Curazzao to Holland, the Jamaican Baptists who emigrated to England and the Latin American women going to Muslim countries among others who have all been part of the migration movement reaching out to other nations, especially to nations with which they (the migrants) shared the same language (inherited from their colonies). Using the example of Latin American believers who migrated to Spain, he recognizes that migrants sometimes can be a challenge to the welcoming church in the host country because "many times they need economic help and solutions to their immigration problems" and that it is not easy for old congregations to adapt to the presence of people with a different culture.[42] The past experience has revealed, however, that these migrant believers bring new missionary enthusiasm and energy that welcoming churches need to respond to contemporary challenges.[43]

The local model of missions in the displacement context of Eastern Congo is not in conflict with Escobar's idea of the migration model, especially by the fact that believers move from rural zones to the city and have actively been part of the urban church life. Whenever war has occurred, displacements have followed. In most cases, people moved from a very insecure zone to seek refuge in safe places within the region or in the city where they were either accommodated by host families or in IDPs or refugee camps. Having a grounded knowledge of the word of God, which participants to this study called "deposit of the word in the heart" (FGDWomenBir [8475–8806]), not only helped displaced Christians to survive in places where there were no churches (i.e. the bush and IDP camps; cf. believers from Goma in Sake-Kitsanga area during the 1994 displacement; FGDWomenBir[8475–8806]), but also watered their initiatives of Christian fellowships in the camps or

---

41. Escobar, *Time for Mission*, 66; Hanciles, "Migration and Mission," 118.
42. Escobar, *Time for Mission*, 66.
43. See Escobar, 66.

host communities (FGDMenKak [17213–17452]) where some later became established churches. The city has, therefore, become a multicultural setting that did not exist in DRC before the war and its church has also become a potential mission force from which, if believers are launched into the world around, they are able to survive the cultural chock as they interact with people from cultural competence similar to theirs.

However, this study has challenged this model arguing that to an extent these migrants are limited to carrying out the gospel to their fellow migrants only because of the imbalance of wealth, wrong worldview and cultural differences between them and their host country's people. Unless the church in the host countries in the West accommodate their church activities, they are likely to become transplanted pastors and not cross-cultural missionaries. The nearest example is the tremendous church planting movement that has aimed at "the resurrection of Christianity in contemporary Britain"[44] in the last thirty years from the third world countries. Its impact was a strong growth of the church in London but by no means across the whole of Britain. What is worse is that "such growth crossed the denominations in large-scale church growth among black, Asian and minority ethnic community and new churches."[45] These church plants from poor countries have not, however, contributed to stopping the problem of British church attendance that is generally in decline.[46] On the contrary, they have contributed to emptying them, for example, with the African Christian migrant community "encountering racism in the workplace and discrimination and cultural differences in existing British churches, they formed churches of their own."[47]

The limitation of the eastern Congolese migration model is that the lack of a mission strategy and the custom of having restricted one-on-one sharing of the gospel to church leaders, "ambassadors" or "evangelism groups," prevented the discipling of mission-minded believers practicing missions as their lifestyle. This explains why no evidence was found of churches that survived the closure of an IDP camp. There is also no evidence of church planting by Congolese refugees leaving the DRC or by Rwandan refugees of the 1994

---

44. Goodhew, *Church Growth*, 253.
45. Goodhew, 253.
46. Burges, "African Pentecostal Growth."
47. Burges, 142.

genocide who were hosted in the area around Goma. In fact, to establish new churches during our research period (1990–2011) Kamuha W'Isuka quotes Muhindo Kasekwa who refers, in his survey, to the CBCA which had to use "a group of Rwandan refugees [that] returned home to Rwanda, where even their former churches were destroyed by the war, they were compelled to start a new church there as a sign of gratitude to the CBCA."[48] Therefore, the praxis of the experiential migration model in Eastern Congo by discipling mission-minded believers will definitely be a very good model to plant new churches in the context of war, if it can be mentored for growth and multiplication following a developed contextual mission strategy.

In addition to the above insight drawn from the comparison between the Escobar view and the eastern Congolese experience, the church has to use believers' migration from warzones to the city to plant multicultural churches whose members are mobilized for evangelism and exercise to give sacrificially for missions. Thus, the church in the city, on the one hand, will be able to prepare migrants on transit to the West for mission. In that case, the sending church should partner with the welcoming church in order to not only coordinate the migration movement of believers from poor counties but also to make sure the receiving churches in the West benefit from the migrants' openness to the gospel and enthusiasm with their faith. This will require an induction of migrant believers concerning the welcoming culture in light with the biblical worldview in order to be able to plant missional churches in the Western world.

On the other hand, the migration model suggested by Escobar fits best the context of internal displacement in Eastern Congo but lacks an approach to the sustainability of planted churches. Migrant believers from rural affected areas plant ethnic churches in the city and therefore, the church, although a strong mission potential already gathered in the city.

The urban churches in eastern Congo, although growing due to migration movement from warzones to the city and a strong mission potential force, might not be capable to serve as a missionary force able to be deployed for missionary work, unless it gets prepared. Furthermore, migrant believers should also be preparing for a reverse missionary task once there's peace in the rural areas and they have to return home.

---

48. W'Isuka, "From Maintenance Christianity," 65, quoting Muhindo Kasekwa.

7.3.3 Stephen Bevans' Model of Constants in Context

Addressing "mission as prophetic dialogue," Stephen Bevans, after presenting six elements of mission as activities also reflects on migration among "issues that concern mission today, and how they too might be understood from a prophetic dialogue perspective."[49] Presenting his catholic position that "mission is first and foremost dialogue . . . [because] one enters into mission with a profound openness to place and to the people in which and among whom one works," hence, he argues that "dialogue is the ministry of presence."[50] For him, "prophetic dialogue (like contextual theologizing) reflects the mission of God whose Spirit pervade the universe and calls us to truth and whose word is found in all human contexts…"[51]

Knowing that, "like globalization (and in some way related to it), migration today forms a major context for church's mission of evangelization and solidarity with the poorest of the earth's poor" and that "greater human mobility is one of the most pervasive features of the current world," he articulates his view based on the fact that "the world contains, in some estimates, fifty-million refugees or IDPs and that the question of migration – forced or unforced – is one of the burning issues today affecting counties in significant ways."[52] He observes that while this migrants' world represents "a vast field for new evangelization to which the whole church is called people from other places have come to our home . . . in contrast to the classic understanding of mission as going to another place."[53]

Therefore, in his model, Bevans suggests two ways of doing missions in the migration context:

> The first being a suggestion to the church to subject migrants to the church's pastoral care and the second being the migrants to call the local church to new ways of being church as themselves become active within the church serving it within and outside their communities.[54]

---

49. Bevans, "Themes and Questions," 2.
50. Bevans, 3.
51. Bevans, "Contextual Theology," 237.
52. Bevans, "Themes and Questions," 12.
53. See Bevans, 12.
54. Bevans, 13.

Toward an Understanding of Church and Mission in the Context of War 249

This is the same model in which Bevans identifies "mission as participation in Jesus' mission in the service of God's reign"[55] and is calling the church to the praxis of the six constants in contexts[56]:

1. Christology with a focus on the historical Jesus in the Gospels, "proclamation and witnessing the reign of God."[57]
2. Ecclesiology (liturgy, prayer, contemplation and the like).
3. Eschatology that is dynamic and oriented toward the future.
4. Praxis of holistic and relational salvation.
5. A positive culture of community.
6. "Work in partnership with God for the full humanization and liberation of thought through forms, customs (cultures)."[58]

According to him "mission in the service of the reign of God will prove to be a key ingredient in the development of the model of mission as a prophetic dialogue."[59]

Apart from the context of migrants, Bevans' model of missions in the context of war is compatible with the various local models that were used by local churches to survive church missions, although none of the churches appeared to have practiced the constants as identified by Bevans. From data it is easy to identify the drama of how proclamation of the gospel was affected by war to the extent that sharing the gospel through sermons from the church pulpit became the main way of proclamation, together with the crusades organized twice a year and used as opportunity for short-term missions, occasional one-on-one events of sharing the gospel with a team of evangelism and elders. Challenges made the prayer life of both Christian leaders and believers to increase. Church attendance increased due to the local theology of eschatology built on the realities that, (1) people flocked to churches during the war because the threat of death resulted in a search for salvation and eternal life, and (2) the church became a refuge for all vulnerable people. This gave room for a contextual discipleship model that mainly focused on teaching church members on current issues. Because the issue of identity

---

55. Bevans, *Constants in Context*, 317.
56. Bevans, 238.
57. Bevans. 317.
58. Bevnas, 321.
59. Bevans, 322.

was one of the causes of involvement in the war, church leaders organized believers into small communities of members to improve cohesion among members. Therefore, church activities such as "Upendo" moving a church service to a vulnerable home of a member, "Likelemba" for help group work and "Kidima," came into being.

Bevans' six constants can be helpful for the development of a mission model that drives the routine church activities in every particular context, thereby helping compile a contextual mission strategy. Unfortunately, the CBCA church as a denomination did not have one although it felt the need to have one[60] and did not use the experience of war to develop it even to help local churches to have contingency mission plans. This is why there is an imbalance of contents between the non-written curriculum of discipleship used on the ground and the official curricula such as the so-called "Kitabu cha Imani Yetu" used by a few people and the Muongozo, a very good trial for a contextual guide for discipleship which unfortunately leaves out the context of displacement and the "ramping" situation that churches experience in the war zone. Moreover, the fact that hymns sung in churches helped build the eschatological hope of believers in Eastern Congo[61] is a factor that calls for the inclusion of music and drama, as well as the other arts in the construction of a mission strategy in the context of war.

Bevans' model of missions, however, conflicts with the local model of missions in the context of migration in Eastern Congo. Data confirms isolation, if not also poor collaboration, between migrant churches and churches in host communities. In host communities like Bwalanda, for example, migrants have their church meetings in a building in the IDP's camp, which is located less than a kilometer from a Baptist church that forms part of the same denomination (CBCA). During group discussion women expressed that they felt "other churches did not like them and they felt like street children who do not belong to any family" (FGDWomenKab) and men recommended that the church denomination should assists churches (FGD MenKab [10956–11222]) while their pastor advocated "for the church regional office to challenge part of the CBCA believers who are neighbors to the IDP church to join their congregation" (I26NyaCKab [33440–33985]).

---

60. Cf. Ngayihembako and Midiburo, "Communauté Baptiste," 10.
61. Cf. Wood and Wild-Wood, "'One Day We Will Sing,'" 145–52.

The above example shows that the lack of partnership between churches in host communities and migrants' churches or existing communities of believers in host communities is a hindrance to helping migrants to become active in serving the church within their small congregation and other congregations as well. It also seems like both churches in host communities and migrants' churches are vulnerable, especially in the war zone, and are in need of pastoral care from outside their zones. Some urban churches came to the rescue of refugees and IDPs around them (e.g. I7MuyCVi [3346–3838]) while others invited them for counselling as they came to seek help from the church (see I43MisBut [12449–13165]).

The analysis of the church practices during war in Eastern Congo in light of Bevans' ideas shows that the church mission is a prophetic dialogue although, to some extent, some practices conflict with his model. The six constants in Bevan's model are insights for church practices to be guided by missiological dialogue with the context of war and violence being experienced by Christian leaders and the members.

7.4 Summary

The purpose of this chapter was to connect the experiences of churches that undertook missions in the context of war in Eastern Congo with biblical perspectives on being church in the context of violence and war, as well as with selected contemporary mission models. It drew attention to the contextualization of missions by local churches and their leaders during the recent wars in the Eastern Congo. It demonstrated that there were essential similarities as well as tensions between the experiences of missions in the Eastern Congo and the biblical and contemporary missiological perspectives. These developments provide new and relevant knowledge about missions, particularly in the context of war.

Some of the local theologies readily align with the biblical command not to fight back but to respond by loving the enemy. Despite the pain and suffering caused by the actions of the enemy, the powerless believers responded with silence. Yet even in that silence, they were convinced that God is present, though silent. They did not agree with the view of the 1970s that "God is present and not silent"[62] nor with Taylor's view of God being absent and waiting to resurrect and commission his disciples.[63] To them, God was silent, yet present as the incarnate God, whose incarnation is represented through the local church pastors' leading their communities and working for their survival while sharing their suffering.

However, in the midst of severe suffering, some church leaders lost their trust in the action of God and chose to either support members' involvement in militia movements or chose to obtain guns so that they could oppose potential enemy attacks. Implicitly they were aligned with the just war position as they allowed or even supported their members to join militia groups. They felt the need to supplement their faith in God's protection with the belief in the power of a gun. Some even went further in acknowledging and fearing the power of witchcraft used by some militia, which is evidence of syncretism gaining a foothold in the church.

Their contextualized eschatology helped the church to survive and enabled their members to endure severe ill-treatment during the war. Rather than focusing on a "the futuristic hope"[64] in the blessings to come (Heb 11:10), the fear of death and judgment motivated individuals to attended church activities (worship services) and seek God. The local pastors responded to that fear of death and judgment by preaching the eschatological hope of eternal rewards to believers, using the experiences of both the heroes of faith (Heb 11) and the experiences of Christian leaders who went through the same suffering, as role models. The church members in Eastern Congo, therefore, did not demonstrate acts of forgiveness and love to the enemy but responded with silence to violence because of this eschatological hope and the expectation of God's judgment (Rom 12:19) to avenge the evil treatment. During the war, therefore, believers silently endured ill-treatment, gaining strength in the incarnated God who was silent but present through the pastor who encouraged them and built their hope for eternal rewards beyond death.

In every situation, the oral proclamation was key, just as the gospel message was discussed (διελέγομαι) in Acts 18. In the context of a war that involved identity conflict, the dialogue moved from individuals to the church

---

62. Schaeffer, *He Is There*, 10.
63. Taylor, *When God Is Silent*, 43–82.
64. Erickson, *Christian Theology*, 1160.

pulpit. The church shifted from being the mission force to becoming the mission field where Christian leaders utilized the opportunity to disciple new members and to reach out to other people. War, therefore, opened a new door to develop the capacity to release church members and involve them in sharing the gospel one-on-one as part of their lifestyle, something that was previously not commonly practiced in CBCA. The pulpit was not only a place of proclaiming salvation but also a force of peace and social justice.

The study found that during the war existing churches were transplanted in Eastern Congo as people moved from less to more secure zones, even though they were not exempted from war. This transplanting stands in contrast to the planting of new churches as we find in the book of Acts. It was also limited by its ethnic character, which hindered interaction between migrant churches and other churches in the host communities.

The situation in the Eastern Congo shows similarities with the emerging model of missions suggested by Bosch. The church struggled to draw the connection between its traditional practices and the church's engagement with the future of missions. This struggle, therefore, caused the church to shift from understanding missions as spreading the good news to a holistic contextual understanding of missions addressing current issues such as peace, reconciliation and discipleship in context. The struggle has led the church to identify its need for a mission strategy, in addition to a trial of a discipleship curriculum and teaching guide which emerged from the felt need during the study period of war.[65] The *kenosis* model of mission from Bosch is similar to the incarnational character of the local church pastor in the local incarnational model of missions.[66] There is evidence that pastors were exposed to suffering and death that he shared with church members.

However, when it comes to church involvement in social concerns the incarnational character of the pastor disproves the hypothesis that the church withdrew from the world and hid behind the pulpit for its survival.[67] Rather, the emerging theology of incarnation identified the presence of needy and spiritually seeking people in the church as an opportunity for the "diakonia missions" through which local church members were giving sacrificially.

---

65. CBCA, *Kitabu Cha Mafundisho Kuhusu Imani Yetu*, 6.
66. Bosch, *Transforming Mission*, 356.
67. Cf. Mwikamba, "Shift in Mission," 12.

Despite this, the church remained isolated due to its stand for neutrality and non-involvement in politics. Some churches encouraged their members not to take revenge. Their passive nonviolence, which pushed leaders to discourage military enrollment, considered the army and politics as evil and caused them to take refuge in the prayer room while leaving politics to others.

While the biblical model from Acts 18:1–4 demonstrates the sharing of entrepreneurship skills by the missionaries in the context of migration, the church in Eastern Congo initiated discipleship classes for young people that were oriented toward professional skills and character development as the church's response to the recruitment of children and youth by the militia and rebellion forces. The church, therefore, contributed to working for peace by educating children and young people for work. In addition to the migration model suggested by Escobar, this study suggests a displacement model which makes the first migrant IDPs and refugees to serve the newcomers while benefiting from their ministry. Furthermore, Bevans' six constants provided helpful direction for the development of a mission model for the church in Eastern Congo through missiological dialogue with the context of war.

A new, contextualized model of missions emerged from the practices introduced by Christian leaders and church members as their response to the war with its accompanying disruptions and suffering. A group of churches were involved in syncretistic beliefs by supporting militia forces that utilized witchcraft against rebels or government forces in their response to the silence of God during their suffering. This group is made of the 24 percent of the participants who indicated that the CBCA survived the war by adopting the just war attitude during the war. Next to this group is the 8 percent of churches who adopted the holy war position. However, the analysis of their reasons revealed that this group was closer to the just war position, since the wars in Eastern Congo did not have a religious character. For 52 percent of the sampled CBCA local churches survival was linked to their pacifist position, "rejecting any kind of war"[68] because of military and militia involvement in evil-doing and mistreatment of the local communities. Yet, there was a clear shift during the war from this position towards supporting military involvement, with support found from the Bible, for example, by referring to the wars of David in 2 Samuel.

---

68. Charles, "Just-War Moral Reflection," 19.

Curiously, 96 percent of the churches supported a nonviolence position. The study has identified that this is the ideal non-documented position of the CBCA church which has less impact on the isolated positions of local churches that experienced war. That is why the analysis of reasons for supporting that position has five categories of churches with three different models of church survival. The first model is that of churches that invested in the proclamation of the gospel message and discipleship in context and taught that the nature of new believers is characterized by love and forgiveness of the enemy. That survival model made a shift in identity from an individual being identified with their ancestral blood[69] and the church becoming a new community with the "Jesus ancestral identity."[70] This category of churches survived the war because it welcomed people based on the biblical character of the church which is a new family (Rom 7:4) and not based on the ethnic conflicts.

The second category were those churches that responded to violence with prayer and taught that the role of the church is to preach the gospel and without getting involved in politics or the military. This category also did not take sides, and therefore, survived the wars. However, the study noticed that this group misunderstood the non-retaliation command in Matthew 5:39 in relation to the role of the legitimate government, be it national or foreign. The latter is illustrated by John the Baptist who "accepted the military service as a legitimate vocation,"[71] the Roman centurion whose faith Jesus praises, and many other examples.[72] This view of military service and politics was a great hindrance for the church in Eastern Congo to utilize the available opportunity for global mission. Consequently, the church failed to shift from a homogenous to a glocal community that would have reached out and discipled militiamen, rebels and their foreign backers' forces and commissioned them for cross-cultural missions and therefore become a mission force in the war zone.

The third category of churches survived using a passive nonviolence position, encouraging its members, for heaven's sake, to endure suffering

---

69. Bujo, "Vincent Mulago," 19.
70. Nyamiti, *Jesus Christ, the Ancestor*, 147.
71. Harries, "Non-Retaliation," 1.
72. Cf. Waus quoted in Harries, "Non-Retalitaion," 1.

and "accept ill-treatment and even death from the groups involved in war."[73] Instead of contributing to peacebuilding, such groups through passivity unknowingly contributed to the prolonging of war in the region.

The fourth category of churches supported militia groups whenever needed for the sake of the advancement of the gospel. These churches survived the war under the protection of militia groups which later were integrated into the FRDC forces.[74] However, when the militia groups in their controlled areas suffered repression, the church and its members were in constant danger because they were incriminated by repressive forces such as the FRDC and rebel groups.

The last category is that of churches that officially adopted a nonviolent position, but still left room for individual members to join and serve in the government's armed forces. However, this group did not allow their members to join local militias, because of the latter's ethnic identity and on ethical grounds, since they rejected the violent actions of the militia. This could be interpreted as an application of a theology of peace in the war zone.

The study found that the survival of the task of missions during the war was the result of the way Christian leaders contextualized the transmission of the biblical message, discipleship and the day-to-day activities of church life. As custodians of the transmission of the Christian message, the leaders primarily used the pulpit to respond to the context of war in conflict areas. In accordance with the church culture, they also organize evangelistic crusades twice a year during baptism festivals. There was little interest in one-on-one evangelism, which had never been a central practice, but was rather seen as the responsibility of evangelism teams. The study found that although the process of discipleship was contextualized during the war, it did not focus on raising up mission-minded believers.

Catechism remained a constant component of the discipleship process before and during the war to which was added contextual discipleship teaching at the local church level, the initiative and encouragement of cell groups and the so-called "Upendo," which encouraged church members to fellowship with one another but also as communities of believers. These initiatives became powerful tools that the church used to promote unity, justice and

---

73. Reed, *Just War?*, 28.
74. Turner, *Congo*, 107.

help to the poor. This confirms that during the war, discipleship went hand in hand with the church's involvement in social concerns for the sake of maintaining the church and surviving the war. Unfortunately, the focus on maintaining the church inhibited and even prevented the expansion of the church through effective mission activities. This provides the background for the request by one respondent (I7MuyCVi [29019–29669]) for proper training and capacity building for church leadership in the context of war.

CHAPTER 8

Conclusion

8.1 Introduction

In this concluding chapter, the researcher provides a summary of the research and synthesizes the results of the church's response in action (ministry and mission) and theological reflection upon that action in the context of the war in Eastern Congo. He establishes the contribution of the study to scholarship, provides recommendations for further studies and presents the implications of this study for the church in the DRC and beyond.

8.2 Summary of Research

This study has examined how the war in Easter Congo between 1990 and 2011 affected the understanding and practice of missions in the CBCA. Through the research objectives (see chapter 1) the study focused in surveyed the relationships between the CBCA's missions before the war in Eastern Congo in the period between 1990 to 2011 as well as the effects of that war on the understanding and practice of missions in the CBCA.

8.2.1 Relationship between the Missions of the CBCA before and during the War in the Period between 1990 to 2011

The exam of the relationship between the CBCA's missions before and during the war in Eastern Congo during the period between 1990 to 2011 was drawn from a clear comparison of the nature of missions during the two periods.

That analysis of the nature of mission also led to the understanding of how the church did survive the war.

In identifying the relationship between the nature of missions before and during the war, the researcher observed significant shifts in the way Christian leaders shared the gospel. The oral witness which, before the war, was mainly through sermons (78 percent), the sharing of the gospel one-on-one (85.6 percent) and two open-air crusades during baptism season every year rose to 100 percent of pastors sharing the gospel trough sermons, with only occasional crusades during baptism festivals which were usually planned and conducted by the regional and head offices of the CBCA. Because of the ethnic character of the war, senior pastors abandoned the one-on-one evangelism, they rather made use of the church setting for sharing the gospel while churches became attractive places for the gathering of believers and non-believers in search of hope, salvation and help.

Second, the practice of evangelism groups or "ambassadors" sharing the gospel one-on-one under the leadership of the associate pastor and in some cases church elders, which existed before the war, continued throughout the war. In their contact with individuals, senior pastors focused their attention on pastoral care for church members affected by the war. Individual believers were also not involved in the "duty of sharing Christ with their relatives, friends, neighbors, and colleagues who do not know him."[1] This neglect of oral witness during war, was a major weakness, showing that churches generally failed with "worship to lead to witness, and witness to worship."[2]

A third observation regarding changes in the nature of mission is the figure of selected churches involved in short-time missions, which dropped from 57.2 percent before the war to 48 percent during the war. This is despite the fact that during the war an additional opportunity was opened up for missions, namely mega-crusades held in partnership with local churches and the regional or head office of the CBCA and involving the sharing of resources with evangelists and choir members being willing to come and help. The experience of kidnappings and the killing of pastors and believers during a baptism festival in Nyamirima (I15KiyCKak [36095–37366]) might have created fear of direct involvement, so that members rather opted for praying

---

1. Stott, *Living Church*, 50.
2. Stott, 51.

for conversions during festivals while remaining at home (I16KerCKak [21639–21988]; I13KiwCBut [17664–18036]).

This format of evangelistic crusades, created to reinforce the existing culture of organizing crusades during festivals, was not effective or appropriate to the context of the war. It only contributed to the maintenance of church life rather than to the development of a mission-minded church in such a context. This was demonstrated by the fact that CBCA had worked to maintain the survival of its routine activities such as baptism and worship services without developing the nature of its oral witness. That is why the majority of churches did not send long-term missionaries, because this was the responsibility of the regional office and because CBCA did not have a missionary support strategy.

Fourth, there also was a significant shift in the nature of discipleship, concerning both the purpose and the means of discipleship. Discipleship practices shifted from running seminars and catechism classes for new believers before the war to a contextual discipleship class where contemporary issues and challenges were addressed and hope was restored. The discipleship curriculum developed during the war by the church leadership was only used by two of the twenty-five pastors interviewed, and they only used it to prepare new believers for baptism. That existing curriculum called "Kitabu cha Mafundisho Kuhusu Imani Yetu" lacked being contextualized to the context of war and probably needs an oral platform rather than textual. The same applies to the Muongozo, a new attempt to contextualize discipleship.[3] While it promoted opposition to the exploitation of women and the environment,[4] it did not address rape directly and did also not give attention to the issue of displacement, which churches in the war zone were still experiencing.[5]

Before the war, the pastor was perceived as the only one responsible for and capable of delivering sermons. During the war, the advanced discipleship class called "Niveau 1" (Level 1) made theological education accessible to ordinary church members. This valuable response of the church strengthened the recruitment for catechism and also laid a foundation not only for church members to raise up and disciple mission-minded believers but most

---

3. CBCA, *Mwongozo Kuhusu Mwaka wa Uamsho*, 133.
4. CBCA, 43.
5. CBCA, 5–8, 132–43.

importantly for the CBCA to integrate lay people into pastoral work through the work of the EVARES.

Another important shift occurred in the provision of the youth with professional skills. Before the war, this was done in order to prepare them for future employment, but during the war, the purpose was to prevent them from being enrolled into militia and rebel armed forces.

The experience of war also positively affected the church's involvement in social concerns. Although there were similarities in the church's involvement to help the poor before and during the war, the task and actions of helping the poor differed in the two periods. The church's involvement in teaching believers how to help the poor was above average (60 percent) before the war. During the war, 76 percent of churches taught their members to love the poor. Only 25 percent of them did this through formal seminars while the rest chose to teach members through actions such as gathering the poor at the church and training them on how to fight poverty. Before the war church actions were oriented toward people sacrificially giving and community work activities to help the widows, the orphans and the aged from among the church members. During the war, in response to the overwhelming needs, the same people gave sacrificially to support the most vulnerable people, including war orphans, victims of lootings, IDPs, refugees and people injured in the war.

During the war, church leaders developed two concepts, namely Upendo and Likelemba. This activity seems to have inspired love and interpersonal relationship and allowed members to fellowship as a community of believers. This was most needed, especially because ethnicity presented the church with such a huge challenge, even before the war. To this should be added the fact that the CBCA, which service to the poor was oriented to widows, orphans and the aged within the church, responded to the crisis by initiating social justice efforts. During war, the work of the JPIC, which is the church's commission promoting peace and justice, together with APRED and World Relief, a Christian relief NGO working in the Rutshuru territory, aimed to create peace and justice cells at the local church level in order to promote conflict resolution and peace among believers. However, it appears that there was lack of cooperation and coordination between JPIC and World Relief.

Dealing with the issue on how the church survived war in Eastern Congo, this study carefully looked at the 96 percent of churches that supported the nonviolence position and concluded that nonviolence, although it seems to have been the general position of the CBCA, which did not get involved in the war, was not the real position on war held locally. Five categories of churches were identified by using the reasons why they supported that position and the five categories constitute or reveal ways through which local churches survived the wars (chapter 6). In addition to those ways of church survival, participants pointed to

1. Eschatological hope preached by pastors during the war,
2. church and members' displacements from the least to more secure zones,
3. discipleship strengthening the belief in the silent presence of God in the midst of their suffering,
4. some churches survived due to pastors and individual involvement in the war, and
5. some survived due to political neutrality of their church leaders.

8.2.2 The Effects of the War in Eastern Congo between 1990 and 2011 on the Understanding and Practices of Missions in the CBCA

The war in Eastern Congo in the period between 1990 to 2011 did affect the church's response, which from Christian leaders' experiences of it, is expressed through mission practices and their understanding of missions, which led to the development of local theologies and attitude toward violence. This section condenses the effects of Christian leaders' experiences of war on church missions, an understanding of mission in that context, as well as suggesting to the CBCA the biblical perspective on missions in that context of war.

Effects of Christian leaders' experiences of war on missions

The researcher found that Christian leaders' experience of war significantly influenced their understanding of, and involvement in, missions. From the Christian leaders' experience of missions in the context of war (see §6.2), a specific understanding of mission emerges, that is, God executes and rescues his mission through the missionary. The focus is on the Christian leader at the center who leads in reconstructing the church's mission in the midst of violence and suffering. Yet the CBCA church is still lacking a mission strategy. The study found that the experience of war positively affected church members' ownership and led to the process of integration of lay church leaders to the extent that today, there are now lay members who have been ordained and taken on pastoral responsibilities.

Christian leaders suffered greatly in fulfilling their mission. Some were killed while on duty, others witnessed the murder of their colleagues and church members, others were abused and exposed their lives for the sake of the church, and others suffered the pain of discipling church members in the context of war. The Christian leaders' families and church members experienced a lot of suffering including the death of loved ones, repeated fleeing and displacement, the so-called "ramping" (sleeping in the bush to prevent nightly raids by rebels and militia), poverty, food scarcity and famine. Their women were subjected to sexual violence, rape, separation from their husbands related to issues of ethnicity, abandonment and many other types of abuse. Their children also suffered terribly, were traumatized, had their education disrupted, were separated from their parents, were orphaned and abused in many other ways. The church faced this kind of tribulation because of believers' hope for eternal rewards (see Rev 2–3).

The Christian leaders understood that their experience of missions in the context of war was a story of God's mission in Eastern Congo, which God was writing as he did with Israel. This made them share the gospel with boldness. The experience of war informed discipleship with a proper understanding of the biblical message in their context of war and they were able to translate it in the context of suffering.

That experience informed church leaders' understanding of missions, which shifted from preaching the gospel to an inclusive, holistic and contextual understanding of what mission is. This includes the prioritization of missions which involved the hard task of mobilization of the entire church, of reconciliation, of pursuing peace and unity and of providing comfort and hope to people in the midst of war. Thus, the study argues that the experience of war has catalyzed the creation and shaping of a contextual theology of missions in the context of war (discussed in chapter 7).

The shift in the understanding of church missions meant changes of practices as church leaders responded by discipling new believers in a context of a war with a strong ethnic character, a response that also limited church missions to the routine of church life. Therefore, participants to the study recommended four major areas of improvement for effective church missions in the context of war, namely evangelism, discipleship, theological education and the need for the church to develop a mission support strategy.[6]

The experience of war has negatively affected the church's position on the war. The manipulation of Matthew 26:52b, separating it from Matthew 5:38–45, has created a misunderstanding of Jesus's command not to retaliate and the law of love. As a result, the proportion of churches supporting the just war position increased from 7.1 percent before the war to 24 percent during the war, thus leading leaders of these churches to support members' involvement in war and some pastors in the region to secretly obtain guns to protect their lives against the enemy. While no church adopted the holy war position before the war, 8 percent of churches supported it during the war. Although the war did not bear a religious character, the churches in that category blamed of the unending suffering and undermining of their freedom by a foreign war. The study also observed an increase of pacifist churches by 10 percent during war. While pacifist churches held on to the freedom for church members to enroll in the military before the war, the same churches restricted the involvement of the church to prayer during war. This was with reference to Ephesians 6:12 and from the experience of the militia groups' misbehaviors on the ground. The 96 percent support to nonviolence position held by participants' churches that supported other positions meant that nonviolence was the general position held by the CBCA, which never involved war, but was not held by local churches.

Towards an understanding of mission in the context of war

Chapter 7 brought together the constituent parts of this book – biblical and missiological perspectives on missions in the context of war, as well as the church in Eastern Congo's experience of the same during recent wars in their area. The researcher found significant continuity between the three and highlighted the processes of integration and contextualization that produced fresh insights for a theology of missions in the context of war. The actions of the church (mission and ministry) and the theology that underlies these actions, therefore, extended existing knowledge concerning missions in the context of war.

---

6. Cf. Ngayihembako and Midiburo, "Communauté Baptiste," 10.

From this interaction, the researcher identified local theologies and models of missions. There was some degree of tension between these contextualized missiologies and the biblical perspectives on missions in the context of war (in chapter 3) and the local experience of church missions (in chapters 5 and 6).

First, it was shown that the local theology of silence, which governed the principle of non-retaliation whenever believers were ill-treated, worked hand in hand with the local theology of incarnation to form the incarnational model with the pastor at the center. Consequently, believers responded to violence with silence, not with love for the enemy. They found comfort in the silent, incarnated God whose presence was actively manifested in the local church pastor who silently shared with them the experiences of violence and suffering as he led them in their quest to survive the war. On the other hand, the research found evidence of syncretistic beliefs in the power of witchcraft in the face of God's prolonged silence while they were suffering. As a result, some church leaders responded to the oppression of the enemy by indirectly getting involved in the war through arming themselves as part of the rebel movements or militia (e.g. the five pastors who possessed guns illegally; I15KiyCKak [40262–41370]) or encouraging church members to join militia groups. This was seen as a form of "syncretistic inclusion."[7]

Second, there emerged an eschatology that differs from the biblical eschatology rooted in "the futuristic hope"[8] of the coming blessings (Heb 11:10). This contextualized eschatology found its motive in the fear of an earthly imminent death caused by war and fear of judgment for eternal damnation and, therefore, led to a marked increase in church attendance. This fear, watered by the Christian leaders' message of eternal reward to build hope, prepared the church for perseverance and survival of ill-treatment and suffering.

Third, the primary task of proclaiming the gospel, as illustrated in Acts 18:1–4, which uses the root διελέγομαι (to argue, to discuss), was accomplished through preaching from the pulpit, addressing the issues with which people were struggling because of the war. The experience of war also released and commissioned individual believers to share the gospel in personal and everyday conversations and interactions, something that was not common

---

7. Hesselgrave and Rommen, *Contextualization*, 1.
8. Erickson, *Christian Theology*, 1160.

before the war when evangelism was seen as the task of special evangelistic teams.

The researcher identified tensions at two levels between the theoretical model suggested by Bosch and the contextualized model of missions emerging during the wars in Eastern Congo. First, Bosch's emerging model of missions in the context of suffering, which calls "the church for theologizing for our own time," supports the contextualized missiologies that survived the war.[9] This is despite the fact that the latter lacked a properly formulated theology and strategy of missions that might have helped "the church to creatively engage with the past and the future, with constancy and contingency, continuity and change."[10] This lack, as already expressed in 2010,[11] resulted in a focus on maintaining traditional, routine missions' activities such as crusades during the baptism festival seasons even these exposed church leaders and members to the risks of raids and kidnapping by the militia.

Second, Bosch's *kenosis* model accommodates both the incarnational character of the local church pastor and the church involvement in social concern.[12] The pastor, as representative of Christ, "shared suffering with members of the community and bears, like them, the scars of suffering as part of his identity."[13] The researcher disagrees with the statement by Mwikamba that "due to suffering the church withdrew from the world and found refuge in sanctuaries."[14] He found that people came to the church in search of refuge, hope and salvation. Church leaders used the pulpit as a secure opportunity to share the gospel and responded to people's needs by guiding members towards sacrificial giving to the poor.

In chapters 2 and 7, the researcher raised criticism of the migration model proposed by Samuel Escobar, which does not address the context of war and is limited to establishing transplanting churches among migrant Christians unless existing churches in the host countries partner with the sending churches to channel cross-cultural missions. The researcher noted that during the recent wars the church in Eastern Congo found ways to adapt their mission

---

9. Bosch, *Transforming Mission*, 363–67.
10. Bosch, 375.
11. See Ngayihembako and Midiburo, "Communauté Baptiste," 10.
12. Bosch, "Vulnerability of Mission," 356.
13. Bosch, 356.
14. Mwikamba, "Shift in Mission, 12.

practices to issues of displacement and migration and that consequently, they can help fill gaps in Escobar's migration model. Whenever believers were displaced, they used their biblical knowledge as they engaged in fellowship and ministry with IDPs and in refugee camps. It is regrettable that the fellowships they started among migrants did not survive the closing of the camps, something that should be attributed at least partially to the lack of a mission strategy and support by the CBCA.

Stephan Bevans suggested that migrants should be involved in missions by "calling the church to new ways of being church as they minister to the church and outside their communities while the host church provides pastoral care to migrants."[15] This study found Bevans' model to be an ideal for realities in the Eastern Congo as the church practiced missions in the context of war and resultant migration. It showed that migrant churches and churches in host communities worked in isolation (cf. FGDWomenKab), since Christian migrants worked to transplant their former home churches in IDP camps or in the host communities. Furthermore, beyond the context of migration, Bevans' "six constants in context"[16] provided the right ingredients for constructing a missiology of "prophetic dialogue."[17] Similarly, the church in the Eastern Congo kept some constants such as evangelism and discipleship in context by refracting them to the church meetings. However, because it lacked a clear mission strategy, the church in the Eastern Congo failed to address or incorporate some of the constants. Even discipleship still faced challenges of contextualization, which was addressed at denominational level rather than in the context of the local congregations where Christian leaders should enter into dialogue regarding the understanding and implantation of these constants.

Biblical perspectives on missions in the context of war

The interviews and focus group discussions reveal disturbing details about the violence, death, displacements and suffering caused by war in Eastern Congo. In chapter 3, the researcher explored biblical perspective on how Christians should behave in situations of violence and war. He focused on

---

15. Bevans, "Themes and Questions," 13.
16. Bevans, *Constants in Context*, 317.
17. Bevans, 322.

three New Testament passages, namely Matthew 5:38–45, Acts 18:1–4 and Hebrews 10:32–34, as well as other biblical passages.

The first one contains Jesus's non-retaliation command and his law of love. These are not new commands and do not contradict the Mosaic law. It should rather be seen as "a Jewish wisdom instruction"[18] that goes against the Hammurabi code, which was the common sense in the Middle East in Moses' time and was still in use in Jesus's time. Matthew had to refer to it in teaching his readers in their context. The assessment found that the non-retaliation command and the law of love go hand in hand with justice, which is the concern of "those with the responsibility for public order,"[19] and there is no tension between teaching on non-retaliation and "the legitimacy of military service,"[20] which is endorsed by numerous biblical texts. However, the non-retaliation command and the law of love in Matthew 5:38–45 give room to both pacifism and nonviolence depending on how scholars interpret the tensions between the command and military service. Therefore, both the OT and NT call for non-retaliation and love as the biblical response to violence, which is exercised as believers take an attitude of forgiveness and as a community of believers practice love of the enemy. That attitude does not contradict the church fighting for justice, particularly when the ruling power is the oppressor.

In light of Acts 18:1–4, the misuse of power and poor leadership in a multiethnic context led to migration affecting families. The exploration of Paul's visit to the migrant couple of Priscilla and Aquila who had a temporary residence in Corinth yielded valuable insight regarding missions in the context of migration. The host family benefited from Paul while they joined efforts as missionaries in their host country. Therefore, the biblical passage suggests that migrants should not feel helpless and only rely on external support but join IDPs in ministry. This idea fits the context of Eastern Congo where migrants are "both an object of pastoral care . . . and calling the church to new ways of being church."[21]

---

18. Harrington, "Sermon on the Mount," 7.
19. Gill, "Textbook of Christian Ethics," 242.
20. Harries, "Non-Retaliation," 1.
21. Bevans, "Themes and Questions," 15.

Hebrews 10:32–24 shed new light on the issue of suffering due to mistreatment and violence in various contexts, suggesting that perseverance and fellowship go hand in hand during hardship. Because of the hope for the eternal reward that "believers are awaiting together with the judgement of his enemies,"[22] "Christians ought to live in peace and avoid to revenge"[23] even in the context such as the one in which the ruling power is involved in believers' suffering. The next chapter of Hebrews lists the heroes of faith from the Old Testament, emphasizing the eschatological hope that enables believers to endure suffering, since they are assured of the presence of the incarnate God in the midst of their suffering.[24] The incarnational character of God in Hebrews is seen from the OT, especially Leviticus. The message is not that suffering qualifies believers for the eternal rewards, but rather that we are called to an exercise of perseverance in the faith while enduring suffering and gaining strength in God's presence. We are also called to remember past experiences of suffering for the sake of participation in "the cooperate relationship of fellowship among believers,"[25] which is the church.

8.3 Contribution of the Research to Missions

This study explored the understanding of church and missions in the context of war. It incorporated information about the experiences of the church of Eastern Congo as it conducted mission in the context of war, as well as biblical and missiological perspectives regarding missions in the context of war. The research brought to light relevant information about mission practices and implicit missiological reflection in the context of war. This contextualized missiology provides new nuances to the "understanding of the God revealed in the Bible and provide a Christian understanding of reality."[26] These insights should enrich contemporary missiology by filling gaps in existing knowledge regarding missions in the context of war.

---

22. Guthrie, *Hebrews*, 220.

23. Chianeque and Ngewa, "Deuteronomy," 252.

24. Cf. Evans and Porter, *Dictionary of New Testament*, 1014; Moore, *Repetition in Hebrews*, 46.

25. Erickson, *Christian Theology*, 949.

26. Erickson, 3.

The researcher engaged, adapted and incorporated insights from the missiological models of Bosch, Escobar and Bevans.[27] He also engaged scholarship on the issue of contextualization in order to strengthen the transmission of the Christian faith.[28] While benefiting from these scholars, he added specific insights obtained from his detailed study of the experiences of the church in Eastern Congo.

Another important contribution to existing scholarship is in the special contextual and missiological approach to the study of selected passages from the New Testament, especially Matthew 5:38–45, Acts 18:1–4 and Hebrews 10:32–34. In the process, the researcher initiated a conversation between experts in biblical, missiological, social-anthropological and intercultural studies on a topic and on passages that do not normally feature prominently in missiological studies. The result of this exercise is an enrichment of current scholarship, especially missiology, by examining its relevance for issues related to war and social identity. In addition to the existing and well-known theories about war (just war, pacifism, holy wars and nonviolence), the study also identified six implicit, contextual theologies of war that contributed to the survival of church and mission in the Eastern Congo.

The study provides the foundation for a contextual theology and strategy of mission for the church in the Eastern Congo, something that is desperately needed in the region. Its value goes beyond its own region, since it provides helpful perspectives for a contextual missiology, inviting others to similarly explore the relevance of Scripture and the shape of missiology in their particular contexts. The eastern Congolese experience of missions, therefore, contributes to the process of the transmission of the Christian faith with its struggles in its "multicultural character in terms of expression and application"[29] and is also a contribution to the global church, which is facing various contexts of wars around the world.

---

27. Bosch, *Transforming Mission*; "Vulnerability of Mission"; Escobar, *Time for Mission*; and Bevans, *Constants in Context*; "Themes and Questions."

28. Bediako, *Theology and Identity*; Hiebert, *Transforming Worldviews*; Ngaruiya, "Multifaceted Genesis"; Sanneh, *Translating the Message*.

29. Walls, *Missionary Movement*, xix.

8.4 Recommendations for Further Studies

This study identified a number of issues and challenges that will need additional study and exploration. A work aiming at the study of missions in a context of war is bound to have limitations and imperfections due to the wide range of components in both the dependent and independent variables. Topics associated with missions in the context of war are, therefore, recommended for further research. For example, dealing with the nature of missions, this study did not place emphasis on the cultural mandate in the context of war. A study to identify how the church can "strive to safeguard the integrity of creation and sustain and renew the life on the earth"[30] in the context of war in Eastern Congo will be of great importance and value. Another study should focus on the ecological impact of war in Eastern Congo and the Christian response to it.

This study found that a group of churches in Eastern Congo survived the war because of its members' involvement in ethnic militia groups and that some pastors were collaborating with negative forces and secretly acquired weaponry for countering violent attacks by their enemies. In this regard, it is important to conduct a theological assessment of the opposing beliefs in light of the sovereignty of God and the real or perceived power of militia groups, and particularly their use of witchcraft. From an ethical perspective, it would also be helpful to explore the conditions, need and – some may say – responsibility for missionaries in dangerous circumstances to make provision for their own protection and that of their families and fellow workers. Such a study might also provide guidelines for missions and other ministry among people involved in military conflict.

During data collection for this study, the researcher noticed that some pastors, who are the pivotal characters in church missions, might have been affected by the traumatic experience of war. This was evident from the amount of time needed to conduct interviews, which may indicate that due to trauma, pastors may have lost some of their intellectual skills. The questions were not difficult to grasp, and most pastors have successfully completed tertiary studies earlier in their lives. Some responses were of such low quality that they could not be included in this study. This may suggest another important field

---

30. Ross, "Introduction," xiv.

for research, namely, the psychological effects of war on the effectiveness of church leaders and the type of pastoral care required to help them recover.

8.5 Conclusion

For two and a half decades, the churches in Eastern Congo had to conduct their mission task in the context of war. The researcher found that the survival of missions through this period depended on the way Christian leaders contextualized the transmission of the Christian message, discipleship and strategically organize the routine of church life.

The experience of war has positively informed the nature of missions, for example, its shift from salvation evangelism to more holistic ministry by Christian leaders. The experience of war stimulated and enforced the contextualization of their ministry in general, and their missions in particular, as they were forced to deal with issues of violence and abuse, displacement and migration and suffering and death. They survived by continuing some of their traditional expressions of being church, such as baptism festivals and short-term mission outreaches, choir groups and evangelistic teams. Yet they also had to adapt the ways they functioned as a church and conducted their mission. In some cases, this included secretly cooperating with or even joining ethnic militia groups and acquiring weapons for the purpose of defense in case of military attack.

This study integrated experiential, biblical and missiological perspectives on missions in the context of war. This initiated a missiological dialogue that identified contextual models of missions and provided the CBCA with contextual missiological perspectives that can help it formulate a relevant theory and strategy of missions. These will also be helpful for missions in other parts of the world, particularly in the context of war with its associated phenomena of violence, abuse, displacement and suffering. This may enable them to see that God continue his mission in those troubling conditions, just as he has done in the Eastern Congo.

APPENDIX A

Face-To-Face Interview Guide

My name is Eraston Kighoma, a PhD in Theology candidate at the International Leadership University in conjunction with South Africa Theological Seminary. I am currently writing a dissertation entitled "Church and Mission: A Descriptive Missiological Study of the Response of the Baptist Church in Central Africa (CBCA) to the War in Eastern Congo between 1990 to 2011." Having served as a pastor in this church, you have been selected to be part of this study. This research will help the church in Eastern Congo to improve its missions in the context of war.

Kindly help to do this research by responding to an interview questionnaire which will provide needed information for the study. All information will be held confidential and the name of the respondent will not be disclosed. Thank you in advance.

Name: _____
Gender: Male _____ Female_____
Age range: a) 15–20 yrs b) 21–25 yrs c) 26–30 yrs, d) 31–35 yrs,
       e) 36–40 yrs, f) 41–45 yrs, g) 46–50 yrs, h) 51–55 yrs, i) 56–60 yrs,
       j) 61–65 yrs, k) 66–70 yrs , l) 71–75 yrs, m) 76–80 yrs, n) 81+ yrs

Contacts
Telephone:_____
Physical address: _____
Email: _____

Marital status   1) Single, 2)Married, 3) Widowed, 4) Divorced, 5) Separated

Church Name: _____
Church District: _____
Church location: _____
Your role in Ministry: _____
Are you a member of the CBCA Church denomination?
R/ Yes___No___ since when? R/_____

I. Nature of Missions

A1. Oral witness before the war

1. How often did you share the gospel through sermons?
2. How often did you share the gospel one-on-one?
3. How often did you have open crusades?
4. How often were your church members involved in sharing the gospel one-on-one?
5. How frequently was your church involved in short-term missions?
6. How many missionaries did your church send for long-term missions?

A2. Oral witness during the war

1. How often did you share the gospel through sermons?
2. How often did you share the gospel one-on-one?
3. How often did you have open crusades?
4. How often were your church members involved in sharing the gospel one-on-one?
5. How frequently was your church involved in short-term missions?
6. How many missionaries did your church send for long-term missions?

B1. Discipleship before the war

1. How did you help new believers to interact with God's word and apply it in their context?
2. How did you involve believers to have a prayerful life?
3. How often did your church members fast organized seek God?
4. Personally, how frequently did you fast to seek God?
5. What did you do to make your church members discover and use their spiritual gifts?

6. What did you do to encourage your church members to fellowship:
   a) with one another?
   b) enroll a community of believers?
7. What discipleship classes were done in your church? What did it require for a person to enroll in those classes?
8. Did the church organize seminars for the purpose of discipleship? How?

B2. Discipleship during the war

1. How did you help new believers to interact with God's word and apply it in their context?
2. How did you involve believers to have a prayerful life?
3. How often did your church members fast in order to seek God?
4. Personally, how frequently did you fast to seek God?
5. What did you do to make your church members discover and use their spiritual gifts?
6. What did you do to encourage your church members to fellowship:
   a) with one another?
   b) as a community of believers?
7. What discipleship classes were done in your church? What did it require for a person to enroll in those classes?
8. Did the church organize seminars for the purpose of discipleship? How?

C1. Involvement in social concerns before war

1. What method did you use in teaching your church members on how to love the poor?
2. What action(s) did you take to the church to demonstrate your love to the poor?
3. Can you share some stories concerning individual believers exercising their love to the poor within your community?
4. What did you do to promote love, interpersonal relationships, peace and unity within the community of believers?

C2. Involvement in social concerns during war

1. What method did you use in teaching your church members on how to love the poor?
2. What action(s) did you take to the church to demonstrate your love to the poor?
3. Can you share some stories concerning individual believers exercising their love to the poor within your community?
4. What did you do to promote love, interpersonal relationships, peace and unity within the community of believers?

II. Experience of Church leaders undertaking church missions during the war

1. Can you share some stories from your experience of missions as you served in this church?
2. What personal suffering did you experience during the war in relation to missions?
3. What suffering did your family experience during the war?
4. What suffering did your church members experience during the war?
5. How did the context in which you served affect your way of witnessing, discipleship and your church's involvement in social concerns?
6. What other experiences would you like to mention?

III. How did the experience of war affect the understanding of church missions in Eastern Congo?

1. What was your understanding of church missions before the war?
2. What was your understanding of church missions during the war?
3. What changed in your understanding of church missions as a result of the war?
4. What are you doing differently now as church missions as a result of your experience of war?
5. What do you think should be improved in terms of missions for your church to be effective in caring out its missionary mandate in the context of war?

IV. What contemporary, contextual mission theory that incorporates experiential, biblical and missiological perspective can be developed based on the experience of the church in Eastern Congo and a biblical model?

IV1. What was the church's theology of war Before the war

1. What was your church's position on war before the war?

Position	Yes/No
Christians should be involved in the war for a just cause and attack the enemy for a rightful intention.	
Christian should respond to war with a peaceful attitude and not enroll in the military.	
Christians should be involved in holy wars.	
Christians should respond to war with non –violence.	

2. Please give reasons as to why you said "yes" to the above questions.

IV2. What was the church's theology of war During the war

1. What was your church's position on war during the war?

Position	Yes/No
Christians should be involved in a war for a just cause and attack the enemy for a rightful intention.	
Christian should respond to war with a peaceful attitude and not enroll in the military.	
Christians should be involved in holy wars.	
Christians should respond to war with nonviolence.	

2. Please give reasons as to why you say "yes" to the above questions.

V. What else would you like me to know?

APPENDIX B

Focus Groups Interview Guide

My name is Eraston Kighoma, a PhD in Theology candidate at the International Leadership University in conjunction with South Africa Theological Seminary. I am currently writing a dissertation entitled "Church and War: A Contextual Study of the Response of the Baptist Church in Central Africa (CBCA) to the War in Eastern Congo between 1990 to 2011." Having served in this church in some capacity, you have been selected to be part of this Focus Group Discussion. This research will help the church in Eastern Congo to improve its missions in the context of war.

Kindly help to do this research by participating actively in the discussion and engage under the guidance of the research team. All information will be held confidential and the name of participants will not be disclosed. Thank you in advance.

1. What kind of witnessing strategies did your church exercise during the war between 1990 and 2011?
2. During the time of war, how was your church involved in disciple-making?
3. Your church is known to have organized discipleship classes during the period between 1990 and 2011. What was then being taught in these classes in that context of war with regard to the poor?
4. How did the church members exercise love to the poor during wartime?
5. During the times of war (1990–2011), which way was your church involved in promoting:
    a) Love?
    b) Unity and interpersonal relationships?

    c) Peace and justice?
    d) Does your church have an experience that stands out which you will be willing to share?
6. How did your church survive the wars?
7. When population movement occurred, how did the members of your church continue with their church lives in a migrant situation?
8. In terms of social concerns, how did war affect the lives of individuals and families?
9. These conditions affected both Christians and non-Christians. How did your church minister to people in these conditions?
10. Which lessons can be drawn from your church experience to other churches in the world facing war contexts?

How did the experience of war affect the understanding of church missions in Eastern Congo?
1. What was your understanding of church missions before the war?
2. What was your understanding of church missions during the war?
3. What changed in your understanding of church missions as a result of the war?
4. What are you doing differently now as church missions as a result of your experience of war?
5. What do you think should be improved in terms of missions for your church to be effective in curing out its missionary mandate in the context of war?

Additional question (specific for CBCA Bunia church)
1. What was your experience of church missions before the ethnic war in Bunia in 2004?
2. The war that occurred here in the year 2004–2005 was an ethnic war which caused much losses and movements. How did the church continue to survive?
3. People say that the church sometimes survives due to ethnic grouping. According to your experience, do you think the same applied to your church during the ethnic clashes?
4. According to you, what are the strengths of ethnicity in the growth of a church in such a context?
5. What else would you like me to know?

Bibliography

Adeyemo, T. "Profiling a Globalized and Evangelical Missiology." In *Global Missiology for the 21st Century: The Iguassu Dialogue*, edited by W. D. Taylor, 259–70. Grand Rapids, MI: Baker Academic, 2000.

Apeh, J. E. *Social Structure Church Planting*. Shipenshburg, PA: Companion Press, 1989.

Arnaut, L. "Letter from King Leopold II of Belgium to Colonial Missionaries, 1883." Online article. Universidade Federal De Minas Gerais. Accessed 16 November 2017, http://www.fafich.ufmg.br/~luarnaut/Letter%20Leopold%20II%20to%20Colonial%20Missionaries.pdf.

Atido, G. P. "Religious Identity and Mobility Among Alur Christians in North Eastern Congo." PhD dissertation, Africa International University, Nairobi, Kenya, 2015.

Augustine, St. *The City of God*. Introduction by Etienne Gilson. Translated by Gerald G. Walsh, Demetrius B. Zema, Grace Monahan, and Daniel J. Honan. Abridged edition. Garden City, NY: Image Books, 1958

Autesserre, S. *The Trouble with the Congo: Local Violence and the Failure of International Peacebuilding*. Cambridge: Cambridge University Press, 2010.

Authaler, Caroline, and Stephanie Michels. "Post-War Colonial Administration (Africa)." *1914–1918 Online*. International Encyclopedia of the First World War. Last updated 8 October 2014. https://encyclopedia.1914-1918-online.net/pdf/1914-1918-Online-post-war_colonial_administration_africa-2014-10-08.pdf.

"Background Variable." *Oxford Reference*. Online article, Accessed 1 July 2017, https://www.oxfordreference.com/view/10.1093/oi/authority.20110803095439564.

Barker, K. L., and W. W. Burdick. *NIV Study Bible*. Grand Rapids, MI: Zondervan, 2002.

Barnett, Mike. "The Global Century." In *Discovering the Mission of God:Best Missional Practices for the 21st Century*, edited by Robin Martin and Mike Barnett, 287–305. Downers Grove, IL: IVP Academic, 2012.

Barrett, D. B. *World Christianity Encyclopedia: A Comparative Survey of Churches in the Modern World A.D. 1900–2000*. Nairobi, Kenya: Oxford University Press, 1982.

Bate, S. C. "Method in Contextual Missiology." *Missionalia* 26, no. 2 (1998): 150–85. http://home.worldonline.co.za/~20058871/Method%20in%20 Contextual%20Missiology.htm.

Beals, P. A. *A People for His Name: A Church-Based Missions Strategy*. Grand Rapids, MI: Baker Books, 1983.

Bediako, K. *Theology and Identity: The Impact of Culture upon Christian Thought in the Second Century and in Modern Africa*. Oxford: Regnum Books, 1992.

Bernard, H. R. *Research Methods in Anthropology: Qualitative and Quantitative Approaches*. Lanham: Atlamira Press, 2011.

Bevans, S. B. *Constants in Context: A Theology of Mission for Today*. Maryknoll, NY: Orbis Books, 2004.

———. "Contextual Theology and Prophetic Dialogue." In *Mission on the Road of Emmaus: Constants, Context and Prophetic Dialogue*, edited by C. Ross and S. B. Bevans, 227–37. London: SCM press, 2015.

———. *Models of Contextual Theology*. Maryknoll, NY: Orbis Books, 1992.

———. "Themes and Questions in Missiology Today." 2009 Mission workshop, Salzburg. Accessed 2 October 2014, https://www.cppsmissionaries.org/download/mission/THEMES_AND_QUESTIONS_IN_MISSIOLOGY_TODAYBevans.pdf.

Boas, Morten. "'New' Nationalism and Autochthony: Tales of Origin as Political Cleavage." *Africa Spectrum* 44, no. 1 (2009): 19–38.

Bosch, D. J. *Transforming Mission: Paradigm Shift in Theology of Mission*. Maryknoll, NY: Orbis Books, 1991a.

———. "The Vulnerability of Mission: A Lecture Delivered on 30 November 1991 to Mark the 25th Anniversary of St Andrew's Hall, Selly Oak, and Reprinted with Permission." *The Baptist Quarterly* 34, no.8 (1992): 351–63. Accessed 17 July 2014, http://www.biblicalstudies.org.uk/pdf/bq/34-8_351.pdf. [1991b]

Bosch, D. J. *The Vulnerability of Mission: A Lecture Delivered on 30 November 1991 to Mark the 25th Anniversary of St Andrew's Hall, the Missionary College at Selly Oak Sponsored by the Baptist Missionary Society, Council of World Mission and the United Reformed Church*. Burmingham: Selly Oak Colleges, 1991c.

Bosela, E. E. "Justice and Poverty in the Democratic Republic of the Congo: A Challenge to the Church." Doctoral dissertation, University of South Africa, Pretoria, South Africa, 2009. Accessed 23 November 2016, https://core.ac.uk/download/pdf/13230849.pdf.

Brown, C. "Rape as a Weapon of War in the Democratic Republic of the Congo." *Torture* 22, no. 1 (2012): 24–37.

Browning, D. S. A *Fundamental Practical Theology: Descriptive and Strategic Proposals*. Minneapolis: Fortress, 1991.

"Brief Survey on the CBCA." Online article. Accessed 16 July 2014, http://www.cbca-kanisa.org/english/pagesweb/Mission.htm.

Bruce, F. F. *The Acts of the Apostles: The Greek Text with Introduction and Commentary*. Eugene, OR: Wipf and Stock, 2000.

———. *The Book of Acts*. Rev. ed. Grand Rapids, MI: Eerdmans, 1988.

———. *New International Bible Commentary*. Grand Rapids, MI: Zondervan, 1986.

Bujo, B. "Vincent Mulago: An Enthusiast of African Theology." In *African Theology in the 21st Century: Contribution of Pioneers*, edited by B. Bujo and J. I. Muya, 13–37. Nairobi: Paulines Publications Africa, 2003.

Burges, R. "African Pentecostal Growth: The Redeemed Christian Church of God in Britain." In *Church Growth in Britain: 1980 to Present*, edited by D. Goodhew, 253–57. Farnham: Ashgate, 2012.

Burrow, S. *Violence against Women in the Eastern Democratic Republic of Congo: Whose Responsibility? Whose Complicity?*. Brussels: International Trade Union Confederation, 2011.

Burtt, E. P. "A Free Translation of the Sermon on the Mount." *The Biblical World* 3, no. 5 (1894): 336–44.

Buttler, M. J. "U.S. Military Intervention in Crisis, 1945–1994: An Empirical Inquiry of Just War Theory." *The Journal of Conflict Resolution* 47, no. 2 (2003): 226–48. Accessed 24 October 2013, https://www.jstor.org/stable/3176168?seq=1.

Cameron, H. *Resourcing Mission: Practical Theology for Changing Churches*. London: SCM Press, 2010.

Cameron, H., and C. Duce. *Researching Practice in Ministry and Mission*. London: SCM Press, 2013.

Carson, D. A. "Matthew." In *The Expositors Bible Commentary*, vol. 8, *Matthew–Luke*, edited by F. E. Gaebelein and J. D. Douglas, 3–602. Grand Rapids, MI: Zondervan, 1984.

———. *The Sermon on the Mount: An Evangelical Exposition on Matthew 5–7*. Grand Rapids, MI: Baker Books, 1978.

Carson, D. A., D. J. Moo, and L. Morris. *An Introduction to the New Testament*. Grand Rapids, MI: Zondervan, 1992.

Carter, Warren. *Matthew and the Margins: A Socio-Political and Religious Reading*. London: Bloomsbury, 2005.

CBCA. *Kitabu Cha Mafundisho Kuhusu Imani Yetu*. Goma, Nord-Kivu: Editions Uzima Tele, 1996.

———. *Mwongozo Kuhusu Mwaka wa Uamsho 2015*. Goma: Editions Uzima Tele, 2015.

Chandran, E. *Research Methods: A Quantitative Approach with Illustrations from Christian Ministries*. Nairobi, Kenya: Daystar University, 2004.

Chapman, T. K. "Expressions of 'Voice' in Portraiture." *Qualitative Inquiry* 11, no. 1 (2005): 1–26. Accessed 13 March 2014, http://www.sagepublications.com.

———. "Interrogating Classroom Relationships and Events: Using Portraiture and Critical Race Theory." *Educational Researcher* 36, no. 3 (2007): 156–62. Accessed 13 March 2014, http://www.jstor.org/stable/4621090.

Charles, J. D. *Between Pacifism and Jihad: Just War and Christian Tradition*. Downers Grove, IL: InterVarsity Press, 2005.

———. "Just-War Moral Reflection, the Christian, and Civil Society." *Journal of the Evangelical Theological Society* 48, no. 3 (2005): 589–608.

Chianeque, L. C., and S. Ngewa. "Deuteronomy." In *Africa Bible Commentary*, edited by Tokunboh Adeyemo. Nairobi, Kenya: WordAlive, 2006.

Christiansen, D. "Wither the 'Just War'?" *America* 188, no. 10 (2003): 1–6.

Clarke, M. "Introduction: Good and God – Development and Mission." In *Mission and Development: God's Work or Good Works?*, edited by M. Clarke, 1–16. London: Continuum, 2012.

Clark, John Frank, ed. *The African Stakes of the Congo War*. New York: Palgrave Macmillan, 2002.

Cockerill, Gareth Lee. *The Epistle to the Hebrews*. Grand Rapids, MI: Eerdnmans, 2012.

Collier, Paul, and Anke Hoeffler. "Resource Rents, Governance, and Conflict." *The Journal of Conflict Resolution* 49, no. 4 (2005): 625–33.

Culy, M., and M. C. Parson. *Acts: A Handbook of the Greek Text*. Waco, TX: Baylor University Press, 2003.

Currie, S. D. "Matthew 5:39a: Resistance or Protest?" *The Harvard Theological Review* 57, no. 2 (1964): 140–45. Accessed 28 March 2015, http://www.jstor.org/stable/1508783.

Dau, I. M. "Following Jesus in a World of Suffering and Violence." *Evangelical Review of Theology* 31, no. 4 (2007): 358–68. Accessed 7 March 2018, https://www.lausanne.org/wp-content/uploads/2007/06/LOP62-2007Limuru-Kenya.pdf.

Deiros, P. A. "Historical Research." In *Introduction to Missiological Research*, edited by E. J. Elliston, 135–40. Pasadena: William Carey Library, 2011.

Diamond, J. M. *Guns, Germs, and Steel: The Fates of Human Societies*. New York: Norton, 1999.

"DR Congo Peacekeeping: UN Votes to Scale Down Mission." BBC News, Africa, 31 March 2017. Accessed from 11 April 2021. https://www.bbc.com/news/world-africa-39456884.

Duku, O. "The Development and Growth of the Moyo Congregations." In *Land of Promise: Church Growth in a Sudan at War*, edited by A. C. Wheeler, 99–141. Limuru, Kenya: Paulines Publications Africa, 1997.

Easter, M. C. *Faith and the Faithfulness of Jesus in Hebrews*. New York: Cambridge University Press, 2014.

Eichstaedt, Peter H. *Consuming the Congo: War and Conflict Minerals in the World's Deadliest Place*. Chicago, IL: Laurence Hill Books, 2011.

Elliston, E. J. *Introduction to Missiological Research Design*. Pasadena, CA: William Carey Library, 2011.

Erickson, M. J. *Christian Theology*. Grand Rapids, MI: Baker Academic, 1998.

Escobar, S. *New Global Mission: The Gospel from Everywhere to Everyone*. Downers Grove, IL: InterVarsity Press, 2003.

———. *A Time for Mission: The Challenge for Global Christianity*. Leicester: InterVarsity Press, 2003.

Evans, C. A., and S. E. Porter, eds. *Dictionary of New Testament Background*. Downers Grove, IL: InterVarsity Press, 2000.

Fiorenza, J., J. Onaiyekan, and M. Sabah. "Other Catholic Views on the War." *U.S. Catholic* 66, no. 12 (2001): 11–13.

Feldman, L. H. "Scholarship on Philo and Josephus (1937–1959) (Continued)." *The Classical World* 55, no. 9 (1962): 278–92 and 299–301.

Ferguson, John. *The Politics of Love: The New Testament and Non-Violent Revolution*. Cambridge: James Clarke, 1977.

Foulkes, F. *A Guide to St Matthew's Gospel*. London: SPCK, 2001.

Fouka, G., and M. Mantzorou. "What Are Major Ethical Issues in Conducting Research? Is There a Conflict between the Research Ethics and the Nature of Nursing?" *Health Science Journal* 5, no. 1 (2011): 3–14. http://www.hsj.gr/medicine/what-are-the-major-ethical-issues-in-conducting-research-is-there-a-conflict-between-the-research-ethics-and-the-nature-of-nursing.pdf.

Gaebelein, F. E., ed. *John-Acts. The Expositor's Bible Commentary with The New International Version of the Bible*, vol. 9. Grand Rapids, MI: Zondervan, 1981.

Galloway, A. "The Judaic Other in Dante, the 'Gawain' Poet, and Chaucer by Catherine S. Cox." *The Review of English Studies* 57, no. 230 (2006): 401–2.

Garrard, D. J. "The Protestant Church in Congo: The Mobutu Years and Their Impact." *Journal of Religion in Africa* 43, no. 2 (2013): 131–66.

Gatwa, T. *The Churches and Ethnic Ideology in the Rwandan Crisis*, 1990–1994. Eugene, OR: Regnum, 2005.

Ghai, Y. P. *Autonomy and Ethnicity: Negotiating Competing Claims in Multi-Ethnic States*. New York: Cambridge University Press, 2000. https://doi.org/10.1017/CBO9780511560088.

Gill, R. *A Textbook of Christian Ethics*. 3rd ed. London: T&T Clark, 2006.

Glasser, A. F., C. E. Van Engen, D. S. Gilliland, and S. B. Redford. *Announcing the Kingdom: The Story of God's Mission in the Bible*. Grand Rapids, MI: Baker Academic, 2003.

Global Witness. "'Faced With a Gun, What Can You Do?': War and the Militarisation of Mining in Eastern Congo." A report by Global Witness, July 2009. Available online, https://www.globalwitness.org/en/campaigns/democratic-republic-congo/faced-gun-what-can-you-do/.

Goodhew, David, ed.*Church Growth in Britain: 1980 to the Present*. Farnham, England: Ashgate, 2012.

Gorman, Franklin H. *Divine Presence and Community: A Commentary on the Book of Leviticus*. Grand Rapids, MI: Eerdmans, 1997.

Grudem, W. *Politics According to the Bible: A Comprehensive Resource for Understanding Modern Political Issues in Light of Scripture*. Grand Rapids, MI: Zondervan, 2010.

———. *Systematic Theology: An Introduction to Biblical Doctrine*. Leicester: Inter-Varsity Press, 1994.

Gudorf, C. E. "Christianity and Opposition to the Death Penalty: Late Modern Shifts." *Dialog: A Journal of Theology* 52, no. 2 (2013): 99–109.

Guthrie, D. *Hebrews: An Introduction and Commentary*. Downers Grove, IL: InterVarsity Press, 2007.

Hagner, D. A. *Matthew 1–13*. World Biblical Commentary 33a. Dallas, TX: Word Books, 1993.

Halej, J. "Ethics in Primary Research (Focus Groups, Interviews and Surveys)." Research and Data Briefing Equality Challenge Unit (2007), 3–12. https://warwick.ac.uk/fac/cross_fac/ias/schemes/wirl/info/ecu_research_ethics.pdf.

Hanciles, J. J. *Beyond Christendom: Globalization and the Transformation of the West*. Maryknoll, NY: Orbis Books, 2008.

———. "Migration and Mission: The Religious Significance of the North-South Divide." In *Mission in the 21st Century: Exploring the Five Marks of Global Mission*, edited by A. Walls and C. Ross, 118–29. Maryknoll, NY: Orbis Books, 2008.

Harries, R. "Non-Retaliation and Military Force: Their Basis." In *The Oxford Handbook of the Reception History of the Bible*, edited by M. Lieb, E. Mason, J. Roberts, and C. Rowland. Oxford Handbooks Online, 2011. Accessed 24 February, http://solo.bodleian.ox.ac.uk/primo_library/libweb/action/search. https://doi.org/10.1093/oxfordhb/9780199204540.003.0018.

Harrington, D. J. "The Sermon on the Mount: What Is It?" *C21 Resources* (September 2008): 6–7.

Harty, S. T. "The Just-War Principles of Augustine: A Theological Essay." Online article, 2011. Accessed 17 July 2014, www.sheila-t-hearty-speaker-editor.com/.

Heil, J. P. *Hebrews: Chiastic Structures and Audience Response.* Washington, DC: Catholic Biblical Association of America, 2010.

Hesselgrave, D. J., and E. Rommen. *Contextualization: Meanings, Methods, and Models.* Pasadena, CA: William Carey Library, 2003.

Hiebert, P. G. *Anthropological Insights for Missionaries.* Grand Rapids, MI: Baker Books, 1985.

———. *Anthropological Reflections on Missiological Issues.* Grand Rapids, MI: Baker, 1994.

———. *Transforming Worldviews: An Anthropological Understanding of How People Change.* Grand Rapids, MI: Baker Academic, 2008.

Hiebert, P. G., and E. H. Meneses. *Incarnational Ministry: Planting Churches in Band, Tribal, Peasant, and Urban Societies.* Grand Rapids, MI: Baker Books, 1995.

Hodge, C. J. "Apostle to the Gentiles: Construction of Paul's Identity." *Biblical Interpretation* 13, no. 3 (2005): 270–88.

Holmes, Arthur F. *War and Christian Ethics: Classic and Contemporary Readings on the Morality of War.* Grand Rapids, MI: Baker Academic, 2005.

Holmes, J. "A Scandal that Needs to End." *Forced Migration Review* 36 (2010): 4–6.

Holt, A. "Early Christian Pacifism?" *Andrew Holt* online article, 2014. Accessed 13 August 2017, https://apholt.com/2014/11/09/early-christian-pacifism/.

Horsley, R. A. "Ethics and Exegesis: 'Love Your Enemies' and the Doctrine of Nonviolence." *Journal of the American Academy of Religion* 54, no. 1 (1986): 3–32.

———. *Jesus and the Spiral of Violence: Popular Jewish Resistance in the Roman Palestine.* Minneapolis: Fortress Press, 1996.

Howley, G. C. D., and F. F. Bruce. *A New Testament Commentary.* Grand Rapids, MI: Zondervan, 1969.

Human Rights Watch. *The Curse of Gold: Democratic Republic of Congo.* New York: Human Rights Watch, 2005.

Hurlburt, C. E. "1860 to 1936 Africa Inland Mission Kenya / Tanzania / Congo." Online article. 2013. http://www.dacb.org/stories/kenya/hurlburt_charles.html.

Hurlburt, P. F. *Engulu Yowene ngoko Yoane Asaka.* London: British and Foreign Bible Society, 1932.

———. *Esiobarua oko banya Galatia, banya Epeso, banya Pilipoi, banya Kolosai.* London: British and Foreign Bible Society, 1937.

Hurlburt, P. F., and M. P. F. Hurlburt. *Engulu Yowene ngoko Matayo Asaka.* London: British and Foreign Bible Society, 1935.

Hurlburt, P. F., and A. C. Mutotoya. *Emibiri Yabakwenda.* London: British and Foreign Bible Society, 1934.

Isaacs, M. E. *Reading Hebrews and James: A Literary and Theological Commentary*. Macon, GA: Smy & Helwys, 2002.

Jackson, B. S. "Lex Talionis in Early Judaism and the Exhortation of Jesus in Matthew 5:38–42." *Journal of Theological Studies* 58, no. 1 (2007): 200–6.

———. "Models in Legal History: The Case of Biblical Law." *Journal of Law and Religion* 18, no. 1 (2002): 1–30.

Jacoby, D. "The Destruction of Jerusalem." Duke University, USA, 1980. Accessed 1 March 2018, https://www.douglasjacoby.com/wp-content/uploads/1986/02/80DestJer.pdf.

Jeffers, J. S. *The Greco-Roman World of the New Testament Era: Exploring the Background of Early Christianity*. Downers Grove, IL: InterVarsity Press, 1999.

Jesse, F. K. "A Missiological Study of the Kimbanguist Church in Katanga." Master's thesis, University of South Africa, 2008. Accessed 17 July 2014 http://hdl.handle.net/10500/2670.

Johnson, Frederick, ed. *A Standard Swahili-English Dictionary*. London: Oxford University Press, 1945.

Johnsson, W. G. "Pilgrim Motives in the Book of Hebrews." *Journal of Biblical Literature* 97, no. 2 (1978): 239–51.

Johnstone, P., and J. Mandryk. *Operation World: 21st Century Edition*. Carlisle, UK: Paternoster, 2001.

Kaiser, W. C. *Mission in the Old Testament: Israel as a Light to the Nations*. Grand Rapids, MI: Baker Books, 2000.

Kassa, T. D. "Hebrews." In *Africa Bible Commentary*, edited by T. Adeyemo. Nairobi, Kenya: WordAlive, 2006.

Kavukal, J. "Christian Mission at the Crossroads of Development: Biblical and Magisterial Perspectives." In *Mission and Development: God's Work or Good Works?*, edited by M. Clarke, 29–50. London: Continuum, 2012.

Keener, C. S. *The IVP Background Commentary: New Testament*. Downers Grove, IL: InterVarsity Press, 1993.

Kehailia, Greg. "Countering Electoral Violence with Electoral Education." In *Elections Worth Dying For?: A Selection of Case Studies from Africa*, edited by Almami Cyllah, 29–45. Washington, DC: International Foundation for Electoral Systems. Available online, https://www.ifes.org/sites/default/files/elections_worth_dying_for_-_a_selection_of_case_studies_from_africa_final2.pdf.

Kighoma, E. "From an Ethnic Church to a Missional One: A Focus on Evangelical Churches in Urban Goma." Masters Thesis, International Leadership University, Nairobi, Kenya, 2013.

———. "Rethinking Mission, Missions and Money: A Focus on the Baptist Church in Central Africa." *HTS Teologiese Studies/Theological Studies* 75, no. 4 (2019): a5102. https://doi.org/10.4102/hts.v75i4.5102.

Kirk, A. "'Love Your Enemies' the Golden Rule, and Ancient Reciprocity (Luke 6:27–35)." *Journal of Biblical Literature* 122, no. 4 (2003): 667–86.

Kirk, J. A. *Mission Under Scrutiny: Confronting Contemporary Challenges.* Minneapolis: Fortress Press, 2006.

Kisau, P. M. "Acts of the Apostles." In *Africa Bible Commentary*, edited by T. Adeyemo, 1323–1373. Nairobi, Kenya: WordAlive, 2006.

Klingbeil, M. *Yahweh Fighting from Heaven: God as Warrior and as God of Heaven in the Hebrew Psalter and Ancient Near East Iconography.* Fribourg: Vanderhoeck & Reprecht, 1999.

Knight, George Angus Fulton. *A Christian Theology of the Old Testament.* London: SCM Press, 1959.

Koenig, H. C. "Christian Attitudes toward War and Peace: A Historical Survey and Critical Re-Evaluation." *The Catholic Historical Review* 50, no. 1 (1964): 73–74. Accessed 22 March 2014, http://www.jstor.org/stable/25017405.

Kombo, D. K., and D. L. A. Tromp. *Proposal and Thesis Writing: An Introduction.* Nairobi: Pauline Publications Africa, 2011.

Kubo, S. *A Reader's Greek-English Lexicon of the New Testament.* Grand Rapids, MI: Zondervan, 1975.

Krey, P. D. S. "Luther in Relation with the Peasant's War: A Historical-Theological Investigation." Unpublished manuscript, 1983–1990. Accessed 18 July 2014, http://www.scholardarity.com/wp-content/uploads/2012/07/Luther-and-the-Peasants-War-Manuscript-I-070412-with-WA.pdf.

LeCompte, M. D., and J. J. Schensul. *Designing and Conducting Ethnographic Research: An Introduction.* 2nd ed. Lanham, MD: AltaMira Press, 2010.

Lewis, G. R., and B. A. Demarest. *Integrative Theology.* Grand Rapids, MI: Zondervan, 1987.

Longenecker, R. "Acts." In *The Zondervan Bible Commentary: New Testament*, vol. 2, edited by K. L. Baker and J. R. Kohlenberger III. Grand Rapids, MI: Zondervan, 1994.

Ludermann, G. *Early Christianity According to the Traditions in Acts: A Commentary.* London: SCM, 1989.

Lukose, W. *Contextual Missiology of the Spirit: Pentecostal in Rajasthan, India.* Eugene, OR: Wipf & Stock, 2013.

Luz, U. *Matthew 1–7.* Edinburgh: T&T Clark, 1990.

———. *Studies in Matthew.* Cambridge, UK: Eerdmans, 2005.

Lwabukuna, O. K. "International Displacement in Africa: African Solutions to African Problems? Challenges and Prospects." *Journal of International Displacement* 1, no. 1 (2011): 131–41.

Mandjumba, Mwanyimi-Mbomba. *Chronologie générale de l'Histoire du Zaïre (des origines à 1988).* Kinshasa: Centre de Recherche Pédagogique, 1989.

Markus, R. A. "Saint Augustine's Views on the Just War." *Studies in Church History* 20 (1983): 1–14.

Marshall, Catherine, and Gretchen B. Rossman. *Designing Qualitative Research*. 5th ed. Thousand Oaks, CA: SAGE, 2011.

Mason, Eric F., and Kevin B. McGruden, eds. *Reading the Epistle to the Hebrews: A Source for Students*. Boston: Brill, 2011.

Mathieu, Paul, and A. Mafikiri Tsongo. "Guerres paysannes au Nord-Kivu (République démocratique du Congo), 1937–1994." [Peasant Wars in North Kivu (Congo), 1937–1994]. *Cahiers d'Études Africaines* 38, Cahier 150/152 (1998): 385–416.

McCullum, H. *The Angels Have Left Us: The Rwanda Tragedy and the Churches*. Geneva: WCC Publications, 1995.

McGavran, D. *Homogeneous Unit Principle*. 3rd ed. Grand Rapids, MI: Eerdmans, 1990.

M. G. T. "Christians – What Does Christ Teach You Concerning War?" *The Advocate of Peace and Universal Brotherhood* 1, no. 11 (1846): 258–60.

Miller, J. G. *Calvin's Wisdom: An Anthology Arranged Alphabetically by a Grateful Reader*. Carlisle, PA: Banner of Truth, 1992.

Mitchell, A. C. *Hebrews*. Sacra Pagina Series 13. Collegeville, MN: Liturgical Press, 2009.

Minani Bihuzo, Rigobert. *Du pacte de stabilité de Naïrobi à l'acte d'engagement de Goma, Enjeux et défis du processus de paix en RDC*. Kinshasa: CEPAS/RODHECIC, 2008.

Minatrea, M. *Shaped by God's Heart: The Passion and Practices of Missional Churches*. New York: Wiley & Sons, 2004.

Montefiore, H. W. *A Commentary on the Epistle to the Hebrews*. London: Black, 1964.

Moore, N. J. *Repetition in Hebrews*. Tubigen: Mohr Siebeck, 2015. https://doi.org/10.1628/978-3-16-153855-1.

Moreau, A. S. *Contextualization in World Missions: Mapping and Assessing Evangelical Models*. Grand Rapids, MI: Kregel, 2012.

Moreau, A. S., G. Corwin, and G. B. McGee. *Introducing World Mission: A Biblical, Historical, and Practical Survey*. Grand Rapids, MI: Baker Books, 2003.

Moreau, A. S., H. Netland, and C. Van Engen, eds. *Evangelical Dictionary of World Missions*. Grand Rapids, MI: Baker Books, 2000.

Morey, R. "The Early Church and War." Online article, 2017. Accessed 13 August 2018, http://www.churchinhistory.org/pages/misc/ch-war-pac.htm.

———. *When Is It Right To Fight?* Minneapolis, MN: Bethany House, 1985.

Morris, Leon. *Understanding the New Testament*. London: Scripture Union, 1969.

Mugambi, J. N. K. *African Christian Theology: An Introduction*. Nairobi, Kenya: Heinemann Kenya, 1989.

———. "Theology of Reconstruction." In *Theologies of Liberation and Reconstruction*, edited by I. M. T. Mwase and E. E. Kamaara, 17–30. Nairobi: Acton Publishers, 2012.

Mugenda, A. *Social Science Research: Conception, Methodology and Analysis*. Kenya: Applied Research and Training Services, 2008.

Mulligan, Kenneth. "Pope John Paul II and Catholic Opinion." *Social Science Quarterly* 87, no. 3 (2006): 739–53.

Musolo W'Isuka, Kamuha. "From Maintenance Christianity to a Holistic and Comprehensive Understanding of Mission: A Case Study of Churches in the North Kivu Province of the Democratic Republic of the Congo." Dissertation, University of South Africa, 2008. http://hdl.handle.net/10500/2658.

Mwase, I. M. T., and E. K. Kamaara, eds. *Theologies of Liberation and Reconstruction*. Nairobi: Acton Publishers, 2012.

Mwikamba, C. "Shift in Mission: An Ecological Theology in Africa." In *Mission in African Christianity*, edited by A. Nasimiyu-Waisike and D. W. Waruta, 11–36. Nairobi: Action Publishers, 2000.

Nasimiyu-Wasike, A., and D. W. Waruta, eds. *Mission in African Christianity: Critical Essays in Missiology*. Nairobi: Acton Publishers, 2000.

Ndung'u, N. "Land as the Source of Economic Sustenance." In *Questions for Integrity in Africa*, edited by G. Waume and M. Theuri, 57–74. Nairobi: Acton Publishers, 2003.

Ngaruiya, D. K. "The Multifaceted Genesis of the 2007–2008 Postelection Violence in Kenya." In *Communities of Faith in Africa and the Africa Diaspora*, edited by C. B. Essamuah and D. K. Ngaruiya, 82–89. Eugene, OR: Pickwick, 2014.

Ngayihembako, S. M., and N. Midiburo. "Communauté Baptiste au Centre de l'Afrique: Compte Rendu ya assemblée Générale ya mara makumi tatu na tatu (33e AG) Iliyofanyika pa Kikyo/Butembo Tarehe 11–15/09/2011, 10." AGM report, Baptist Church in Central Africa, Goma, DRC, 2011.

Ngolet, Fançois. *Crisis in the Congo: The Rise and Fall of Laurent Kabila*. New York: Palgrave Macmillan, 2011.

Nguyen, vanThanh. "Migrants as Missionaries: The Case of Priscilla and Aquila." *Mission Studies* 30, no. 2 (2013): 194–207.

Niringiye, Z. "Proclaim the Good News of the Kingdom (ii)." In *Mission in the 21st century: Exploring the Five Marks of Global Mission*, edited by A. Walls and C. Ross, 3–24. London: Darton, Longman and Todd, 2008.

Nyamiti, C. *Jesus Christ, the Ancestor of Humankind: Methodological and Trinitarian Foundations*. Nairobi: CUEA Publications, 2005.

Noonan, J. T. "The Metaphors of Morals." *Bulletin of the American Academy of Arts and Sciences* 42, no. 2 (1988): 30–42.

Nye, J. S. *Understanding International Conflicts: An Introduction to Theory and History*. New York: Pearson Longman, 2007.

Nzogola-Ntalaja, G. "The International Dimensions of the Congo Crisis." *Global Dialogue* 6, no. 3–4 (2004): 116–26. Accessed 24 November 2016, https://projectcongo.org.

Oden, T. C., ed. *Ancient Christian Commentary on Scripture: New Testament 10: Hebrews*. Downers Grove, IL: InterVarsity Press, 2005.

OCHA. "Democratic Republic of Congo-North Kivu." Situation report no. 17, 2012, 1–17. Accessed 13 August 2017. https://reliefweb.int/report/democratic-republic-congo/north-kivu-situation-report-no-17-11-december-2012.

OECD. "Mapping Support for African Infrastructure Investment." Report 2012. Accessed 26 May 2016. http://www.oecd.org/daf/inv/investment-policy/MappingReportWeb.pdf.

———. "Responsible Supply of Minerals from the Great Lakes Region: How Can Donors Support Host Governments." Report 2012. Accessed 26 May 2016. https://www.oecd.org/investment/investmentfordevelopment/50531057.pdf.

Okosun, T. Y. "War and Spiralling Injustices in Africa: In Search of a Transformative Response." *Contemporary Justice Review* 10, no. 3 (2007): 323–50.

Okoye, J. C. *Israel and the Nations: A Mission Theology of the Old Testament*. Maryknoll, NY: Orbis Books, 2006.

Oulton, J. L. E., and H. Chadwick. *Alexandrian Christianity: Selected Translations of Clement and Origen with Introductions and Notes*. Philadelphia: Westminster Press, 1954.

O'Riordan, S. "Towards a Theology of Peace." *The Furrow* 30, no. 3 (1979): 144–54. Accessed 22 March 2014, http://www.jstor.org/stable/27660707.

Ott, C., ed. *The Mission of the Church: Five Views in Conversation*. Grand Rapids, MI: Baker Academic, 2016.

Ott, C., S. J. Strauss, and T. C. Tennent. *Encountering Theology of Mission: Biblical Foundations, Historical Developments, and Contemporary Issues*. Grand Rapids, MI: Baker Academic, 2010.

Oucho, J. O. *Undercurrents of Ethnic Conflict in Kenya*. Leiden: Brill, 2002.

Partner, P. *God of Battle: Holy Wars of Christianity and Islam*. Princeton, NJ: Princeton University Press, 1997.

Paton, L. B. "The Original Form of Leviticus xvii.–xix." *Journal of Biblical Literature* 16, no. 1/2 (1897): 31–77. http://www.jstor.org/stable/3268866.

Peach, L. J. "An Alternative to Pacifism? Feminism and Just-War Theory." *Hypatia* 9, no. 2 (1994): 152–72. Accessed 23 March 2014, http://www.jstor.org/stable/3810175.

Pennington, J. T. *Heaven and Earth in the Gospel of Matthew*. Grand Rapids, MI: Baker Academic, 2007.

Perdue, L. G. "*The Problem of War in the Old Testament* by Peter C. Craigie." *Journal of Biblical Literature* 99, no. 3 (1980): 446–8.

Peters, G. W. *A Biblical Theology of Missions*. Chicago, IL: Moody, 1972.

Polat, N. "Peace as War." *Alternatives: Global, Local, Political* 35, no. 4 (2010): 317–45.

Priest, D. "Holding Down Two Jobs." In *The Gospel Unhindered: Modern Missions and the Book of Acts*, edited by D. Priest, 143–56. Pasadena, CA: William Carey Library, 1994.

Punch, Keith F. *Introduction to Social Research–Quantitative & Qualitative Approaches*. London: SAGE, 2005.

Punt, J. "Hebrews, Thought-Patterns and Context: Aspects of the Background of Hebrews." *Neotestamentica* 31, no. 1 (1997): 119–58.

Reed, C. *Just War?: Changing Society and the Churches*. London: SPCK, 2004.

Reeves, Celia. *Quantitative Research for the Behavioral Sciences*. New York: Wiley and Sons, 1992.

Reyntjens, Filip. *The Great African War: Congo and Regional Geopolitics, 1996–2006*. Cambridge: Cambridge University Press, 2009.

Robben, A., and C. Nordstrom. "The Anthropology and Ethnography of Violence and Sociopolitical Conflicts." In *Fieldwork Under Fire: Contemporary Studies of Violence and Survival*, edited by C. Nordstrom and A. C. Robben, 1–24. Berkley, CA: University of California Press, 1995.

Robinson, P. H. "Competing Conceptions of Modern Desert: Vengeful, Deontological, and Empirical." *The Cambridge Law Journal* 67, no. 1 (2008): 145–75.

Ross, C. "An Exposition and Critique of the Five Marks of Mission." In *Ecclesiology in Mission Perspective*, edited by C. Ernst. Leipzig: Evangelische Verkagsanstalt, 2012.

———. "Introduction: Taonga." In *Mission in the 21st Century: Exploring the Five Marks of Global Mission*, edited by A. Wall and C. Ross, xvi–2. London: Darton, Longman and Todd, 2008.

Rubin, B. R. "Central Asia and Central Africa: Transnational Wars and Ethnic Conflicts." *Journal of Human Development and Capabilities* 7, no. 1 (2006): 5–22.

Sanneh, L. *Translating the Message: The Missionary Impact on Culture*. Maryknoll, NY: Orbis Books, 1989.

Schaeffer, F. *He Is There and He Is Not Silent*. London: Hodder and Stoughton, 1972.

Schaff, P., ed. *Lange's Commentary of the Holy Scriptures*. Grand Rapids, MI: Zondervan, 1980.

Schreiner, T. R. "Interpreting Romans 4:1–8: The Theological and Exegetical Contribution of Psalm 32." Paper presented at the 2002 Evangelical

Theological Society in Toronto. Accessed 23 March 2018, http://d3pi8hptl0qhh4.cloudfront.net/documents/tschreiner/Romans4_1-8.pdf.

Schreiter, R. J. *Constructing Local Theologies*. Maryknoll, NY: Orbis Books, 1985.

Simon, Xolile. "Mission as Frontier-Crossing and Identity Formation: An Integrating Contextual Missiology." *Scriptura* 100 (2009): 89–103. Accessed 10 March 2017, http://scriptura.journals.ac.za/pub/article/viewFile/657/654.

Stacey, W. D. *Groundwork of Biblical Studies*. London: Epworth Press, 1979.

Stassen, G. H. "The Fourteen Triads of the Sermon on the Mount (Matthew 5:21–7:12)." *Journal of Biblical Literature* 122, no. 2 (2003): 267–308.

Stott, J. *The Living Church: Convictions and Lifelong Pastor*. Nottingham: Inter-Varsity Press, 2007.

Sheils, W. J., ed. *The Church and War*. Studies in Church History 20. London: Basil Blackwell, 1983.

Smith, K. G. *Academic Writing and Theological Research: A Guide for Students*. Johannesburg: South African Theological Seminary Press, 2008.

Sökefeld, M. "Reconsidering Identity." *Anthropos* 96, no. 2 (2001): 527–44.

Son, K. *Zion Symbolism in Hebrews: Hebrews 12:18–24 as a Hermeneutical Key to the Epistle*. Milton Keynes: Paternoster, 2005.

Stackhouse, M. L. *God and Globalization*. Vol. 4, *Globalization and Grace*. New York: Continuum, 2007.

Steffen, T., and L. M. Douglas. *Encountering Missionary Life and Work: Preparing for Intercultural Ministry*. Grand Rapids, MI: Baker Academic, 2008.

Stetzer, E. *Planting Missional Churches: Planting a Church that's Biblically Sound and Reaching People in Culture*. Nashville, TN: B&H, 2006.

Schensul, J. J., M. D. LeCompte, B. K. Nastasi, and S. P. Borgatti. *Enhanced Ethnographic Methods: Audiovisual Techniques, Focus Group Interviews, and Elucidation Techniques*. Lanham, MD: Atlamira Press, 1999.

Schensul, S. L., J. J. Schensul, and M. D. LeCompte. *Essential Ethnographic Methods: Observations, Interviews, and Questionnaires*. Vol. 2. Walnut Creek: Atlamira Press, 1999.

Stearns, J. K. *North Kivu: The Background to Conflict in North Kivu Province of Eastern Congo*. London: Rift Valley Institute, 2012.

Stremlau, J. *Presidential and Legislative Elections in the Democratic Republic of the Congo, November 28, 2011, Final report*. The Carter Center, Atlanta, USA: One Copenhill, 2012.

Stuhlmueller, C., and D. Senior. *The Biblical Foundations for Mission*. Maryknoll, NY: Orbis Books, 1983.

Swartley, W., and A. Kreider. "Pacifist Christianity: The Kingdom Way." In *Pacifism and War – When Christians Disagree*, edited by O. R. Barclay, 38–60. Leicester: Inter-Varsity Press, 1984.

Taylor, B. B. *When God is Silent*. Cambridge, MA: Cowley Publication, 1998.

Taylor, M. L. "Derrida, the Death Penalty, and the Theologico-Politico." *Theology Today* 72, no. 1 (2015): 100–8.
Taylor, W. D., ed. *Global Missiology for the 21st Century: The Iguassu Dialogue.* Grand Rapids, MI: Baker Academic, 2000.
ter Haar, G. T. "Who Defines African Identity? A Concluding Analysis." In *Uniquely African? African Christian Identity from Cultural and Historical Perspectives,* edited by J. L. Cox and G. ter Haar, 261–74. Asmara, Eritrea: Africa World Press, Inc, 2003.
Terry, J. M., and E. C. Smith. *Missiology: An Introduction to the Foundations, History, and Strategies of World Mission.* Nashville, TN: B&H, 1998.
"The Code of Hammurabi." Online. http://uruk-warka.dk/news/09-2014%20 Specail/code%20of%20hammurabi.pdf.
"The Queen and the Church of England." *Royal.uk* online. Accessed 24 October 2013. https://www.royal.uk/queens-relationship-churches-england-and-scotland-and-other-faiths.
Titeca, K., and K. Vlassenroot. "Rebels Without Borders in the Rwenzori Borderland? A Biography of the Allied Democratic Forces." *Journal of Eastern African Studies* 6, no. 1 (2012): 154–76.
Tienou, T. "The Great Commission in Africa." In *The Great Commission,* edited by M. I. Klauber and S. M. Manetsch, 164–75. Nashville, TN: B&H, 2003.
Tsehle, A. R. "An Evangelical Contextual Missiological Approach to Mission Praxis in Africa: An Indigenous South African Perspective (1950–2005)." MTh thesis, South Africa Theological Seminary, Johannesburg, South Africa, 2009.
Turner, T. *Congo.* Cambridge: Polity Press, 2013.
———. *The Congo Wars: Conflict, Myth and Reality.* New York: Zed Books, 2007.
Upham, T. C. "Forgiveness and the Love of Our Enemies." *Advocate of Peace,* New Series 2, no. 21 (1970): 1847–1884. Accessed 30 March 2015, http://www.jstor.org/stable/27904782.
Vaus, W. *Mere Theology: A Guide to the Thought of C. S. Lewis.* Leicester: Inter-Varsity Press, 2004.
Verweijen, J. "From Autochthony to Violence? Discursive and Coercive Social Practices of the Mai-Mai in Fizi, Eastern DR Congo." *African Studies Review* 58, no. 2 (2015): 157–80.
Vlassenroot, K., and K. Büscher. *The City as Frontier: Urban Development and Identity Process in Goma.* Crisis States Working Papers Series 2. London: London School of Economics and Politcal Science, 2009.
Wallace, D. B. *Greek Grammar Beyond the Basics: An Exegetical Syntax of the New Testament.* Grand Rapids, MI: Zondervan, 1996.
Walls, A. F. *The Missionary Movement in Christian History: Studies in the Transmission of Faith.* Maryknoll, NY: Orbis Books, 1996.

Wenham, J. W. *The Elements of New Testament Greek*. Cambridge: Cambridge University Press, 1965.

Wheeler, A. C. "Church Growth in Southern Sudan 1983–1996." In *Church Growth in Land of Promise: Church Growth in a Sudan at War*, edited by A. C. Anderson, 11–36. Limuru: Paulines Publications Africa, 1997.

Wild-Wood, E. *Migration and Christian Identity in Congo (DRC)*. Leiden: Brill, 2008.

Williams, D. J. *New International Biblical Commentary: Acts*. Peabody, MA: Hendrickson, 1985.

Wimmer, A. *Nationalist Exclusion and Ethnic Conflict: Shadow of Modernity*. Cambridge: Cambridge University Press, 2002.

W'Isuka, K. M. "From Maintenance Christianity to a Holistic and Comprehensive Understanding of Mission: A Case Study of Churches in the North Kivu Province of the Democratic Republic of the Congo." MTh in Theology, University of South Africa, 2009.

Wood, P., and E. Wild-Wood. "'One Day We Will Sing in God's Home': Hymns and Songs Sang in the Anglican Church in North-Eastern Congo (DRC)." *Journal of Religion in Africa* 32, nos. 1–2 (2004): 145–80.

Wright, C. J. *The Mission of God: Unlocking the Bible's Grand Narrative*. Downers Grove, IL: IVP Academic, 2006.

———. *The Mission of God's People: A Biblical Theology of the Church Mission*. Grand Rapids, MI: Zondervan, 2010.

Yoder, J. H. *The War of the Lamb: The Ethics of Nonviolence and Peacemaking*. Grand Rapids, MI: Brazos Press, 2009.

Zink, J. "Five Marks of Mission: History, Theology, Critique." *Journal of Anglican Studies* 15, no. 2 (2017): 144–66.

Langham Literature, with its publishing work, is a ministry of Langham Partnership.

Langham Partnership is a global fellowship working in pursuit of the vision God entrusted to its founder John Stott –

> *to facilitate the growth of the church in maturity and Christ-likeness through raising the standards of biblical preaching and teaching.*

Our vision is to see churches in the Majority World equipped for mission and growing to maturity in Christ through the ministry of pastors and leaders who believe, teach and live by the word of God.

Our mission is to strengthen the ministry of the word of God through:
- nurturing national movements for biblical preaching
- fostering the creation and distribution of evangelical literature
- enhancing evangelical theological education

especially in countries where churches are under-resourced.

Our ministry

Langham Preaching partners with national leaders to nurture indigenous biblical preaching movements for pastors and lay preachers all around the world. With the support of a team of trainers from many countries, a multi-level programme of seminars provides practical training, and is followed by a programme for training local facilitators. Local preachers' groups and national and regional networks ensure continuity and ongoing development, seeking to build vigorous movements committed to Bible exposition.

Langham Literature provides Majority World preachers, scholars and seminary libraries with evangelical books and electronic resources through publishing and distribution, grants and discounts. The programme also fosters the creation of indigenous evangelical books in many languages, through writer's grants, strengthening local evangelical publishing houses, and investment in major regional literature projects, such as one volume Bible commentaries like the *Africa Bible Commentary* and the *South Asia Bible Commentary*.

Langham Scholars provides financial support for evangelical doctoral students from the Majority World so that, when they return home, they may train pastors and other Christian leaders with sound, biblical and theological teaching. This programme equips those who equip others. Langham Scholars also works in partnership with Majority World seminaries in strengthening evangelical theological education. A growing number of Langham Scholars study in high quality doctoral programmes in the Majority World itself. As well as teaching the next generation of pastors, graduated Langham Scholars exercise significant influence through their writing and leadership.

To learn more about Langham Partnership and the work we do visit **langham.org**

www.ingramcontent.com/pod-product-compliance
Lightning Source LLC
Chambersburg PA
CBHW070234240426
43673CB00044B/1784